HERB COHEN
THE CHOICE IS NON-NEGOTIABLE!

"No one goes very far in life without negotiation. Herb Cohen makes the trip easier, more successful, and more fun, whether it's convincing someone to marry you, give you a loan, or release some hostages."
—MARIO CUOMO

"Knowing Herb Cohen for decades, I was surprised that a book could capture his unique style and sense of humor. [This book] will not only help you get what you want, it's a joy to read. Almost every page is hilarious, so that profound aspects of human behavior become pure entertainment."
—LARRY KING

"There's an art to deal-making and negotiating, and it's an art that few people possess. Herb Cohen is one of those few people. He knows what is involved in negotiating, as well as the indispensable tools required to be effective."
—DONALD J. TRUMP

"Folksy anecdotes, sagacious observations."
—*Miami Herald*

"NEGOTIATE THIS! brilliantly captures what makes Herb Cohen the world's best negotiator. He is articulate, genuine, and profound. You will be a better negotiator (and parent) after reading this book. Share it with the other side—better yet, buy them a copy—and you'll find that you'll both do better."
—BARRY NALEBUFF, Milton Steinbach Professor, Yale School of Management, and coauthor of *Why Not?*

"Whether you are negotiating with your teenager or a terrorist, Herb Cohen's new book should come in very handy. It's packed with practical insights based on decades of negotiating experience and filled with humorous stories that drive the points home. A sheer delight!"
—WILLIAM URY, coauthor of *Getting to Yes*

Also by Herb Cohen

You Can Negotiate Anything

HERB COHEN

Negotiate This!

By Caring,
But
Not
T-H-A-T
Much

WARNER
BUSINESS
BOOKS™

NEW YORK   BOSTON

Copyright © 2003 by Herb Cohen
All rights reserved.

Warner Business Books
Warner Books

Time Warner Book Group
1271 Avenue of the Americas, New York, NY 10020
Visit our Web site at www.twbookmark.com.

The Warner Business Books logo is a trademark of Warner Books.

Printed in the United States of America
Originally published in hardcover by Warner Books
First Trade Edition: January 2006
10 9 8 7 6 5 4 3 2 1

The Library of Congress has cataloged the hardcover edition as follows:

Cohen, Herb.
    Negotiate this! : by caring, but not T-H-A-T much / Herb Cohen.
        p. cm.
    Includes bibliographical references and index.
    ISBN 0-446-52973-7
    1. Negotiation. I. Title.

BF637.N4C545 2003
302.3-dc21   2003043281

Cover design by Andrew Newman
Cover photo by Herman Estevez
Book design by Giorgetta Bell McRee

ISBN 0-446-69644-7 (pbk.)

FOR MY BESHEERT,
who helped me understand
that he who laughs—lasts!

CONTENTS

ACKNOWLEDGMENTS

"There is no present or future—only the past, happening over and over again—now."
EUGENE O'NEILL

This book has been incubating in me for some time. To be sure, if you believe in the academic axiom "publish or perish" I would be long dead.

Since *You Can Negotiate Anything* appeared in 1980, hundreds of publications have been devoted to this subject to the point where negotiation is now virtually regarded as the new mantra or "the nimbus of salvation." This flourishing body of knowledge has, for the most part, carried the subject beyond timeworn tales, aged anecdotes, impromptu insights, and gut feelings. Thus, this work attempts to integrate some of these available insights along with my own personal experiences in a form that I trust you will find both entertaining and eminently readable.

What is different about this book? To begin with, it is written in my own unique and recognizable style: the distinct manner I have used to communicate with almost one million people in speeches, lectures, and seminars over the years. Mistakenly or misguidedly, I have once again deliberately tried to be myself.

Next, the distinctive quality of this work is not primarily derived from the discovery, invention, or revelation of new things. Instead, by using allegorical stories, metaphors, and simple models I have tried to get you the reader to view your own experience, behavior, and relationships in a different light.

Lastly, as you proceed I hope you will be smiling and amused by the examples and illustrations. Humor, of course, is no laughing matter. If nothing else, it is a tranquilizer without side effects. But more, if used well it can deepen your understanding, so that you are better able to appreciate yourself as a subject interacting with others in a changing chaotic world.

Many of the ideas and concepts set forth in the pages that follow took their earliest form in 1963 during a three-week negotiating course that I developed and conducted for claims adjusters and attorneys under the auspices of Allstate Insurance Company. It was back then that I used the expressions "win-lose" and "win-win." Since that time, however, I have been personally involved in thousands of negotiations, having benefited immensely from exposure to many thinkers and doers in the field. Moreover, while formally educated in history, international relations, and law, I have spent endless hours in my formative years reading about various means of strategic interaction, in such diverse fields as game theory and social psychology.

In the same manner, for decades I have been an inveterate reader of *Time, Newsweek, Commentary, The New Republic, The Nation,* and preeminently *The Economist,* which has greatly affected my thinking and outlook.

Accordingly, this volume, like any other, though signed by one person, carries the presence of many. "We are in the world," playwright Arthur Miller once wrote, "but the world is also within us." As a result, I have come to believe that what is often represented as "total originality" is frequently the unconscious forgetting of one's sources. For what is recollection, if not the manipulation of memories?

Having said this, I would be remiss if I did not mention some of the individuals who contributed to my growth and development. Special thanks go to Eugene Emerson Jennings of Michigan State University, a thinker who was always ahead of his time. Also, I owe a debt of gratitude to Saul D. Alinsky, Hannah Arendt, Maureen Berman, Harlan Cleveland, Norman Cousins, Robert Dahl, Morton Deutsch, Viktor Frankl, Jay Haley, Eric Hoffer, Fred Iklé, George Kennan, Henry Kissinger, Morrie Leibman, David

Mamet, Marya Mannes, Hans Morgenthau, George Odiorne, Dean Pruitt, Anatole Rapaport, Edward Rowny, Bertrand Russell, Tom Schelling, and I. Willliam Zartman.

To others who left their imprint on my life and so on these pages, I extend my appreciation—particularly Al Carzoli, Harry Chapin, Wes Cornish, Ralph Coppeto, Henry Drewes, Tammy Haddad, Ruzka Korczak-Marle, Vitka and Abba Kovner, and Walt Sirene and Ed Tully of the FBI. I am especially beholden to Larry King for his dedication to bringing this project to fruition. As he often said, "In view of the popularity of *You Can Negotiate Anything* you have a ready-made audience for this book." Then came the caveat: "However, in view of the time lag, half of them are already dead."

Likewise, this work comes to you because of the help I received from Julie McCarron, Paul McLaughlin, Deborah Raffin, and especially, Ed Victor. Above all, I am grateful to my editor, Rick Wolff, a person of infinite patience and understanding, and the encouragement and assistance I received from my agent, Michael Viner.

Also, I have the gift of friendship from so many over the years: Betty and Forrest Belcher, Alice Ginott and Ted Cohn, Matilda and Mario Cuomo, Asher Dann, Ellie and David Drachman, Robin and Sol Gittleman, Ted Greenberg, Barbara and Jerry Greenbaum, Joan and Jeff McGrath, Janine and Jon Miller, Susan and Maxwell Soll, Sid Young, and the very special Judy and Stan Sporkin.

More personally, I am thankful to have had a supportive family:

My parents, Esther and Morris Cohen, who taught me by example that one should not try to be a success but rather a person of value. Verily, one is considered successful who takes more out of life than he gives. But a man of value will contribute more than he receives.

My sister, Renee Blumenthal, the family intellectual, who upon reading my first book remarked, "It was written for the ages—between ten and twelve."

Our children, Sharon, Steven, and Rich, and eventually, Bill

Levin, Lisa Melmed, and Jessica Medoff, who have enriched our lives.

Most of all, I wish to thank my partner, adviser, and now and then critic, Ellen, for over four decades of encouragement.

Let us turn now to some "administrivia" before proceeding further. For one thing, in writing this book I was confronted with what I consider the bias or limitations of the English language: the question of pronoun usage. Finding pronouns and principles an uneasy mix, I decided in favor of clarity and simplicity, trusting that the majority of readers would understand that no slight is intended. For another, to make this offering readily readable for the public at large, I have chosen not to furnish potentially disconcerting footnotes. For those who wish to view this subject from other perspectives, I have provided an extensive bibliography.

Finally, I believe my manner of expression is somewhat impressionistic, in that I tend to suggest rather than state. As it is, I'm more comfortable describing, rather than prescribing, behavior. The problem with general prescriptions is that each of you is a special case. You have your own separate and unique destiny to fulfill. And the road toward fulfillment lies in questioning everything, including what others tell us, and even what we think we know. The person in charge of you is . . . you.

When the French diplomat Talleyrand was told that the Russian ambassador died in his sleep, he is reported to have said, "I wonder what his motive was." To dispel any lingering doubt about what provoked me to write this tome, let me give it to you straight.

While some people still see negotiating as a spectator sport—confining it to collective bargaining, diplomacy, or "big ticket" deal making—it is being used in an ever increasing number and range of social situations. Sure enough, one of the most pervasive signs of our time is the widespread acceptance of negotiation as a means of decision making in which two or more parties communicate in an effort to resolve their divergent desires and interests.

Like breathing, negotiating is necessary to our continued existence. The quality of our life, indeed our very survival, may depend upon how well we engage in this process. Put it this way:

Each day, every day, we communicate with others in an attempt to affect their behavior, both on and off the job. Hence, this skill is not only desirable but also, more to the point, it's acquirable. Surely, it is an axiom of this book that negotiators are made and not born.

My purpose is to afford you, the reader, insight into vexing human problems and situations, along with timeless and tested advice for handling them. What you will get as you turn these pages are commonsensical and satisfying techniques that can be comfortably used. Very simply, by seeing new possibilities and realities you will feel more confident, empowered, and liberated.

The timeless truth is this: It's surprising how much more anxious some people are to extend their life than to improve it.

Though President Ronald Reagan once said, "It takes two to tango," it takes only one to alter the nature of an outcome. For in any "negotiable relationship," you determine my response just as I determine yours. By changing your behavior you can very often alter the way the other side reacts or responds.

It is negligence, arguably even mild masochism, to permit your life to just happen or to live by what somebody else thinks you should be doing. Playing the negotiating game is the respectable means to bridge the gap between creed and deed, who you are and what you might achieve or become. But more, it is the most practical mechanism to affirm a person's freedom against all attempts to reduce him to an abstraction, an automaton propelled by conventional wisdom, peer pressure, circumstances, or unbridled authority. "There can be no darker or devastating tragedy," Saul Alinsky wrote, "than the death of a man's faith in himself and his power to direct his future."

Which brings us back to square one: the epigraph at the very beginning. Reflecting on the deterministic quote, we know that if we continue our "repetition compulsion"—to do more of the same—the future will arrive like the past, only using a different entrance. The French proverb had it right: "The more things change, the more they remain the same."

Although it goes without saying, I'll say it anyway: I believe that negotiating skill can give an individual the freedom to act—to begin anew—to create consequences that may be endless and even unpredictable. Consider: Andrei Sakharov, Nelson Mandela, Lech Walesa, Ralph Nader, Mother Teresa, Kemal Ataturk, and Martin Luther King Jr. They are not alone; each of you is a potential creator who can, if you wish, shape and alter the nature and the quality of your interpersonal dealings and relationships.

The very act of writing this book is in itself an expression of optimism, a demonstration of assurance that awareness plus negotiating strategy and savvy can be sources of success and satisfaction. For I believe we can exercise our capacity to create and invent new outcomes that are mutually beneficial, rather than simply repeat ourselves.

CHAPTER I

THE JOY OF DETACHED INVOLVEMENT

The one human freedom that cannot be taken from you is the capacity to choose your attitude in any given set of circumstances—to choose one's own way.

VIKTOR FRANKL

1

A GAMING MECHANISM

Negotiation is the game of life. Whenever you attempt to reconcile differences, manage conflict, resolve disputes, establish or adjust relationships you are playing the negotiating game. Truly it is the lifeblood of relationships. While people accept the importance of this learned skill in diplomatic dealings and labor relations they sometimes fail to see the opportunities that exist for them to gain a better mastery in their everyday lives via negotiating know-how.

For all of us, life is a continuing process of trying to influence others, whether it be your boss, a client or customer, a landlord, a neighbor, a banker, a broker, a medical or legal professional, an insurance or utility company, a salesperson, a car dealer, an HMO, an IRS auditor, or even a family member. We seem forever absorbed in trying to get others to agree with us. Whatever the case or cause, whenever you communicate with an objective in mind, engaging in social exchange to affect someone's demeanor or behavior, you are playing the negotiating game. Inevitably, your attitude and actions often have the potential to determine the distribution of available resources, the satisfaction of those involved, and even the nature of the relationship.

Please note that I refer to negotiating as a gaming mechanism or game, because if you see it in that light you will perform much better. Since a game is where you care—really care, but not t-h-a-t much.

Now why do I say that? Well, who is the worst person you negotiate for? Of course, I believe the answer is: yourself. That's not only true in your case; I know that's my own reality. Actually, to be completely candid with you, in the past three decades I have earned a lucrative living negotiating on behalf of others. Indeed, I try to have as my clients very wealthy entrepreneurs or large corporations with money to spend, who employ me to operate on their behalf in deal making. The way I am compensated is that I get a meager or modest percentage of an enormous deal. Would you believe that this formula works out well for my family and myself? So I must be pretty good at doing that.

Yet, when I negotiate on behalf of myself it's not a game anymore, it's my life, my legacy. So the result is often plainly pathetic. Now why is this the case? Do you believe it is because I'm lacking in self-esteem? Let me assure you that this is not so. Really, I like me one heck of a lot. In fact if I could be more effective for myself and less effective for you I would prefer it that way. But in truth I am better for you. Why? 'Cause I don't even know you.

Naturally I care about you, but not t-h-a-t much. It's that attitude that gives me perspective when working on your behalf. Indeed I suspect you already know that the best way to make a good deal is to convey to the other side that you are capable of living without the deal—that you have other options or alternatives. So as the "great negotiator" Kenny Rogers once said in a song lyric, "You got to know when to hold 'em and know when to fold 'em" and walk away. Succinctly put, the operative approach for success and satisfaction in all of life's interpersonal exchanges is to really care—but not t-h-a-t much.

Let me further illustrate this concept. About twenty-five years ago I was retained by a Chicago executive to help him finalize an agreement with the French government. We flew out of John F. Kennedy Airport heading for Paris. We sat next to each other in first class. Apparently, for him this deal was a vital matter that would have a substantial impact on the bottom line of his business. I learned this on the way over, because he frequently turned to me and said, "You know, this is a large financial transaction and I've got a great deal at stake." He must have used the same language about five times, so I eventually figured out that this was "a large financial transaction with a great deal at stake." From all indications he was under stress and he repeatedly asked, "What's our game plan?" In response, I found myself saying things like, "Well, we'll get in there and see how it goes." He kept shaking his head. "No," he blurted out. "We need more structure—you know, detail, specificity, meat—pith." At the time, never having heard the word "pith," I was somewhat alarmed.

Unimpressed by my vague replies, he took the initiative. "Maybe we should open up by blitzing the French officials. You know, take them by surprise, red dog 'em. We could even send out a flanker, and when they follow the flanker, we blindside them." It took me a while to realize that this man was speaking to me in an arcane, esoteric language. He was using American football terminology.

As you know, in any attempt to communicate with an objective in mind or any purposive social exchange, you should begin by determining the other party's frame of reference. As young people used to say, "Where is this person coming from?" Clearly, my traveling companion's paradigm was professional football.

"Okay, I got it," was my response. "In this culture, we don't want to appear overly aggressive or offensive, so at the outset we'll go with a flex defense." Surprisingly, he nodded like he understood this. Encouraged, I went on: "We'll give up yardage but we won't let them put any numbers up on the board." Presumably, this satisfied him and the rest of the trip was uneventful.

The next day, we met with the French authorities and from all indications my client's initial reservations appeared prescient. Right at the outset I made a substantial error. Note that I refer to my faux pas as an "error." Though responsible for the misstep I select a suitable word to describe what happened. Thus when I bungle I always call it an "error," because "To err is human and to forgive divine." In contrast, when you mess up, that's a "mistake," which could well be the product of gross stupidity and sheer incompetence.

As a consequence of my miscalculation my client was in an untenable position, which unfortunately he realized. He was upset— but not I. Of course, I'm caring—but not t-h-a-t much, 'cause I'm getting paid by the day. Unquestionably, because of this attitude, things turned around the next day and we concluded the deal with my client doing twice as well as he expected.

I now returned home to my family feeling rather triumphant. Walking into my household I was expecting that wonderful greeting that I have been expecting for decades. Only this time I noticed the atmosphere was particularly strained. Approaching my significant other, my wife, I asked the obvious: "What's wrong? What's going on here?" Quickly I learned that in my absence the family had organized against me. In effect, I had my own little "Solidarity Movement" operating here. It was like a welcome to Gdansk.

Well, what's the problem? Quickly I learned that they all wanted me to speak to our youngest child about cleaning up his room. To me this was trivial, as I try to concern myself with broader problems—like nuclear proliferation. (By all accounts the pubescent Amy Carter and I were the only people who worried about that issue.)

"Okay, let me give all of you another option. Get the kid to close his door." They didn't buy that. Successively they were on my back assaulting me with a verbal barrage: "Dad, things are growing in his room that have never been planted . . . Your son is a slob who takes after you . . . He's corrupting the family chromosomes." And then came the final kicker, "Forget all the stuff you're involved in, Mr. World Traveler, this is the only heritage you're leaving behind."

Amid all this I became passionately involved with a twelve-year-old child. No longer was this a mere game. It was my life and my legacy. As it happened, I became so emotionally enmeshed with this kid and his siblings that I not only got out-negotiated but also humiliated in the process.

All this is to say that whenever a social interaction looms so large in your mind that you view it as a watershed event in Western Civilization, you're in trouble. You're caring too much and with that you lose the requisite detachment necessary for success.

There's a prosaic saying that when a person is overcome with feelings, be it anger or desire, he or she "can't see the forest for the trees." Oddly, or maybe fittingly, when that happens you move in so close that you might even swear, "There is no tree, only a knothole right here." In other words, what you must do is train yourself to step back, so you can see the pattern, relationships, and interconnection of things.

ITEM: In the fifth century B.C., the Chinese military and political strategist Sun Tzu commented about the wisdom of perspective. In essence he wrote that "during an engagement a leader should not be in the midst of his forces but a little distance apart. Otherwise, his outlook will be distorted and he will misjudge the situation as a whole."

Earlier, I said that negotiating often involves the managing of conflict. At times, however, some conflicts that come your way need not be confronted but should be avoided. If you have some perspective you can see things beginning to develop and use your lead time to adopt a blueprint of avoidance. Another strategy that comes with distance is to diffuse or reconcile differences before they even come to a head. Finally, a third option is to confront the problem directly looking for alternate solutions that will provide for joint gain and build mutually beneficial relationships.

So, although negotiation is a game, it is best played as one of *addition, not subtraction or exclusion.* This means that we must often dampen our adversarial urge and drain some of the emotional content from life's strategic interactions. Recognize that this encounter which seems so important right now in the long run will be no more than a blip on the radar screen of eternity or a walnut in the batter of your life.

Perhaps you are wondering whether the author of this book, someone with some negotiating savvy and experience, ever gets bested in business dealings. Interestingly enough I only have to recount an event that transpired last year to make the point.

As you may know, for at least three decades I have been on the lecture circuit, getting paid to speak on subjects ranging from international terrorism to professional selling to dispute resolution. When prospective clients want to use my services they either call a speaker's bureau or sometimes my office. When they contact my office directly to work out the terms of the booking they never get to speak to me on that first call. There is, of course, a reason for that. You see, my speaking fees are astronomical and there's no way I can honestly justify earning the kind of money that I do.

However, the people in my office who make the initial arrangements don't have my compunctions. When you call, they care about booking the date, but not t-h-a-t much. Consequently, without batting an eye they throw out that astronomical number. Usually the fee we quote is immediately accepted without negotiations. Understandably, it's due to our presentation. Consider, for example: "Here's Herb's standard fee. Now you would like his standard performance wouldn't you?" The retort is almost always predictable: "And what does that include?" Our answer is always the same: "First and foremost a guarantee that he'll show up. You would want that, wouldn't you?" At this point the prospect is transformed into a client when they blurt out "Oh yes." This occurs 90 percent of the time. In the case of the small minority, they occasionally become indignant and say something like "Forget it, I can get Henry Kissinger for less." Given this scenario I don't even know who these people are since I never work for them.

Which brings me to the phone call received this past year from a large information technology company in Silicon Valley, California. As the events were recounted to me, a female executive phoned to inquire about my fees for a specific conference to take place in San Francisco. To be sure, the dialogue followed a routine pattern. After discussing the length of the talk, the composition of the audience, and so on, there's invariably an inquiry along the lines of, "What will this cost? How much is Herb's remuneration?" or the standard rhyming couplet, "So what will the fee be?" At this juncture those in my office quoted the standard "astronomical fee" knowing that on occasion this might produce a contentious reaction, at least from that unknown 10 percent.

However, the woman executive on the other end of the line went against the norm and our expectations. What she did was creative, differentiating herself and her conference from all others. Alas, she was applying the theory that "A nose that can hear is worth two that can smell." While I'm not exactly sure what that means, nonetheless I know it works.

Instead of saying "How much does he want?" or "What do we have to pay?" she inquired softly, "So what would Herb's honorarium be?" Our initial reaction was, "Honorarium? What the hell is that?" Being somewhat familiar with Latin I know that when you translate it into English it means "You're getting less." And the reason I know that, is when people are offering me more honor that's going to leave over less "arium." Fortunately, the people in our office don't know Latin so they came back with the standard astronomical fee.

The other side's rejoinder was not emotional, nothing like, "Who does he think he is? Nobody merits that!" Rather she said, "We know he's worth what you're asking. What's more, our executive VP heard him speak previously and said his value is at least twice that amount. And if we had that kind of money it would indeed be our privilege, our pleasure, and our honor to offer him that. But regrettably this is all we have in our budget." Did that work? Well, six months later I was on stage at the San Francisco Sheraton fulfilling my commitment.

ITEM: In the golden age of television, Jackie Gleason's show was one of CBS's highest rated programs. William Paley, the network's CEO, was anxious to re-sign him, only Gleason wanted to be paid a then unheard of sum of $11 million a year. During the final bargaining session, the Great One, who was hungover, fell asleep during the argument over money. Paley, observing his condition, said, "Okay, if that's his attitude [caring but not t-h-a-t much], give him what he wants."

2

VOLUNTARY DECISION MAKING

Fundamentally, what negotiating is all about is voluntary decision making. Unlike the great growth industry of our time—litigation—negotiating in the final analysis requires two parties to say "yes." The difficulty, however, is that at least one of these entities starts out by saying "no," or at best they are not sure or profess reluctance to say "yes." So your basic task as a negotiator is to help move someone from "no" to "yes" or from reluctance to commitment.

Occasionally I am asked, "Herb, in your career have you ever encountered a situation where two people are saying 'yes' from the outset and they call you in?" And the answer to that question is "No!" Why would they call me?

You don't have two people sitting around a table in Dallas and one says to the other, "I think we would be willing to pay $8 million for your business." And the other remarks, "I concur, I think we've got a deal here. Now let's give this guy Cohen a call on the East Coast, bring him out so we can give him a portion of the sale price." Nope, I don't get those calls. I don't know who does, but it's not me.

Let me tell you when I get involved. Those two people are meeting in Dallas and the first party opens with the same proffer of $8 million. However, the response is drastically different. "Are you kidding!" the second guy retorts. "I'm offended by that

11

chintzy, niggling, paltry, and pitiful offer, which I regard as personally insulting. Do you know my grandfather started this company, which by any measure is worth $80 million? Hey, the only way I might even be forced to respond," he continues, "is if you threaten to rip the tongue from the roof of my mouth. If you threaten to tear the eyeballs from my skull. If you threaten to maim, murder, and destroy my family, whom I love dearly, and that were a viable threat. Only then might I consider it. But as far as you're concerned right now, shove it."

Not long after, the person who was the recipient of that tirade may call my office. Interestingly, he presents the problem in a matter-of-fact manner. "We have some differences here in Dallas about perceptions. Perhaps Herb might come out and serve as a catalyst to facilitate things." By my reckoning I have made too many of these hopeless journeys.

Nevertheless, when I arrive at the DFW Airport, as I stride off the plane to be welcomed by the parties, I do not say, "Hi there, here I am, hotshot negotiator from the East ready to take command." Indeed to be honest with you the picture on this book's jacket is about as good as I ever look. Check out that photo and you know right away that I'm not a big believer in "dressing for success." Never have I been in a situation where people are saying "no," "fuhgeddaboudit," or "never," when suddenly I appear on the scene, immaculately and fashionably attired. Do you believe they look up and say, "Hey I love the way that guy's put together. Wow, that matching ensemble, the power tie, the cut and fabric of his garment. Gee, I was going to say 'no' but based on his clothing, make that 'yes.'" The opposite may actually be true. Somehow if you look too good they expect you to make concessions. So my strategy in negotiations is generally to make the other side feel superior to me. In so many instances you have to work so very hard but nevertheless it pays off.

3

AN OTHER WORLDLY UNDERTAKING

Whenever you face off with someone in this process of voluntary decision making you're in an association with a dissimilar organism or a symbiotic relationship. By that I mean there are both elements of cooperation and competition involved—shared interests and issues in conflict. What is clear is that without commonality there is no reason to try for a resolution of the problem. So too, without discord there is nothing to negotiate about. Therefore, whenever someone says, "All right, I'll meet with you, but not to discuss this matter or God forbid to negotiate," you should regard that as an opening bargaining position. Unless you are exceptionally attractive or a professional entertainer, why are they spending their valuable time in your company? Evidently, they either recognize some commonality that exists or realize that an outright rejection of the meeting has the potential of producing detrimental consequences for them.

Generally what appears to take place in the customary negotiating encounter is that the parties first verbalize contradictory demands and then try to move toward agreement by concession making or possibly a search for new alternatives. This may suggest that the game may be sufficiently superficial to lend itself to a mathematical solution. Yet the truth is that what appears to be happening on the surface can be misleading. Implicit but often neglected is that the parties involved in this dynamic process through the trial and error of reciprocal communications are attempting to satisfy their needs.

There's the rub. We are dealing with sentient beings, unique complex creatures who are both malleable and resilient and who are capable of changing their minds but only if given enough acceptable reasons, time, and social support. As a matter of fact, a human being is motivated by his or her individual interests, but their "rational decision making" normally embodies some degree of intuition, emotion, habituation, and arbitrariness.

So when we run into conduct that deviates from our expectations, underlying it are experiences and a system of values and beliefs that we do not understand. This is true because all behavior, no matter how bizarre, makes sense from the standpoint of the actor. In this regard we could easily be talking about a spiteful ex-spouse, disobedient child, problematic in-law, revengeful former associate, or a callous bureaucrat.

Each of us is so bound by our own parochial assumptions, behaviors, and experiences that we frequently do not recognize differences. This is so even when we are in the midst of another culture. In short, you and I do not see things as they are. We see things as we are. We are truly captives of the pictures in our brain. Hearing words and observing behavior we construct a map only to learn later that our map does not depict the actual terrain. The point is this: Although automatic stereotyped behavior is prevalent and perhaps even convenient in a complicated and chaotic world, an individual human being defies classification. Each person is unique—one of a kind. Think of it this way: If there was anyone here exactly like you, there'd be no reason for you to be here.

All of which should suggest that if you want to be effective in selling your ideas, persuading others, or exercising leadership, you must start out as other-directed. That is to say: It is important that you see any purposive interaction as an opportunity to acquire information about the other side's beliefs, motives, attitudes, and values. All this means is that you want to see yourself as "other worldly."

Which brings me to one of the first full-time jobs I had while an undergraduate student. It was during the Korean War and there was a recession in the United States. Only in those days, they never told you that the economy was in the tank. When you couldn't find a job you thought, "What's wrong with me?" This fact was underscored when I ended up working as a commission salesman for a national life insurance company.

As I recall, the training program lasted three days and we were told to "dress to impress," display "zeal for the deal," and take control of the prospect by talking and telling. According to our instructor, selling was a high-pressure ritual dance of courtship, an assertive seduction pure and simple. When asked about listening to the customer he gave us the impression that silence on our part was a symptom of muted imbecility.

Surrounded by signs that read, "There Is Only One Thing in Life More Important Than a Little Money and That's a Lot of Money," we were encouraged to chant in unison, "I feel great, I want money." Despite our encyclopedic ignorance of our company's products and services, we were advised to use hyperbole as part of our stock-in-trade and when answering questions to remember that "a lie is not a lie if the truth is not known." (Parenthetically, this was a novel ethical formulation that came to mind years later when Marion Barry, the mayor of Washington, D.C., said "There are two kinds of truths: real truths and made-up truths.")

Our guiding principle was to control the discussion with an opening sales pitch, to be followed by twenty-two surefire ways of overcoming objections, and finally eighteen guaranteed techniques to close the deal. As young and inexperienced as I was at the time, even I realized that there was less here than met the eye.

How long did I last in this company? Very much like a dead fish, after about five days the smell got to me. Although this took place over forty years ago, there is still a misguided minority who believe that persuasion and selling is about erudition, audacity, appearance, and taking charge.

4

NEW COMMUNICATION APPROACHES

Quite to the contrary, if you want to impact favorably on the other side's decision making, you've got to be other-directed, understanding their values, beliefs, experience, and mind-set. Businesspeople call this being "customer- or client-focused." The same is true in Arthur Miller's play *The Price,* where the octogenarian appraiser Gregory Solomon explains, "If you don't understand the viewpoint, you don't understand the price."

Beyond a doubt all human beings perceive, discover, and create their realities according to the maps or paradigms they have in their minds. Hence it is natural to ascribe our beliefs, values, concerns, and aspirations to those with whom we negotiate. But we must guard against this inclination. Such "mirror imaging" or projection on our part will only produce discomfort and discord.

Recognizing this problem, common sense might tell us that when engaged in any attempt to influence behavior we must start out asking more questions than giving answers and listening more than talking. Needless to say, too many people cannot resist the urge to immediately inaugurate the discourse with a generic sales pitch that extols the technical features of their services, products, ideas, or proposals. Instead, viewing yourself as a problem solver, you should try to elicit from the other party their underlying concerns, interests, preferences, and needs.

Given this approach the basic formula works like this: First off, you should *begin by asking questions even if you think you know the answers.* Not only listen to what they are saying, but convey that you are engaged in active listening. How do you do this? Well, when they speak, look at them, and smile and nod when it's appropriate. Do not mask your reactions with a poker face, even if you've heard it all before. Try to display empathy and understanding, since people want to know that you truly care about their situation.

Second, *write down what they are saying.* Often people ask, "But what if their comments are gibberish, asinine, and moronic?" To which I say, "In that case it's even more important for you to record their claptrap; you may be the only person who has ever taken them seriously." Remember, people want to be in a relationship with those who respect their point of view.

Third, *while taking notes, pause occasionally to read back to them what you have written.* In all the years I have been doing this, never once has the other side said, "Gee you got that perfectly." Usually their reaction is, "You left something out" or, "I believe you mischaracterized that." At this point, I willingly change what I have, conforming to their wishes so that we may establish a consensus of their concerns.

Fourth, I *allow them to tell their story in their own way, which means that they sometimes digress and meander.* Never do I interrupt to keep them on track, because I know that ultimately their willingness to say "yes" will not be based only on facts, hard evidence, and rational thinking. Certainly, decision making will also be affected by gut instincts, comfort level, emotions, feelings, predilections, learning ability, risk tolerance, pride, past experiences, and perceived consequences. Make no mistake: Persuasion is more complicated than it may look at first blush.

Fifth, although opinionated and judgmental to some extent, I *try to control my words and reactions.* Consequently, even if I disagree strongly with what's been said, I qualify my objections by saying, "I think I understand your position, but from my narrow perspective, limited as it may be, I see it this way . . ."

Finally, I never spend any time arguing or debating with people. I don't show them where they are wrong, foolish, stupid, or misinformed. Even if I might overcome their arguments and prevail, such a victory would prove self-defeating inasmuch as my potential partner may be thinking, "Do I want to enter this relationship where I regularly meet with him in the future for further humiliation?" It would take a strange person to willingly acquiesce to such an arrangement.

Reduced to essentials, you want to always see yourself as a problem solver, someone with very sensitive antennae who is probing deeper and listening louder to acquire information. This will help you overcome the potential barriers to gaining agreement and making a deal. Here's a rule of thumb: See every negotiation, whether it's with your child or a business transaction, as a cross-cultural encounter where you start out sensitive to a differing perspective. Consequently, gather intelligence with the attitude of knowing that you don't know because individuals not only reveal but also conceal information.

5

APPLYING CONSCIOUS INATTENTION

Let's now consider two world headline dramas where using negotiating savvy I attempted to influence the course of events. In retrospect these efforts did not produce national acclaim nor was my reputation especially enhanced. But you can judge for yourself.

THE SEIZURE OF THE JAPANESE EMBASSY IN LIMA, PERU, IN DECEMBER 1996

On the week before Christmas in December 1996 over five hundred members of Peru's elite had gathered at the Japanese embassy to celebrate the birthday of Emperor Akihito. Among the guests were Supreme Court justices, ministers, generals of the National Police, diplomats, and business executives. While they were sipping cocktails and swallowing sushi an explosion shattered the surrounding wall and fourteen masked men and women (some of them teenagers) started firing their weapons and announcing, "We are the Tupac Amaru and you are our hostages." The Tupac Amaru Revolutionary Movement was a group that espoused political violence and had as its mission the establishment of a Marxist regime. It had gotten its name from the last emperor of the Incas, who was executed by the Spanish in 1572.

That's what I knew about this situation until I received a phone call to come to the White House a few days after the occurrence. Since I was one of those involved in the FBI's Hostage Negotiating Program in Quantico, Virginia, and was constantly warning our government about the scourge of international terrorism, I was looking forward to a long meeting with the President where I would share my thoughts and philosophy.

Upon arriving I met with a national security expert who gave me a concise review of the situation and asked whether I would be willing to go to Peru to afford President Alberto Fujimori the benefit of my experience. Answering affirmatively, I was putting away my pad when the door to the briefing room opened partially.

Looking up I noticed the head of President William Jefferson Clinton popping in. It was just his head, not his body. To this date, I have never seen his body in person—only his head. So don't ask me anything about his body 'cause I'm not acquainted with it. However, I do know the head and it spoke to me. "Good luck, Herb," it said, and, "Remember, this matter involves plausible deniability." Which after translation into English means, "When you screw this up, we don't know who you are." So it was with this vote of confidence that I was on my way to Lima, Peru.

When the plane landed, I didn't even go through customs but into a large limousine that took me to the Presidential Palace, where I was greeted by President Fujimori. He shook my hand, offered me a cup of tepid tea and a plate on which rested one cracker. At the time I remember looking for something to put on the cracker; which tells you a lot about my personal needs and priorities. While I gazed about, the President excused himself saying, "I'm not involved in the details of this, but the military is." As if on cue the door swung open and three army generals strode in, marching in lock step. They were wearing uniforms and caps with fruit salad on the beaks. Down their uniforms they had an abundance of service ribbons, and medals were around their necks. Noticing their appearance I remember thinking, "Did I miss a big war down here? Because I've got to be in the presence of some of the world's bravest people."

At the outset, following the dictates of my charge from the

White House, I began to detail my credentials as I shared my experiences with the generals. Looking back now, I must have been talking one helluva lot, because I soon realized that they were staring at the ceiling. The only time I paused was when the general with the most decorations held up his hand and said, "You want to know about hostage negotiations? I'll tell you what I've been through. I came from a small town, Alca. Once a nine-year-old boy took a dog that didn't belong to him and ran into a wooden shack. And do you know what we did? We surrounded the shack and counted to ten for him to come out." Although thinking to myself that this culture is slower because in America we do "one-two-three," I leaned forward and asked, "What happened next?" Shrugging, he replied, "We burned down the shack." Somewhat bewildered, I inquired, "What happened to the boy?" He answered indifferently, "The dog jumped out and ran free."

Was he just putting me on or was this a metaphorical story to communicate how they deal with hostage takers? At the time I remember thinking that just spending time with these guys would cause the loss of brain tissue and a precipitous drop of my IQ.

In hindsight I realize that my problem was that I had forgotten the advice that I gave you previously about questioning rather than telling. I had put myself in the role of "gringo expert" talking down to the common people. Conspicuously absent up to that point in my demeanor was any sense of humility and humanity.

Recognizing that I was losing credibility, I changed course and began to focus on them: their families, their travels, their tastes, and their lives. In short, to stop the skid I let go of the wheel.

Surprisingly after a time, our relationship changed and the generals gradually revealed what was going on. From them I learned that President Fujimori was infuriated by the takeover. Not only was this a humiliation for him and his government, but also his mother, sister, and brother were among the hostages. As a result, they had already started digging a rescue tunnel and preparing 150 commandos for an imminent attack. In addition, the President, who was dedicated to eradicating terrorism, wanted this to end forcibly by Christmas, as he would not negotiate with "this band of outlaws" under any circumstances.

Eventually I was able to get the generals to understand and to agree that time was in our favor if we wanted to safeguard the lives of the civilians. Respecting Fujimori's wishes that there be no formal negotiations, a Commission of Guarantors (consisting of the head of the Red Cross, the Canadian ambassador, and a re-spected Peruvian archbishop) was formed to engage in "prelimi-nary conversations" with the hostage takers. It was through these contacts and the relationships that developed between the captors and their captives that a great number of hostages gained their freedom, culminating with the release of 225 as a "goodwill ges-ture" just before Christmas.

When I left Lima fewer than one hundred hostages were still being held and the crisis had calmed considerably. Both sides had reduced their demands and they had settled into a contest of wills, playing to audiences at home and abroad. Significantly, the Peru-vian government was using the tunnel excavations as a means of gathering intelligence and were willing to be patient "even if it took three months." Perhaps more telling was that Nestor Cerpa Cartolini, commander of the operation, was starting to worry about his image and did not want to be compared to the more vi-olent Shining Path terrorist group.

The denouement, which is still somewhat controversial, came after a 126-day siege. While the rebels were playing indoor soccer without their shirts and weapons, they were surprised by a massive commando onslaught. Making use of the intelligence that was collected over time, the security forces were able to safeguard the lives of almost all of the remaining hostages. The one exception was a businessman who sustained a heart attack during the assault and died on the way to the hospital. In essence, it was the passage of time, which allowed them to gather information, that saved the day for the remaining captives.

Although many who were directly affected by these events have melancholy memories, on occasion when I think back to my visit to the Presidential Palace I remember Edward R. Murrow's dictum: "The obscure we see eventually, the completely apparent may take longer." But godfather Michael Corleone may have been more to the point when he said, "The one thing I learned from Pop was to try to think as people around you think."

THE IRANIAN HOSTAGE CRISIS—NOVEMBER 1979

Doubtlessly many of the West's difficulties with the Muslim world had at their genesis, or were at least exacerbated by, the Ayatollah Khomeini, the godfather of hate directed at America. Indeed, the handwritten words left behind by Mohammed Atta, the leader of the kamikaze nineteen that gave us the atrocity of September 11, 2001, are almost identical with the instructions Khomeini furnished to the thousands of children who were given the "keys to paradise" before exploding themselves on landmines during the Iran-Iraq War.

You may recall that this problem was first brought forcibly to our attention when a multitude of Iranian students seized the American embassy in Teheran in November 1979 and took fifty-two diplomats hostage. Despite the provocation of this Persian version of *Dog Day Afternoon*, President Jimmy Carter responded with admirable initial restraint and patience. But then, from my scape we seemed to engage in mirror imaging—applying our standards and values to the muddle and mobocracy that was developing in Iran. We publicly observed that the holding of our citizens was a violation of international law and a breach of diplomatic tradition. Also, President Carter informed us that he was praying for the hostages morning and night. And, oh yes, embarking upon the "Rose Garden Strategy," he would not actively campaign against Senator Ted Kennedy in the Democratic presidential primary. As might be expected, despite all the media fanfare and public outrage, the hostages remained.

The upshot was that I ultimately met with President Carter and Secretary of State Cyrus Vance in mid-December 1979 to discuss my observations on how to influence the behavior of the Iranian mullahs.

Presumably what brought this about was my experience, which seemed especially apropos for the crisis. Formerly, I mentioned that I worked with the FBI and was knowledgeable about hostage negotiations. But there was more: To begin with I had spent considerable time in Iran involved in commercial dealings. Second, I was a student of Islam and Shi'ism. Third, I knew a great deal about Persian history and culture. Last of all, when I was with the United States army in West Germany, I had met Ayatollah Behesti, then an adviser to Iranian students, but now the leader of the Islamic Republican Party in Iran. Based upon this background, I saw my task as explaining to the Carter administration how the mullahs viewed this situation. Our purpose I thought should be to get into *their* world and furnish them with incentives, both positive and negative, to gain the freedom of our citizens.

When the meeting began I started to explain how our adversaries come from a bargaining culture, which is different from ours. At the outset, I remember saying something along these lines: "How do Americans feel about negotiating? We don't even like the word, calling it haggling or chiseling. My own wife has even said to me on many occasions, 'I do not lie for money.' Of course, the implication is that I do. But in Iran everything is bargained for.

"Think of your own experience. Have you ever purchased a Persian rug retail? Even if you wanted to, they wouldn't let you. It would be a cultural sin.

"From their bargaining mind-set the mullahs see this as a buy-sell transaction." I continued, "They have fifty-three hot rugs for sale (one was later released) and are trying to obtain as much as they can for their illegally obtained merchandise. So when President Carter walks into the rug sellers' bazaar and tells the prospective seller how much he wants and needs the merchandise, the price is not going down. In fact, this may even raise the ante.

"What's happening is that by the behavior of the administration and our massive media coverage we are creating more demand for the rugs. Since the supply is limited, the cost is going up. So, quite unintentionally we are prolonging the captivity of the hostages."

At this point the President cut in: "Herb, I don't think you understand. You, myself, and the mullahs, we're all from the same Abrahamic tradition." When I first heard that I didn't even know what he was talking about. But then I sort of figured it out and it struck me that the President and I may have been from that religious tradition, but not the mullahs.

Resisting the inclination to get sidetracked, I continued. "Okay, let's look at Americans. What is the largest single purchase we make in our lives?" Without waiting for the answer I blurted out, "Yes, it's a residential home. Now even if that prospective house is in a tract area, a development where all the homes look alike, how do we know what to pay?"

Again acting as if this was a rhetorical question I moved on. "Indubitably we look for the big sign in the sky. You know the one that's 150 feet up there that says in big block numbers $179,226. Yup, that's what we're paying, the same as everyone else, what it says on that sign. So what if we're getting ripped off at that price? We don't care, 'cause everyone's getting screwed at that price. Hey that's the American way, equality of screwing across the board."

Undeterred by the apparent lack of enthusiasm for my presentation, I never paused. "And surely when we make this purchase we are going to do it quick. You know, fast. Because in our culture, time is money, so it's in and out.

"Meanwhile how about the Iranian mullahs? Well, first of all they will bargain *everything*. From their experience, you *can* negotiate anything. Furthermore, if you're a mullah, by dint of your occupation you're unemployed. Other than your obligatory prayers five times a day, the remainder of your activities are spent looking to kill time. So, we are coming from a different place."

President Carter interjected, "I don't think you understand the Ayatollah, Herb," he went on. "By all reports he's not like you and me. He's a martyr. He wants to die. Chhooomayne doesn't care about his own life." The President always strung out the name, prolonging the CH sound as if clearing his throat. It was like he knew Farsi and I didn't.

Shaking my head, I remarked, "A martyr, not exactly. How old is Khomeini?" The President, who had an exceptional grasp of details, responded, "Eighty-six years and eight months."

"Okay," I said, "that proves it. How can you have an eighty-six-year-old martyr? On the face of it the life expectancy of a martyr is probably 19.2 years. Certainly when you get into your twenties or thirties you need another career."

The inevitable result was that when I returned home from meetings like this in Washington, I was generally pessimistic, maybe even depressed. Walking into my household I would be greeted by my wife, Ellen, who is an upbeat, optimistic person. She'd say with a big smile, "Hey, how'd it go?" At the time I re-member saying, "Do we have any United States Savings Bonds? Well . . . *sell!*"

And there you have it: Fortunately President Jimmy Carter brought the fifty-two Americans safely back from captivity. Unfor-tunately it took 444 days to achieve the result.

After the White House meeting, I continued to work with the administration attempting to obtain the release of our diplomats. In the subsequent months I wrote a number of memorandums and frequently met with members of the State Department and National Security Council, but all to no avail. Of these meetings, it cannot even be said that we were ships that passed in the night. I don't even think we were sailing in the same waters. For what-ever reason I could not get the decision makers to understand the mentality and mind-set of the Iranian mullahs.

Of course, what these criminals were doing was in violation of international law, but considering their objectives, frame of refer-ence, and mental set, their behavior made sense to them and should have been predictable to us. Almost without exception you don't change people's behavior through rhetoric but only by alter-ing their ways of looking at things. This means that if we wanted to facilitate the release, we should have had a coherent action strategy that made the Ayatollah realize that it was not in his interest to allow the status quo to continue. In other words, in the cost-benefit calculus of our adversary, the disadvantages of retaining the hostages would far outweigh the benefits of keeping them.

But instead of getting into the head of the ruling mullahs and being other worldly, we were invariably looking for a quick fix. This being the Middle East, the magic potion was usually someone who we thought knew someone who knew someone. That in turn led to Teheran visits by Ramsey Clark, Yasser Arafat, Kurt Waldheim, and even cleric Valerian Cappuci. As you doubtlessly know, they all failed.

After about three months of frustrating trips to our nation's capital, I returned to earning a living. Thereafter, much to my amazement, I was contacted by Republican party stalwarts who were concerned that a Jimmy Carter "October Surprise" would alter the presidential election's outcome in the final weeks. Ultimately, I met with Governor Reagan's campaign manager, William Casey, and finally the candidate himself at a home he was renting in Virginia. Before even doing this I had one major concern and condition, and that was that the plight of the hostages not be introduced into the political campaign. Once this was agreed upon, I gave Governor Reagan my viewpoint on the situation, much of which was memorialized in a confidential memorandum sent to him on October 25, 1980. (The appendix of this book contains this document along with the Jack Anderson syndicated column of February 12, 1981, which refers to it. Presumably, after the presidential inauguration in January 1981, this writing was given to the media. It's worth reading, because using the approach discussed I actually predicted the date that the fifty-two hostages would gain their freedom.)

In the intervening years, I have been asked numerous times, "How were you able to analyze this matter and foretell the outcome with such certainty?" My best answer is that, unlike others whose intellect and intelligence were superior, I didn't have a career or reputation invested in this crisis. And I was less inhibited by a desire for acceptance or fear of disapproval. Not knowing any of those held captive, my vision wasn't obscured by emotion. Most significant perhaps was that as an outsider I was able to see what more accustomed eyes overlooked—to observe in an unhabitual way.

This applies to you as a negotiator. While in the midst of fervent discussion and emotive people, you must try to remain aloof from the turmoil, so as to be able to see the unfolding pattern. Imagine if you would, that at the same time you are participating, you are also above the fray, listening with a third ear and observing with a third eye, much like an out-of-body experience.

What you are striving for is the perspective of an outsider. This will enable you to care, but not t-h-a-t much. What seems certain to me is that satisfaction in life is often best achieved by finding the proper balance between effort and relaxation. In the final analysis it's not what happens but your view of what happens that counts. For what you and I see is often determined by what we already believe and think we know. Surely we don't see with our eyes but with our brain. And to further complicate what we call "objective reality" may be our relative position in space and time. Conceivably, that's why in Antarctica the temperature at which water freezes is called the "melting point."

Picture it this way: Effective negotiating requires balance. That means everything in moderation . . . including moderation. You want to care but not t-h-a-t much, just as you want to trust, but not t-h-a-t much.

It is in this sense that Islam's Hadith, which are the sayings and teachings of the Prophet Muhammad, declares, "Trust in Allah, but always tie up your camel."

PROMINENT POINTS

- Whenever you engage in any purposive social exchange or negotiation, detach yourself emotionally to gain perspective, so you can see the pattern, relationships, and interconnection of things.
- To be effective in influencing behavior, start out by trying to acquire information about your counterpart's beliefs, motives, values, and underlying needs.
- Always view yourself as a problem solver, searching for creative alternatives that can satisfy both sides' real concerns and interests.
- Since all behavior makes sense from the standpoint of the actor, attempt to see the problem through *their* eyes and experiences.
- In dealing with avowed opponents, realize that getting them to change is in direct ratio to their pain threshold. Behavior won't be altered until they believe that the danger of intransigence outweighs the cost of accommodation.
- When we care too much our adrenaline starts flowing, causing us to become doped up and dumbed down.
- Even when subjected to irrational discourse, emotional diatribes, or the threat of an impasse, strive for a balanced attitude of caring, but not t-h-a-t much.

CHAPTER II

SALVATION BY NEGOTIATION

Your destiny may not be in the hands
of the gods, but in your own head.

1

AN AGELESS PHENOMENON

Negotiating, in the sense of one human being attempting to affect another's behavior, is older than recorded history. It was common in the earliest, most primitive cultures, where ritualistic interactions took place to build bonds of friendship that held communities together. From time immemorial people have been playing this game. Just look at the earliest pieces of literature or the most venerable religious texts and you will find them replete with anecdotes and episodes involving negotiations.

Early in the Book of Genesis of the Old Testament there is a story that you may recall. It's when the Lord informs Abraham that he intends to destroy the sinful Twin Cities. In other words, Sodom and Gomorrah must go. Which is to say, they're history.

From what occurs subsequently we know that Abraham does not agree with the Lord's solution. Although this is not exactly an equal or symmetrical relationship, Abraham tries to question the decision. Actually, in doing so he is in a rather awkward, tenuous, or precarious position. Why? He is after all trying to negotiate with the Almighty. I call this operating from a position of less leverage. Hey, whenever anyone says to you, "Okay, get out there and negotiate with the Almighty," it doesn't take a lot of smarts to figure out that the power may be on the other side.

Now it is instructive, at least to me, how Abraham goes about this task. Does he tell the Lord, "You know in the past your decision making was outstanding. Your judgment, impeccable. So, I always went along. But I think you may have blown this one!"

No, no. If you go back to your Bible you will see Abraham's humble, low-key, deferential approach to persuasion.

"Gee, you know, I was just thinking about what you were saying," he utters. "Overall, another judicious decision on your part, so eminently fair, as I knew it would be. No surprises there."

Abraham pauses, then softly declares, "However, a question sort of popped into my head. I was just wondering, what if we were to come up with fifty good and decent people there, amidst all the evil and corrupt?" Then answering his own question with a question: "Do you think it would be right to kill the fifty good along with all the wicked? . . . Just asking!"

Assuredly, the Lord will respond. Why? Because all negotiations embody action and reaction. Think of your own experience. You make a proposal to someone and what do they do? Usually they return with a counterproposal. There's a demand, which is followed by an offer; a bid that follows the asking price. But sometimes when given a proposal, the other side doesn't even respond. Yet, you also understand that not to respond is still a response.

Why is this so? Because we're talking about a paradoxical game. It's an enigma or conundrum, where things on its face make absolutely no sense, yet at an underlying level it somehow does. It's like Chicago's O'Hare Airport, where more planes land than take off. Which, parenthetically, many of us can't figure out. It's like answering the question, "What do you say to God when he sneezes?" Presumably a paradox of sorts.

Which brings us back to the negotiation with the Almighty and Abraham's proposal. "Well what if I came up with fifty good and decent people there among all those wicked?"

The Lord reacts, "All right, Abraham, you find those fifty and I'll spare all of Sodom and Gomorrah."

"Gee, I really didn't do a count," Abraham hesitates. "What if I'm five short? How would you feel about forty-five?"

"Okay, Abraham, locate those forty-five and the cities will survive."

"But, Lord," Abraham pleads, "I'm speaking figuratively. For all I know, there may be only twenty-five."

"Absolutely, Abraham, find just twenty-five, and I will spare everyone in those places," the Almighty responds.

Ultimately the Bible tells us how Abraham brought the Lord down to ten, which I personally feel is damn good negotiating. The only problem was that Abraham could not come up with the ten. (Ironically, that may be another subject entirely.)

2

FAMILIARITY BREEDS CHILDREN

In relating this example, I have two purposes in mind. For one thing I want to emphasize that you know more about negotiating than you realize. Chances are you have children or occasionally come into proximity with nephews or nieces who choose this process in an attempt to further their interests. Never mind that you yourself were once a child—a little person in a big person's world. Yet even though small fry are without formal power or authority, kids seem to get a heck of a lot of what they want: a few with extravagant demands and blatant manipulative maneuvers, while others employ more subtle means of persuasion. How do these petite persons do it?

Number one, kids have high aspiration levels. They aim high, somehow knowing that we ultimately attain what we think we can attain. Their motto: "If you expect more, you get more." Fact is that empirical evidence supports this idea. On this last point you may remember the German scientist Wernher von Braun, who developed the V-2 missile and after World War II came to the United States to develop rockets for the Army and then NASA. Fittingly, a movie based on his life was called *I Aim at the Stars*. Well, he never hit the stars, although he hit London an awful lot. Granted, it pulled up his performance. Accordingly, youngsters with their unreasonable requests do surprisingly well.

Number two, children understand the decision-making process

within their family organization. Initially they may approach their mom with a request. Rejected, they don't stop there but go to their dad, only to be similarly spurned. Up against a united front, you might think that the child would give up. But no, they appeal to the grandparents. After all, despite the hefty generational gap, it's easy to build a coalition against the common enemy: the parents.

Number three, kids recognize in their gut that "no" is an opening bargaining position. They appreciate instinctively that it takes a while to get used to a new idea. So they are willing to wait and wear you down with sheer tenacity and persistence.

Last of all, your progeny, these little nippers, have been interacting with you for years, shaping your behavior. This makes them bold because "those who carve the Buddha never worship him."

My wife and I are the parents of three children. With the oldest child, our daughter, I remember we used to have principles. And we insisted that she adhere to these standards. Then came the second child, her brother. Sure, we had the same standards, but many more exceptions. Unknowingly, we had become a bit more flexible. Finally, the third child came. By then, having been through all of this stuff before, we were tired people. Actually, I remember saying to the youngest, "Why don't you ask your sister or brother, they'll tell you how it used to be around here."

By virtue of these kinds of encounters you may be more versed in this subject than you realize. When confronted by a situation of potential conflict at home or in your career, recognize that you've probably been there before. Certainly the cast of characters, the setting, and the issues at stake are different, but try to conceptualize from your past experiences. If you can do that, you'll relax and build your confidence.

3

GETTING FRAMED

The second point I wish to make is that one of the reasons we are disappointed with a negotiation outcome is that all too often we accept the way the other side has framed the issue or formulated the problem. At the "endgame stage" they will ask one of the "surefire closers": It's now up to you! Yes or no? Is there a deal or do I walk? Is this a go or no-go situation? Do you or don't you want my business? What's it going to be, A or B?

At the time we evaluate what we've heard and think: "Gee, A is terrible for me, but B on the other hand is only poor." Now if that's the range of my alternatives, I think I'll go with poor. Obviously, it's much better than terrible. Except if you contemplate for a moment, you will realize that you're virtually never limited in this way. Even an ultimatum that appears on its face to be a twofold choice is not. Remember, this is "The World of Illooshin" where "things are seldom what they seem, even skim milk masquerades as cream." Sure, you can take it or leave it, but there's a third choice. In any ultimatum, unexpressed but understood is that you can always come back with another option. So it's never between A or B. Out there somewhere there's a crucial C, maybe an M, perchance a P, or the omen of an omega. In short, there may be a more suitable alternative or even a more creative selection that was not presented.

In the realm of politics, pollsters, pundits, and spinners practice this art of impression management. They know that what really matters are not the facts themselves but the name you succeed in imposing on the facts.

ITEM: My son Steve pulled a slight variation of this forced choice, or entrapment ploy, when he was about eleven years old. Concerned about how I would react to his disappointing grades, he handed me his report card and asked, "Dad, what do you think my problem is? Nature or nurture?"

But why do we get caught in this rut? Well, part of the problem I suspect is that if you went to grade school in North America, the teachers communicated how they recognized the gifted student. First, if called upon, they had the correct answer. The second way they could be identified was when the teacher asked a question of the whole class. Here the bright student was the one who got his or her hand in the air first. For the impressionable young, the conclusion was inescapable: Speed of response puts you on the fast track to success.

4

SPEED KILLS

What's more, this behavior of hustle and dispatch is reinforced in a culture where change and acceleration are signs of progress. Conversely, those who appear reflective or thoughtful are sometimes labeled "ignorant."

Interestingly enough, to underscore this point is the popular television program *Who Wants to Be a Millionaire,* credited as the salvation of the ABC network. Having watched the show, it strikes me that the questions are not that difficult (except for pop culture) but I myself would never be able to earn the coveted contestant's seat across from the host, Regis Philbin. Oh sure, I might qualify for the trip to New York City where it's taped, but that's as far as I would get. Because in order to be singled out to answer the money questions, you must put four choices in chronological or geographical order in 2.6 seconds. Are you kidding? Not even my fingers work that fast.

5

"WHAHDJA SAY?"

While rote memory and speed will pay off on *Millionaire* or *Jeopardy!*, the same may not be appropriate in life. As a matter of fact, in negotiating the opposite is desirable. Sure enough, dumb is really better than smart and inarticulate is preferable to articulate. You actually want to train yourself to say, "I dunno" . . . "I don't understand" . . . "Gee, I'm sorry, you lost me" . . . "Could you please repeat that" . . . "Where are we?"

In the tradition of the Socratic pose of ignorance and the Bible, which commands us, "Teach thy tongue to say I do not know," try to divest yourself of preconceived notions, biases, and prejudices. Ignorance, even if feigned, would produce curiosity, humility, open-mindedness, and ultimately innovative ideas that may bring people together.

ITEM: About five years ago I was called to Milwaukee, Wisconsin, to try to help settle a labor dispute at the eleventh hour. Since this was a rush call, I hardly had the time to familiarize myself with the issues involved or the history of labor-management relations in the industry. So I spent my time listening to both sides trying to find meaning in their words. On one occasion, after hearing an emotional account of a grievance, I remember saying, "Wow, I understand why

41

you're upset and how you must feel." When asked what I thought, I just threw up my hands and said, "I dunno." By the way, this was no playacting on my part, I really didn't know. In a little over a day, the matter was settled just prior to the deadline.

While we were gathering our things and shaking hands all around, the union steward took me aside and remarked, "You realize, Herb, that in one day I've come to like and trust you. You know why?" He didn't wait for my reply. "It's because you're a damn modest guy." My face was starting to feel flush when he hit me with the zinger. "But then, you have a lot to feel modest about."

What I'm saying is, if "ignorance is bliss," why pretend to be wise? Slow down, control your response, and tread softly. Qualify what you have to say. If someone asks you a question, you do not have to respond immediately. Take your time. Teach yourself to dwell amidst silence and ambiguity. Don't be in a hurry to clarify things. Remember, this is not commercial television where you are paying for airtime.

Get in the habit of answering questions with questions. Whenever you're stuck, ask the other party, "If you were me what would you do?" No matter how they respond you are never in trouble because you can always come back with, "Gee, it's too bad you're not me." And you're back to where you were.

6

LEND ME A HAND

There is an inescapable truth about relationships: People appreciate hearing the words "Help me." No matter what you may be talking about, the other party has information, expertise, knowledge, or experience that you do not possess. Thus we need them to willingly share what they have, which will facilitate getting to yes. Moreover, there is always the subject of implementation and commitment to what was agreed upon. Here you don't want them to just go through the motions but you need their assistance and support. Evidently, Saint Paul recognized this dilemma when, discussing mere literal compliance, he said, "The letter kills but the spirit gives life."

As you read this, some of you will be going into negotiations or selling situations where you feel you are overmatched and overwhelmed. Why? Well, you may be a woman and they're all men. You are just out of school and she seems to be seasoned and experienced. You operate a small business and they represent a Fortune 500 company. Your bald head is reflecting light and he has flowing, styled hair. You have despair and doubt, and she has assurance and aplomb. You are open and straightforward, and he is devious and overbearing. You are diminutive in stature, and they are tall and imposing. You have a large bulbous nose, and he has picture-perfect nostrils. Whatever the reason, you're permitting

yourself to enter this situation feeling disadvantaged and disheartened.

Before I go further, allow me to make a point of personal privilege. What you and I look like and even to some extent our personality come to us courtesy of life's genetic crap shoot. In other
words, we shouldn't receive credit and certainly not accept blame
for the cards that we have been dealt. However, each of us has a
great deal of free will in determining how we play our hand.

Take my last illustration, the silly cultural fixation on nose size
and shape. Apparently, from what I hear and observe, there are
better noses and worse noses. I don't understand it. If the purpose
of a nose is to smell, you would think the bigger the better. So the
best proboscis would be a schnozzle about the size of an eggplant.
But no, the late Tip O'Neill's bulbous smeller was not held up as
perfection. Rather, if you look at magazine covers seen by susceptible youth, there are models and celebrities with ever-smaller
snouts, like Michael Jackson. It's as if perfection will ultimately be
two holes drilled right into your skull.

So if you ever feel hindered or hobbled by physical factors, inexperience, or just plain lack of bargaining leverage, reveal that
right at the outset. Turn to the other party and say, "Look, I'd like
to apologize for my inexperience" or, "I really appreciate that you,
representing Microsoft, are taking the time to see me" or, "Perhaps I shouldn't be saying this but I'm feeling awkward because . . ." All of these openers should then be followed by the
wondrous words—"Please help me." If you are able to carry this
off with sincerity and goodwill you may be surprised by the reaction. Almost half the time you will transform what might have
been an adversary into an ally and in some instances even a men-
tor.

1

ATTUNED TO THE MUSIC

Please do not mistake the thrust of my remarks. I am not a pacifist, nor one who believes in the sacrifice of ethical principles and values for the expediency of even a profitable deal. What I am saying is that if faced with a situation where you are uncomfortable and trust has not been established, a softer demeanor can favorably affect the negotiating climate. It should be borne in mind that you do not have to overtly counteract each tactic or redress every ploy.

Arguably, the most influential individual in the history of our world was the carpenter from Nazareth, who left a legacy that has affected the lives of billions of people. His impact in three short years was so great that we measure time itself being before (B.C.) or after (A.D.) his life.

Jesus Christ came not to judge but to help. He had a vision to change the world, teaching new ways of thinking that produced a new testament. By my definition—using information and power to affect behavior—he was a negotiator par excellence. Not only did he negotiate to gain the support of his disciples and followers but also he negotiated with the Almighty on behalf of the poor and powerless.

Yet when Jesus stepped into the public arena, alone and unknown, he was confronted by the military might of the Roman Empire. Instead of trying to counter force with force, he used an accommodation approach or what could be called a "meekness maneuver." In a nutshell: turning the other cheek. As stated in the Gospel of Luke, "So unto him that smiteth thee on the one cheek offer also the other."

Think of it: What satisfaction can be derived from defeating a defenseless opponent? When an aggressor strikes a helpless victim and his blows are not returned, what is the after-effect? In most cases the upshot is an assailant overcome with frustration and regret. As you know, this "meekness maneuver" later became Gandhi's "nonviolent resistance" and was adopted by Martin Luther King Jr. in the civil rights movement. From all indications, these three champions of passive resistance achieved their objectives but not without cost. Still, if the opponent were amoral or immoral, the likes of Hitler, Stalin, Pol Pot, Saddam Hussein, or a "true believer," the outcome would be disastrous.

8

ABRACADABRA

Let me share with you the magic words of effective negotiating. Words I trust you will memorize and make part of your vocabulary for use in life's strategic interactions. These utterances or jargon should become part of your lexicon to make the initial pose of ignorance credible.

They are wee words, each three letters. The first is spelled H-U-H and pronounced HUH. Second word is spelled W-H-A. Note there is no T on this and it is pronounced WHA. Now what you want to do is integrate the two, so you can utter HUH . . . WHA . . . or maybe even UH . . . HUH . . . WHA. Instantly you will find that all your social exchanges will become more fun and satisfying.

Quite conceivably some of you at this point may be shocked. Perhaps you are thinking, "Before acquiring this book I was doing fine in my life and profession. I only started reading this to polish a few skills. But if I listen to this guy and start blurting out HUH and WHA, my whole life could go down the drain."

For those of you who feel that way, let me assure you that I can relate to those sentiments. For that reason, I will furnish you with an alternate option, a maneuver slightly more sophisticated than HUH and WHA. Remember, my overall purpose is to try to get you to slow down, because in negotiations quick is risky. And it is especially hazardous for those less prepared, who cannot determine equity in a given situation.

For instance, suppose you are embroiled in a prospective deal with someone who is more familiar with the details than you are. Suddenly they change the terms or specifications or introduce something unexpected. He or she looks to you for an immediate reaction. What do you do? Surely you need to delay, to stall until you can evaluate the consequences of this new idea.

If you are with someone, a member of your team, you can always say, "Excuse us for a moment, we're going to the rest room together, it's our team tradition." Naturally, you withdraw from the meeting place and jointly discuss what transpired before returning with your response.

But what if you are alone and you don't want to leave the room, but need time to think? Well, here's what I do. Unexpectedly, I develop a rapport with the pen that I have in the inside pocket of my jacket. I think about this particular writing instrument that has been by itself for hours since I got dressed that morning. Identifying with it, I know it's dark in that pocket. It's lonely. It's humid there. Bending my head to see how it's doing, I even imagine odors coming from that pocket.

So what do I do? Sympathetic to its predicament, I liberate the pen, freeing it from its confines. Holding it in the air, I spin it around in my hand. Then pulling off the cap and exposing the tip, I proceed to purse my lips and blow, furnishing it with an even greater sense of freedom. Finally, with the completion of this emancipation ritual the pen is returned to the pocket.

Watching this rite performed, usually in stunned silence, is the other side. Typically, I turn to them and say, "Where were we?" At the very least this gives me time to contemplate. And more often than not it lightens the atmosphere by providing an amusing diversion.

9

A HOLLYWOOD EXEGESIS

As mentioned previously, negotiation has always been an important feature of human relationships. Anthropologists tell us that as early as 5,000 B.C., family units, kinfolk, and then later entire tribes traveled together for mutual assistance and protection from enemies. Although these groups had norms, rules, and codes of behavior regulating common interests, disputes would still arise over relationships and the division of labor. When this occurred, the revered tribal chief might intervene or, if not, the parties would attempt other conflict resolution methods—ranging from combat to negotiating. Yet there are few recorded details about these transactions.

The earliest documents that we have that specify complex purposive social exchanges come to us from the Bible. Previously, we discussed how in the Book of Genesis, Abraham established the precedent of reasoning with the Lord in an attempt to achieve justice. In my opinion, however, the most vivid examples that employ actual negotiating techniques still viable today can be found in the Book of Exodus. While we cannot be certain of the exact dates of the events that I will be describing, most scholars believe they occurred roughly three thousand years ago, when Shirley MacLaine was born in Egypt during one of her previous lives.

The central character in this chronicle is Moses, who, acting on behalf of the Almighty, liberates thousands of Hebrew slaves from bondage and brings them to the Promised Land. In the course of the journey he must bargain with Pharaoh, interact with the Children of Israel, and most important of all, negotiate with the Lord. Surely, their ultimate rescue and deliverance is a saga of salvation by negotiation.

For our purposes, let me begin the narrative with our protagonist. Moses was born in Egypt at the time it was ruled by a bloodthirsty pharaoh. His mother, Jochebed, and father, Amram, were both slaves as was his older sister, the eight-year-old Miriam, who worked in the palace for Pharaoh's youngest daughter. Completing the family was Moses' brother, Aaron.

Perhaps at this point I ought to inform you that I am far from being a biblical scholar. In truth, the version of events I am offering may not be totally authoritative. It comes primarily from having seen Cecil B. DeMille's epic motion picture *The Ten Commandments* at least twenty times. Honestly, when I say Moses I see Charlton Heston. Writing "Pharaoh" brings Yul Brynner to mind. Even Pharaoh's daughter for me is Nina Foch, just as Aaron is John Carradine. As you know he's Keith's and David's father. With this qualifier out of the way, let's get back to the story.

Just months prior to the coming of Moses, Pharaoh learns of a prophecy circulating among the Israelites: "A male Hebrew child will soon be born and he will become a brilliant liberator and leader who will cause Pharaoh big problems and much tsorris or worry." Reacting immediately, Pharaoh issued an edict that said, "Every Hebrew boy-child born will be thrown into the Nile and drowned." Quite naturally, Moses' mother was reluctant to go along with the program. Jochebed fed the infant for three months in secret and when he became too big to hide, wrapped him in a blanket, which she placed in a basket she floated down the river. Eventually the basket was found in the bullrushes by Pharaoh's daughter, Nina Foch, who decided to keep him.

That night when Pharaoh returned to the palace he heard the child crying. Immediately he recognized that this male infant was of the Hebrew persuasion. Likely he knew this because of the distinct design of the blanket. Ordering that the child be put to death, he was confronted by a sobbing Princess Nina, who said, "Please let me keep him. He's like a toy . . . a diversion." Though Pharaoh's immovable at first, Nina persists. "It's so boring here, there's nothing to do. I'm tired of watching slaves get whipped. Pleeease?"

After endless "pleeeases," Pharaoh finally relents somewhat. "Enough," he says. But remembering the prophecy, he continues, "You can keep the Hebrew kid providing he fails a simple IQ test."

So Pharaoh orders that two dishes be placed before the infant Moses: one containing glistening gold and the other red-hot embers. "If the baby reaches for the red-hot embers, we will let him live," Pharaoh states. "But if he should be so bright that he would go for the gold (which could be where that expression comes from) we go for the kid. He's dead."

Hence the scene is set for the life-or-death choice. Sages tell us that the infant Moses started to reach for the glistening gold, which sparkled and shimmered, but God intervened, directing his hand toward the scorching coals. Grasping the torrid embers, Moses, like all children his age, had a suckling reflex, so he placed the fiery coals to his lips and tongue. From that day on, the great liberator, lawgiver, and leader stuttered and spoke with a lisp.

Thereafter Moses was raised as one of Pharaoh's grandsons, brought up in luxury and educated as an Egyptian prince. But all this ended when Moses intervened when he saw an Egyptian overseer beating a slave. Accidentally killing the assailant, Moses was forced to flee for his life, crossing the Sinai into Midian. There he received safe haven from Jethro, where he married his daughter, Yvonne De Carlo, had two sons, and became a shepherd. Years passed and he had become so much a Midianite that thinking back to his prior royal life was like trying to recall a dream.

10

AN ATTENTION GRABBER

One day while grazing his sheep, Moses saw what appeared to be a burning bush. Approaching, he noticed that though flames flared around it and he could feel the heat, neither the branches nor leaves were getting singed. Trying to get closer, he was shocked by a booming voice that seemed to be coming from the heavens.

"Moses, go no further! This is holy ground. Take off your sandals."

"Whu, Whu, Who ar, arr, are you?" Moses stammered.

"I am the Lord, the God of Abraham, Isaac, and Jacob. Because I have heard my people's cries and seen their misery, I will deliver them from servitude. You will take them from Egypt to the Promised Land. Now go at once to Pharaoh and tell him to let my people go."

Moses stood there dumbstruck. The Lord, however, did not just dismiss him assuming that he understood and would carry out his wishes.

Obviously God is not just omnipotent and omniscient but also an expert in "attribution theory." Ergo, he said to Moses, "Now what did I just tell you to do?" Putting it in lay terms, he asked for feedback.

Moses tried to respond. "I wi . . . wi . . . will . . . g . . . go . . . to . . . th . . . the . . . wand . . . of . . . Ph . . . Ph . . . Pha . . . oh . . .

Pharaoh . . ." Recall that Moses had a speech impediment, which he got as an infant when Pharaoh tried to assay his intelligence.

God at this point does not remark, "Well, speechcraft is obviously not your strong suit" or, "Before you go, work on your elocution" or possibly, "Forget it, I'll just send Pharaoh a note myself written on papyrus." No indeed, the Lord wants this man for the strength of his character. Meanwhile, aware of Moses' sensitivity to his rhetorical difficulty he presents a face-saving alternative.

"By the way, Moses, is there anyone that might accompany you on this long arduous trek?"

"There, there's my br . . . br . . . brother Air . . . Aar . . . Aar . . . Aaron," he replies.

"Good," the Lord responds. "You take Aaron along. Let him speak for you and that will be your team."

Thus Moses left for Egypt, where he met Aaron and they embarked upon the first hostage negotiation in the annals of history.

11

AXIOMS FROM ABOVE

Although recognizing that we still have not arrived at the heart of this drama, certain negotiating truisms may have already been revealed to us by none other than the Almighty. First of all, the Lord selects Aaron to do the actual bargaining with Pharaoh. Moses will be present but his brother will do the talking. This is in accordance with the principle that ultimate decision makers should stay out of the nitty-gritty of deal making.

Basically, there is a twofold explanation for why we often do not achieve our potential as negotiators. One, as we've seen, is that we are too emotionally involved, caring too much. The second reason is that we have too much authority. What I'm saying is that the last person who should negotiate for a country, corporation, or business is the chief executive officer. Take that one step further and realize that the worst person to negotiate for you is—you. Clearly this presents a practical problem that can be solved by limiting your own authority. Always give yourself room to say, "That sounds good to me but I'll have to check with my board." If you don't have a board, then substitute the word banker, attorney, adviser, boss, or even spouse.

A decade ago I was involved in many negotiations with a woman whose husband and business partner was never in town. Every agreement we made, though, was tentative—subject to his final approval. Years later I learned that she was never married nor did she have a business partner. What I'm urging is that you not make precipitous decisions in the heat of activity under the pressure of time. Allow the opportunity for reflection by circumscribing your ability to say "yes."

Second, it occurs to me that by contemporary standards and tastes Moses would not be in the running for chief negotiator. Fact is, he didn't really look like Charlton Heston or for that matter George Clooney. Probably his appearance was closer to that of Dustin Hoffman in *Rain Man*. More to the point, in today's politically correct terminology, we would say he was "oratorically challenged."

Certainly, the Lord knew that it would take more than glib verbal skills to change the heart and mind of Pharaoh. He understood that, then as now, outstanding negotiators are innovative, patient, dogged, self-reliant, calm under fire, and flexible in thought and action. Evidently these were key qualities that affected the selection process.

Above all I suspect that God, who is all knowing, realized that extracting the hostages from Egypt would be the least of Moses' problems. Much more troubling would be his mission to transform thousands of despairing former slaves into a nation of believers and freedom fighters. Indeed, Moses would ultimately be judged based upon his ability to get these ex-slaves to do voluntarily those things that would have to be done. And that's leadership by negotiation.

Last is the accepted gospel that you have an advantage if accompanied by an associate or companion. Having a sidekick reduces stress, furnishes a sense of support, provides the opportunity for feedback, and allows for more flexibility in tactics. So the inclusion of Aaron, who will be at Moses' side for his entire life, is a deliberate decision. Let me remind you that even the Lone Ranger had his Tonto.

12

BARGAINING WITH A BASTARD

Both in negotiation and drama, conflict is vital to the development of the action. It establishes character, illuminates differences between people, moves the process forward, underscores the issues at stake, and reveals ironies. The confrontation of the forces of God and that of the cruel Pharaoh engage both our intellect and our emotions.

Seeing the movie spectacle as an impressible young person I especially remember the scene where Moses and Aaron stand before the truculent King of Egypt, who sits high above them on his throne bedecked in regalia. At the time I expected to observe the Almighty's model or method for dealing with difficult people.

Unexpectedly, with all the powers of the Lord behind them, Moses and Aaron start the negotiation in a congenial manner. Instead of opening with a threat, they approach Pharaoh in a respectful fashion, explaining why they have come to see him. Only then does Aaron inform Pharaoh (Yul Brynner) of God's request that he free the Israelites.

Still, Yul reacts angrily, "Who is this God? . . . Hey I'm a god myself so how come I never heard of him?" Continuing his rant, Pharaoh especially harangues Moses, who at one time lived as his adopted brother in royal splendor. Finally Moses responds, "This is not me speaking. God says, let my people go."

Pharaoh is about to dismiss them when Aaron asks for a short recess so he might confer with Moses (Charlton Heston). During this brief time-out they decide to answer Pharaoh's question by displaying proof of the true God's power.

Back in Pharaoh's presence, Aaron flings his staff to the ground and it becomes a hissing snake. Recognizing this as the old vaudeville "stick shtick" or stick trick, Yul has his magicians duplicate it. Even when Aaron's snake eats all the others before his eyes Pharaoh is not moved.

Next, Moses points his staff at the river flowing behind them. Aaron speaks, "Do you see that river where you drink and bathe?" Yul nods. "The Almighty as his first plague hereby turns it into blood." Sure enough the river's color is changed from azure blue to dark red. Again, Yul is not swayed. Possibly he's thinking, "Hey this is 1,200 B.C. so we're not that big on hygiene. Also we can get fifty cases of Perrier delivered to the palace daily."

But changing the river to blood, the initial plague, proved little more than an inconvenience. Very much like hearing, "This is the first offer," which you never accept because there's more to come, so too it was with the misery heaped upon Pharaoh and his people. From the second affliction (the nuisance of the frog proliferation) through the ninth plague (the torment of constant darkness), God tightens the screws by increments, making the keeping of Hebrew slaves more burdensome and oppressive.

Although Moses and Aaron started somewhat amiably, this has become a bitter adversarial confrontation. Upon reflection, I have come to believe that what we have been given in this tale is a prototype for dealing with obstinate people. To this day when I'm facing someone who has a reputation for being callous and hard-boiled, I always start cooperative with the hope that they will respond in kind. Put it this way: It's easier to go from cooperative to competitive; whereas it's virtually impossible to reverse this process and maintain your credibility.

Meanwhile, Pharaoh is still defying the command of God. After each plague he promises to allow the slaves to depart only to renege when the scourge ends. Still, there is the final negotiating session as Charlton Heston and Yul Brynner confront each other, their tempers at trigger point. "For the last time," says Charlton, "let my people go."

"The last time," scoffs Pharaoh. "If I see your face again, you die."

"That will not happen," Moses replies, "because at midnight tonight the tenth plague will come, killing all the firstborn sons of the Egyptians. It will take this tragedy for you to let God's people go."

You know what happens. Yul Brynner remains unyielding until faced with the death of his oldest son. Only then does he allow the Hebrew slaves to depart, but not without one last calamitous attempt to recapture them when the Almighty parts the Red Sea. Arguably if the tale ended at this point we might have the proverbial Hollywood happy ending. But it does not.

13

THE ROAD LESS TRAVELED

While the mind boggles at the miraculous escape of the Hebrews, this, however, was only the beginning of their journey. At first they are elated by their deliverance and the Egyptians' fate, but after months of trudging in the hot sun they become discontented and disillusioned. Although the Lord has provided them with food from the sky (manna—"the breakfast of champions"), and Moses brings them to where they can find water, they are not happy campers.

Finally Moses (or Charlton) takes them to the foot of mountains where clouds swirl overhead and lightning is flashing in the sky. "God is here," he said. "Let's build him an altar and maybe he'll come down to us."

When the people heard this they shook with fear. "No, no, if we see the Lord's face we could die," they begged, "please climb the mountain and speak to him for us."

The next morning Moses leaves camp and takes Joshua or John Derek (Bo's late husband) with him. He has him wait halfway up the mountainside. To Charlton Heston and John Derek their time away passed quickly, but for the Hebrews down below weeks went by. Unbeknownst to them, Moses is up there getting instructions and receiving two flat stones upon which God has written the Ten Commandments.

Day after day, the Hebrews waiting for Moses and Joshua sat in the rain and grew more impatient. And as in all Hollywood movies of that era whenever the natives are left alone for too long they become restless and agitated. Troublemakers like Edward G. Robinson spring to the fore.

"Hey what's the story here?" he shouts. "Moses has deserted us. He schlepped us all this way and he's not coming back." Addressing Aaron, he explains, "This is a damn sham. We don't even know where we are. We need a map and there's not a Shell station in sight."

Turning back to the clamoring crowd, he brays, "Nya, life in Egypt was hard, but at least there was a nightlife. Here we got nothing. What we need are options. Yeah, that's it—options. We need a backup God—yeah, in case this one doesn't work out."

The crowd was becoming a mob. Things were getting out of hand. They demanded that Aaron make a God that they could see and touch.

Undoubtedly you recall that Aaron, bowing to this pressure or stalling for time (since I'm a direct descendant, maybe I'm going easy on him), goes about collecting bracelets, earrings, and gold from the Israelites and fashions a Golden Calf for the people to worship. Which they did.

At the same time, though, Moses is at the top of Mount Sinai having just received God's law and oblivious to anything else. Especially ironic is that the first commandment as originally written stated, "I am the Lord your God who brought you out of slavery. You will have no other Gods before me. You will make no images to worship, of animals, people or other living things." So the Israelites are literally and figuratively breaking the leading law of God.

14

NEGOTIATING WITH THE ALMIGHTY

Thus we have Moses, unaware and unknowing about the idol worship taking place among his own people. The Almighty, of course, knows. Suddenly and surprisingly he confronts Moses, as the following indicates:

> Moses, go get thee down: for thy people
> which thou brought out of the land of
> Egypt has corrupted themselves.
> They have turned aside quickly
> out of the way, which I commanded
> them. They have made a molten calf,
> and have sacrificed to it and have
> said these be thy gods, O Israel, which have
> brought thee out of the land of Egypt.
> And the Lord said unto Moses,
> I have seen this people, and, behold it
> is a stiff-necked people.
> Now therefore let me alone, that my
> wrath wax hot against them, and that I may
> consume them: and I will make of thee a great
> nation.
>
> EXODUS 32:7–10

Imagine how Moses felt after hearing this. Initially the revelation of what his followers were doing came like a bolt out of the blue. But the Lord's proposal had to leave him thunderstruck.

Consider this: Moses at this point is about eighty years of age. He's got arthritis, sciatica, and gingivitis. In one year he has gone from the calm of a shepherd's life to the aggravation of dealing with Pharaoh. For months now he's been dragging himself around in the hot sun arguing with these complaining Hebrews. Indeed, he finds himself thinking, "Why am I doing this at my age? I'm tired. I should be with *my* chosen people in a condominium in North Miami Beach."

Upon reflection here's what is going through his mind: You know, I never asked for this job. I was minding sheep when the burning bush starts talking to me. Now the Big Guy is saying "*thou* people" which "*thou* broughtest." Wait a second. I never chose these people and it wasn't my idea to free them. Besides, what's his solution? Sure he doesn't like the stubborn Hebrews. He wants to get rid of them. But then I'm supposed to find a new Chosen People? Oh boy, I'm going to have one helluva recruiting problem. Can you see me on a scouting trip to the Amalekites, Midianites, or Canaanites. What do I say to them? Hey there, how would you like to be the new Chosen People? We march you around the desert for six months then wipe you out. Any volunteers? No, no. No matter how bad these Hebrews are we know their faults. Why go from the known to the unknown?

Having surmised all this, it follows the Lord's plan does not meet Moses' needs. From what we know now, he did not have a knee-jerk reaction to just go along. Believing that you can at least attempt to negotiate anything and bolstered by God's previous dialogue with Abraham over the destruction of Sodom and Gomorrah, let's speculate on Moses' strategy. Essentially he must adapt to satisfy the Almighty's underlying concerns and interests.

So here's the "Mosaic" for negotiating with a much more powerful entity:

1) Get the other side to realize that this is a mixed-motive situation. While there is an initial difference as to how to solve this particular problem, the parties have a great deal in common as to their ultimate goals. Instead of viewing this as Moses versus the Lord, it should really be both of them versus the problem to be solved.

2) There is a need to formulate this matter differently, to reframe the issue so that a mutually satisfying solution can be found.

3) The overture should display humility and respect. Due deference and recognition must be given to what the might and power of the Almighty has already accomplished.

4) Seek to subtly remind God of the investment that he has in his chosen people—what they have previously been through together.

5) Try to have the Lord identify with the Hebrews as his people. Remind him that he made the selection and he brought them forth to freedom.

6) Attempt to have the Almighty ponder the consequences of his initial decision to consume the Israelites. What will his enemies think? Remember this is the Middle East where "the enemy of my enemy is my friend."

7) Reminisce with God about the admirable ancestors of these people whom he liked and to whom he made promises. The implication, of course, is that the Lord would never go back on his word.

With this strategic thought process in mind let's move to the next portion of our biblical text:

> But Moses pleaded before his God.
> Lord, why doth thy wrath wax hot against *thy* people,
> which *thou* has brought forth out of the land of Egypt
> with great power and a mighty hand?
> Wherefore should the Egyptians speak, and say,
> For mischief did He bring them out, to slay them in
> the mountains, and to consume them from the face

of the earth? Turn from thy fierce wrath, and repent
of this evil against *thy* people.

Remember Abraham, Isaac, and Israel, thy servants, to
whom thou swearest by thine own self, and saidst unto
them, I will multiply your seed as the stars of heaven,
and all this land that I have spoken of will I give unto
your seed, and they shall inherit it forever.

And the Lord repented of the evil which He thought
to do to *His* people.

EXODUS 32:11–14

Most of us know the rest of the story. For their transgressions
the Hebrews had to spend the next forty years in the wilderness.
But the laws given to them during that time formed the ethical
foundation for the three major monotheistic religions of Judaism,
Christianity, and Islam.

PROMINENT POINTS

- Because there is a correlation between aspiration level and outcome, set high goals.
- In the language of negotiation, "no" does not mean never. Instead, it is a reflexive reaction to the unexpected or an opening
  bargaining position.
- Don't necessarily accept the way the other side has framed an
  issue or formulated the problem.
- Since fast responses can produce detrimental consequences,
  slow down, ask questions, and seek clarification.
- Especially if you are taken by surprise and cannot determine
  equity, find ways to stall or delay, ranging from calling a recess
  to identifying with your pen or wristwatch.

- The best response to those who have all the answers is to say, "I dunno" or, "I don't understand" or, "Please help me."
- Generally, begin negotiations in an amiable fashion using the Socratic pose of ignorance.
- Keep the ultimate decision maker out of the nitty-gritty of deal making. If that's not possible, convince him of the need to circumscribe his own capacity to say "yes"
- Where practical, have an associate with you when you go into a bargaining session.
- Always begin all strategic interactions in a congenial and respectful manner in the hope that your counterpart will respond in kind. If they don't reciprocate, it's easier to move from a mode of cooperation to one of competition than vice versa.

APPLYING MOSES' MOSAIC

- Display humility, deference, and respect, commending the other side for what they have previously accomplished.
- Remind your negotiating partner of your shared history that is worth preserving.
- Because negotiating is a mixed-motive game, instead of initially focusing upon areas of disagreement, start with mutual interests. While differences exist, point out how both sides' ultimate goals are compatible.
- View the conflict as an opportunity to solve the problem creatively where everyone's needs are satisfied.
- Subtly remind your negotiating partner of the investment they've already made.
- Call attention to the ultimate distasteful and problematic consequences of their proposal that perhaps they have not considered.
- Delicately mention the commitments previously made and your faith that your partner would never go back on his or her word.

CHAPTER III

PLAYING THE GAME

The singer counts for more than the song just as the players are more important than the plays.

We have just seen how one human being affected the behavior of a much more powerful entity. Implicit in this account is the style Moses used in negotiating with the Almighty. By this I mean his demeanor or way of communicating. From what we know, it consisted of a soft voice, deferential bearing, and humble attitude. In the end it may be that this demeanor more than the substance of his request was what carried the day.

1

STYLE SUPERSEDES SUBSTANCE

Today in the era of negotiation your approach can have the same effect. For the way you put your thoughts into words and the language of your behavior combine to mirror your character. It's from this that people make an initial assessment of your sincerity and trustworthiness. Remember, throughout this process they are asking themselves, "Is this the type of person we want to do business with?"

By style I mean *how* you negotiate. It's your approach and manner. Be assured that it counts for more than *what* you're talking about or the content of the discussion. Beneficial aspects of style are characterized by displays of the following: active listening, warmth and sensitivity, patience, sharing of feelings, and consideration for others' worth and self-esteem. Thus, *how* you engage in this process will affect emotions, feelings, perceptions, rapport, trust, and expectations.

What, on the other hand, deals with things that are openly discussed and can be quantified like quality, delivery dates, amounts, price, technology transfer, or contract wording. Although we talk about these items, which are easy to verbalize, ultimately it's style that supersedes substance in decision making.

Having said this, I am not suggesting that you transform yourself into something you are not. Too many people in this age of celebrity try to be someone else. Their life becomes a comic or tragic mimicry. More precisely, I am saying that you should be yourself on purpose. In fact it's the celebration of your singularity that will enable you to relax and give you freedom to play the game.

As you read this, many of you who have been exposed to my speech pattern and attitude know that, if nothing else, I'm distinct. Ponder if you will Bella Abzug, Mel Brooks, César Chávez, Perry Como, Katharine Graham, Katharine Hepburn, Barbara Jordan, David Mamet, Thurgood Marshall, Golda Meir, Harry Truman, John Wayne, Paul Wellstone, and even G. Gordon Liddy. What they have in common is that each prospered. And did so precisely because they remained true to their authentic selves.

All this is significant because you and your style can make a big difference. Make no mistake, you the singer count for more than the song. Just as in sports, it's the players not necessarily the plays that affect the final outcome.

Why is it that this timeless truth has not received wider recognition? By way of answering, let me share a story from my own life.

Many years ago when I was working in the corporate world our district office received a visit from a home office auditor. After spending days sitting there in his green eyeshades counting beans or whatever he was doing, we were told his wrap-up conference would be held that afternoon from 2:00 to 4:00. Unfortunately that morning I had made a commitment to pick up one of my children at school and take him to the doctor at 3:30. Before the meeting started I informed the auditor that I had this scheduling conflict. When advised what it was, he frowned and rolled his eyes.

More troubling was that during the session itself, when asked to explain a particular finding, he remarked, "Well, I'd love to, but we don't have time, thanks to Herb." But he did have the time to preach to us and sermonize. At one point he even said, "If you people spent more time working, you wouldn't have some of these discrepancies." Clearly I felt this little caustic comment was aimed directly at me.

Suffice to say, I found his words to be inane, inaccurate, and inappropriate. But more, he personally was dumb, despicable, and disgusting. Although knowing rationally that *he* had the problem and not me, I found myself tightening and churning inside. Indeed, my first reaction was to strike back and achieve at least some verbal retribution.

But even back then I knew that for the sake of my livelihood I would have to mask these primitive urges and don the executive facade, which I did. Then, about 3:20, I excused myself and left to fulfill my obligation.

That evening when my wife came home, I couldn't wait to tell her what happened at the afternoon meeting. Still seething inside and needing to unburden myself, I felt she would appreciate my sacrifice and stoicism.

As soon as she walked through the door, I began telling her what I went through that day. At the same time she was hanging up her coat and went into the kitchen to make some tea. She was listening all right—but not t-h-a-t much. After I finally concluded my passionate recounting of events, her first reaction was, "Well that's the way life is. They never promised you a rose garden." "Hey," I said to myself, "when it comes to giving empathy, she was stopping at nothing."

Annoyed at what looked like apathy I said, "Would you listen to what I'm saying because I'm going to tell you this one more time." Would you believe that I actually told the story again? Only this time I myself was listening. Surprisingly it didn't sound that bad even to me.

Exasperated I eventually said, "Look, it's not *what* he said, it's the *way* or *how* he said it. If you would have been there you would understand."

The question is, why was it so difficult for me to get across the depth of my feelings? The answer, of course, is that this is a bottom-line culture where if you can't quantify something, we believe it doesn't exist. And because it's so arduous to put the whole *how* into words, we tend to think it's of little significance.

But it's not. You show me someone who is admired and influential and without doubt it's a person whose style commands respect. These are individuals who cause things to happen and whose lives leave an imprint upon the planet.

A case in point would be Pope John Paul II, who has imparted the values of peace, freedom, and faith to the world. To my mind he was one of the crucial few who helped bring about the peaceful implosion of the Soviet empire.

As you no doubt know, the central doctrine of this Pontiff is his reverence for life. Hence, the Roman Catholic Church in his time has strongly emphasized its stand against capital punishment, abortion, and even the use of birth control devices. In spite of these prohibitions, polls of practicing Roman Catholics in the United States inform us that a substantial majority are for the death penalty and employ contraceptives to limit the size of their families. Yet these same believers hold Karol Wojtyla and his teachings in the highest regard. Inconsistent? Not at all. They are simply expressing appreciation for his self-sacrifice, noble intentions, and—not the least—his style.

2

THE WAY OF THE GIPPER

Perhaps an even more vivid example is the most prominent President of our lifetime, Ronald Reagan. Some political savants have suggested that his popularity was due to his policies and programs. Except that when I worked for him, I wasn't even sure what they were. Not that anyone else knew either!

Yet, President Reagan was a political giant who possessed firm convictions and unerring instincts. He was a man of boundless optimism and faith in the American people. In the course of eight years he faced down the "Evil Empire," changed the direction of government, presided over the restoration of patriotism, and caused a resurgence of the national economy. No mean feat.

Ironically enough, when the Gipper was beginning his political career no one expected much. In fact, when Hollywood's Jack Warner heard that the Republicans were thinking of running Reagan for governor, he is reported to have said, "No, no. It's Jimmy Stewart for governor, Ronald Reagan for best friend."

When Reagan became our fortieth President, complaints continued about his lack of intellectual substance and his advanced age. Even when he nominated the first woman, Sandra Day O'Connor, to the Supreme Court he didn't get much credit. Here again they joked, "Being hearing-impaired he probably thought he was appointing Sandra Dee." Certainly, the media's impression was that he was not a man of substance—all facade with a hollow core. Likewise, Edmund Morris in his authorized biography, *Dutch,* compared Ronald Reagan to the planet Jupiter, "a diffuse amorphous object with a huge gravitational force."

In reality what enabled President Reagan to achieve his objectives was his style. And this was communicated to his constituency via television. What they saw was idealism, optimism, congeniality, self-assurance, and above all self-deprecating humor. He just looked and behaved in a way that Americans understand and respect.

Embodying these style characteristics that are very American, it was relatively easy for President Reagan to relate well to the national electorate and they to him. You may even say it was close to a perfect fit.

3

AN OUTSIDER'S VIEW

Truly I say this because in 1831 an aristocratic French sociologist by the name of Alexis de Tocqueville came to this country, where he traveled about meeting and interviewing Americans. He took extensive notes, so when he went back to France he was able to write *Democracy in America,* a two-volume study in which he explained us to ourselves. Now, how come this foreigner could explain me to me? Why haven't I been able to figure me out? Well, it's difficult for me to really know myself. For in trying to gain this self-awareness, I've got to look at me through me, which creates distortion. That's why it's often said that "it takes two to see one." Actually, as I would say, "Does the fish know it's in the water?" Have you ever wondered about that? Presumably not.

But candidly, I'm obsessed by this. Throughout my life I find myself constantly watching fish swim through water. They are so graceful. But then the fish makes its last move. Its final mistake. Yeah, it lunges for food, which we term bait. The food is always impaled on a hook, so the fish not only gets the food but the hook as well. When this happens I'm usually with a child who is mercilessly reeling up his catch. In all these years I've noticed that when fish break through the water, their behavior and befuddlement is ever the same. Their body is contorted and their eyes bulge. Their mouth opens and closes as if to say, "What the hell . . . I was in the water!" Now what did they think—that blurred vision was the norm? Thus it's hard for us to know ourselves. Often it takes a third party to edify us.

So what did this outside observer Tocqueville tell us about Americans?

There were three characteristics, he said, that he did not find prevalent among other peoples.

Number 1, we prefer issues that are pure and simple—framed in black and white.

Number 2, we are an almost blindly optimistic people, always upbeat and hopeful.

Number 3, we relate to and respect regular and authentic guys, those who come across as fallible and human.

4

LESS IS MORE

For one thing, we like things simply put, believing in good and bad, right versus wrong, for me or against me, friend or foe. Americans then and now are reluctant to embrace nuances, gradations, or subtleties.

About 1993 I was interviewed on a national television program and asked whether I thought the United States would be sending ground forces to fight in Bosnia-Herzegovina. My response was immediate, "Absolutely not."

Taken aback the host inquired, "How can you be so certain?"

"Well," I said, "there are two reasons. One, Americans don't know geography. Since we can't locate Yugoslavia on the map how can we figure out where Bosnia-Herzegovina is? Then there's the main reason, which is that this is a three-party struggle." The questioner looked puzzled, so I continued. "Americans don't get involved in three-party disputes. The only way we might be drawn into this matter is if it were a two-sided war, where it's clearly virtue against evil."

Why are we this way? Probably it's our history, geography, and our social and political system. Maybe there's even some mythology in the mix. Nonetheless, all of this has been reinforced by Hollywood motion pictures, which have given generations of Americans their values. Let me remind you that the films young people see today are not the movies that Ronald Reagan and I saw in our formative years. In my day before we went to a movie we knew what to expect. It wasn't necessary to look in the newspaper or call the theater for show times. We could come in during the middle and still know what was going on. If you walked in and saw on the big screen two horses outside a saloon—one a good horse and the other a bad horse, you knew what was to follow. It was predictable.

John Wayne may have had a wardrobe change but he was the same Duke from role to role. He never let you down. Gary Cooper, who I thought was a fine actor, also was consistent. One year he made eight motion pictures. People said, "Gee how could he memorize all that dialogue?" Well, it wasn't that difficult because the dialogue was always the same: "Yup . . . nope . . . hmm . . . naw . . . aha . . . giddyap . . . yep."

Today, when I go to one of these multiplex theaters or even rent a video it's different. I cannot recognize Meryl Streep from one role to the next. To me that woman is a human chameleon. Robert De Niro and Tom Hanks expand and contract before my very eyes. As for Dustin Hoffman and Robin Williams, I can't always be certain of their gender.

Ronald Reagan is a product of my time, a different, less complicated era. So mirroring the Hollywood heroes of his time he came across as natural, modest, unaffected, and unpretentious. Thus he let people know what he stood for in simple terms, using undecorated language that stirs emotions. Often accused of "the facile categorization of complex issues," who can forget the turning point in the televised presidential debate when Ronald Reagan asked the electorate, "Are you better off now than you were four years ago?"

On another occasion, there was Reagan's seemingly effortless but brilliant framing of what was at stake during the air traffic controllers' (PATCO) strike. At the time, I received a phone call from a top official from PATCO. He asked, "How long do you think the strike will last?" My response was, "Ahhh . . . probably forever."

He said, "No you don't understand. We didn't go out yet."

"That's what I'm trying to tell you," I said. "Don't go." In making this analysis I figured that these guys had made every possible blunder that could be made. Almost without exception, they hit every rut on the road. Presumably the only way this could be done was to double back. In truth, however, the single biggest mistake they made was to let Ronald Reagan frame the issue. Which he did in his own simple way. In effect, he asked the American people, "Is it okay for a government employee to disregard a sacred oath, to strike against the interests of all Americans, in violation of the law of the land?"

Are you kidding? How can anyone win with this issue? The President wrapped himself in the American flag, apple pie, and a hot lunch for orphans. From that moment on, PATCO was perceived by the public to be a greedy, selfish union. Ironically, those who were experts in airplane collision avoidance didn't understand how to apply it to the collective bargaining process.

Ronald Reagan understood at a gut level that people will not necessarily make sacrifices for positive ideals. For instance if I were to say to you, "Will you and I agree to die for liberty?" you might flippantly remark, "Hey why don't you die first, tell me how it was, and then we'll talk about it."

All the same, people will endure suffering if it's against some tangible iniquity. Hence by labeling the Soviet Union the Evil Empire and discussing the threat it posed to our way of life, Reagan was able to get the American people and Congress to go along with a costly military buildup at the expense of social programs.

In the aftermath of the catastrophic terrorist attacks of September 11, George W. Bush was faced with a similar dilemma. Clearly, the strategy of al-Qa'eda was to draw the United States into an immediate, indiscriminate, and massive retaliatory response that would attract Muslims around the globe to fight a holy war.

However, the president was not precipitous but used time to make overtures to the Islamic community, thereby building a broad coalition against terrorism. Moreover, his choice of language, like "evildoers," "you are for us or against us," and so on galvanized the American people and even the Western allies for the struggle that was to come.

5

ALL'S RIGHT WITH THE WORLD

The second thing that Alexis de Tocqueville observed is that we are the most optimistic people he ever encountered. Indeed, even to this day Americans believe that all problems can be solved in our lifetime and all obstacles overcome. We are the only country in the history of this world that has ever declared war against poverty. Poverty has been in existence since the beginning of time. Not only did we declare war against it, but we also had a deadline for knocking it off—giving ourselves three years. Then we would go on to something else.

Al Smith, the Democratic party's presidential candidate in 1928, observed, "Americans don't need umbrellas—we walk in eternal sunshine."

Decades ago there was a Broadway musical that later became a film called *Annie*. The hit song from that musical sold millions of records in North America. Surely you remember it, though I suspect some people wish they could forget it. It's called "Tomorrow" and it had these upbeat lyrics, "The sun will come out tomorrow, bet your bottom dollar that tomorrow there'll be sun . . ." Yet, this recording sold millions of copies in the United States and Canada, despite the fact that it had no beat. Total overseas sales, however, were nineteen. They had no idea what the hell it was about. This is an especially American song made for a country that has always been about becoming, not being; about the outlook for the immediate future and not the legacy of the past. Truly, this is a Polly-annaish place where we're hopefully optimistic about tomorrow, or next week, or next year.

Astonishingly, after being elected to our highest office, Jimmy Carter forgot this characteristic of his constituency. During his presidency he had his "malaise period." When he finally came down from the "mountain," it seemed as if he took political advice from Howard Cosell and he decided to "tell it like it is."

And he did. In effect he told the American people, "Let me be candid with you. Our future is behind us. In fact, the current generation will be the first whose standard of living may be lower than that of their parents. As far as owning your own home, the prospects are bleak, because interest rates are out of control. Actually, we're working hard to get a handle on what's happening. As far as educating your children beyond high school, don't count on it. The likelihood is they won't be going to college because by that time the costs will be prohibitive . . . so vote for me!" Obviously, not the best approach to win the favor of this electorate.

Ronald Reagan, on the other hand, for all his years in politics was always hopeful, congenial, self-assured, and confident. His "Morning in America" TV commercial was not just a political slogan but also a personal expression of optimism that was almost religious in its fervor. So, here was a man who appeared joyful, carefree, enthusiastic, and exuberant. Realistically, however, the man never had a right to be that happy. Why do I say that?

Well, two and a half months into his first term as president there was an assassination attempt that almost killed him. His wife, Nancy, whom he loved dearly, had a mastectomy. Members of her family Reagan was personally close to died while he was in office. He also developed skin cancer, which meant that almost monthly he'd go to the hospital where they would snip off a little piece of his nose. But foremost as a source of aggravation had to be that he had some of the most disappointing children you could wish on any parent.

Notwithstanding all this, for eight years Ronald Reagan exuded ebullience, affability, and optimism. During this time, I was working a great deal in Western Europe. Inasmuch as this was prior to the proliferation of CNN, it meant that while over there I was without my daily fix of national and sports news. Hence, I would take a midday flight on Friday and rush home to watch the network news on CBS, NBC, or ABC. Every week I'd turn on the set and no matter what was happening in the United States (events that may have been good, bad, or neutral), the report always opened with a shot of Ronald Reagan walking toward a helicopter. By the way I never knew where he was going, but he was always smiling, waving, and seemingly happy. As if to say, it's been another great week for me, America, and the entire free world. There he was, an affable man with a very old face and very young miracle hair. Right behind him was Nancy, who came across as a woman being pulled by a dog.

Now just short of the helicopter the President would stop and turn to the pool of White House reporters, in order to take a question from the omnipresent Sam Donaldson, whom I personally felt was chained to him. How did we the viewers know it was ABC journalist Sam Donaldson? Well, Reagan would cue us by saying, "Yes, what is it, Sam?" No one actually saw Sam and no one seemed to hear him, except for the President. This was especially remarkable since at the time our commander in chief was wearing a hearing aid in each ear. The man could not hear, which may have accounted for his congeniality. Cupping a hand over his ear, Reagan assumed a listening stance and muttered "Yes, ah . . . huh." As reporters looked futilely for the questioner the President began to speak. In the midst of his response, however, the helicopter blades started to rotate, drowning out his words. Waving and smiling, Reagan gave his professional military salute before he was spirited away for the weekend. Still, the imagery of this performance was that our commander in chief was visibly dealing with the problems, interacting with the media, and exercising leadership.

6

EQUALITY—VALUED OR TAINTED?

The third distinctive quality that Tocqueville found among Americans was the belief in the virtues and wisdom of the common people. From the earliest days until today there has always been an egalitarian strain in our nation. This conviction appears in the adage, "Though not all of us can hit a home run, still everyone should have a chance at bat."

Knowing the attraction of populism in this culture, aspiring politicians often go to extreme lengths to show that they are one of the people. In Robert Penn Warren's classic book *All the King's Men,* candidate Willie Stark, in a thinly disguised portrait of Huey Long, greets the voters with, "Friends, red-necks, hicks, and fellow-suckers." This ambitious candidate is letting us know something vital—that he doesn't feel superior to the average person.

Although only a handful of those who comprise the national government were born and raised inside the Beltway, there exists a pervasive view that when men or women spend time in Washington, D.C., something sinister occurs. Whether elected or appointed, there is a belief that Lord Acton had it right when he said, "power tends to corrupt." It's as if formerly respectable, dependable, and unassuming folk risk being debased or stricken with "Potomac fever," an ailment whose symptoms are arrogance, aloofness, and the sudden acquisition of expertise.

Problem is, Americans don't like experts, who are seen as people who know more and more about less and less until they eventually know everything about nothing. Typically, the derogatory stereotype of those who are part of the federal system is that they are know-it-alls who come across as didactic and patronizing.

It follows, therefore, that the way to run successfully for political office is to position yourself as an outsider and complain about the central government. Candidate Reagan did exactly this when he said, "I don't know of any place where prayer is more needed than in the nation's capital." In the same vein, a few days later he followed with, "There are two ways of doing things: the right way and the way they do it in D.C." Likewise even after his election he carried on, "When you mention common sense in Washington, you cause traumatic shock."

> ITEM: Back in 1987 during the Iowa Republican presidential primary, Bob Dole, a great public servant who had been in Washington for decades, vied with Vice President George H. W. Bush for the nomination. Repeatedly when speaking to crowds in the snowy cornfields, Dole attempted to call into question Bush's upper-class elitist background by saying "I'm one of you."

All in all, Americans identify with regular people, those who are modest, gracious, and willing to laugh at themselves. When critics said he was a nine-to-five President, Reagan's retort was, "It's true, hard work never killed anybody, but I figure why take the chance?"

Belittled because of his advanced age, Reagan faced the issue directly, making it part of his speeches, as he recalled his friendship with Betsy Ross and Thomas Jefferson. Addressing a medical convention he told them, "Should I ever need a transplant my problem is that I've got body parts they don't make anymore."

If Ronald Reagan has taught us anything it's the value of self-deprecating humor. For one thing, it humanizes the speaker, helping the listener to identify with him, creating a sense of oneness. For another, it can deepen the audience's feeling of dignity and worth. Lastly, it enables people to see things in a different light, giving events new meaning.

But there was a time when President Reagan got into big trouble. Do you remember the Iran-contra scandal? When the episode became public, the print media went wild. One newspaper, in particular, lashed into Reagan with apparent glee. "Finally, we caught him," their editorial said, "the Teflon Presidency is over because there's only two possible explanations. Number 1, the man was actively involved orchestrating criminality. Once again we have a President who is a crook. Or number 2, he's so distant, dull and dopey that he didn't even know what was going on around him."

Presumably, they were waiting for the President to select from one of the two. But not Reagan, he just kept moving about, smiling and waving. Another "morning in America." Finally, when the media cornered him, he appointed the Tower Commission to impartially look into this matter. So now he couldn't discuss the situation since he didn't want to prejudice their findings.

Meanwhile, the Democrats who controlled Congress made a political blunder. Seizing upon the issue, they preempted the field by appointing a joint committee of Congress, headed by Senator Daniel Inouye of Hawaii. It turned out that the committee went whole hog, conducting an exhaustive investigation of documents and witnesses and holding televised hearings. Afterward, they wrote a thorough report that was very disparaging of President Reagan's role in the affair.

When the pejorative findings became public, there was enormous pressure on the President to get on television and explain how this could have happened. At the time I was in Washington when I learned that President Reagan would be on television that night to clear up and expound upon the matter.

I was excited, just anticipating how he would untangle himself from this mess. Expecting a memorable or even historic speech, I rushed out and purchased ten legal-sized pads and fifty sharpened No. 2 pencils. Sitting in front of my TV set I could hardly wait.

At the appointed hour the President came on. He did that long hallway walk to the podium, building up suspense. Although the room was packed with media people from all over the world, Reagan seemed to be looking beyond them to his real constituency across the vast land.

"I don't know," he said. "I didn't understand. I don't know whether I knew and forgot . . . or maybe I never even knew." Now how did people react to that? Surprisingly, they didn't even get upset. Invariably they said, "Well you can't know everything. C'mon, the guy's getting old. Give him a break."

What Reagan did was relate to an old American cliché or chestnut. So those watching were thinking, "Hey you know, this is still the land of opportunity. Anybody can be President around here." Indeed, if at the time a viewer was having a problem with a teenage child, he or she might envisage that there was even hope for their offspring. There you have it: Ronald Reagan humanized himself and tapped into the values of those he was trying to influence.

Today as Ronald Reagan the man dims, his star shines brighter than ever. For even those who did not agree with his politics admire the class and spirit he displayed in *how* he announced his illness.

Now, as I look back on President Reagan, policies aside, he was a unique individual who was unassuming and warm. Indeed, listening to him sometimes made your heart skip a beat like Marlon Brando did in *On the Waterfront* when he said, "I coulda been a contenda."

What is most striking about this is that by and large Americans do not relate well to the highfalutin, to those with a masterful and magisterial manner. Most of us like people that are not affected but humble. Fact is, we don't even mind if they mess up as long as they own up to messin' up.

No one understood this concept better than Ronald Reagan. Think for a moment . . . what were the areas where he claimed special expertise? Watching him over the years it seemed to me that he never claimed to know anything. On the other hand, he was a man of convictions—an unshakable belief in a few simple truths.

Actually, we admire women and men who have convictions, core values that make them predictable. Though occasionally believing they are wrong, we still have a certain grudging respect. After all it's a matter of conscience and who can argue with that.

ITEM: Moon Landrieu, the legendary mayor of New Orleans, once told me that "All a politician needs to be elected is 50 percent plus one of the votes cast. If you achieve a greater number than that, at the expense of doing what was right, you have sacrificed your integrity needlessly."

Years later, I was reminded of this when Governor Mario Cuomo of New York, a man of conviction not consensus, would veto legislation to reinstate the death penalty. To my way of thinking his was a "Profile in Courage." By his actions he was saying in effect, that while a politician should respect public opinion and obey the law, anything beyond that is the willing submission to the tyranny of ambition.

7

THE OPTIMUM STYLE

From the prior examples it should be evident that I believe it's always advisable to begin every negotiating encounter in a cooperative fashion. More precisely, that means in an amiable manner with a congenial low-key pose of calculated incompetence.

Although my intention throughout this book is not to be authoritative, experience tells me this is the best way to open. Here's why:

First of all, if you start cooperative, there's a good chance the other side will respond in kind. The reason is that in most civilized cultures there is a strong norm of reciprocity. What we call "tit for tat." Consider if you will what your mother and my mom told us as children, "If you'll be nice to people, they'll be nice to you." A platitude perhaps, but it works about 85 percent of the time.

As for the remaining 15 percent, who are Soviet style win-lose ("rat for tat") operators, they are most likely to behold your decency as weakness and lick their chops. This minority tends to observe a soft style and easygoing attitude as a bull notices a red cape. What usually happens with these dog-eat-dog types is that they charge, trying to wrap things up quickly. Often they become hostile and confrontational and use all sorts of tactical ploys. But as you know, the countermeasures for any adversarial gambit are to slow down and not to react the way they expect you to. Even if a threat is made, smile and nod your head up and down as if you're acknowledging a compliment.

As an aside, let me say that the toughest individual to negotiate with is a crazy person. The second most difficult is someone who is irrational. And the third is the "toilsome dummy" who can't even comprehend when he or she is being threatened. So, should the other party become hostile and hard-nosed, a tincture of insanity, a dash of irrationality, and a dose of dumb make for a tasty countering recipe.

The implication of what I'm saying is that when cornered by an offensive bully, don't go with your first two options: *fight* or *freeze*. But there is a third option that I recommend, which is to *flow*. By this, I mean lighten up and say to yourself, "This is a game. Hey it's showtime . . . I'm in the World of Illooshin." In my own case, when someone has tried to intimidate or manipulate me with a stratagem from "good guy–bad guy" to a last-minute nibble, my usual response is, "Hey I love the way you did that, could you do that again—only a bit slower?" Remember, this is show biz!

While all of these games are being played out, time is passing and the other party is investing in this relationship. And once they invest, it's hard for them to divest. Indeed, rats and human beings have this in common: The more energy expended in pursuit of a particular goal, the more desirable that goal becomes. Once faced with the reality that their competitive approach will not work and confronted with the prospect of having to start all over again with another mark or target, they often modify their behavior. Remarkably, they then say to you, "Hey, I was just playing the game. You can't blame me for trying."

The second reason you should be cooperative at the outset is, as I said formerly, it's virtually benign to move from collaborative to conflictive, whereas to reverse the process is exacting, to say the least.

Remember when the Almighty sent Aaron and Moses to negotiate with Pharaoh, they did not start with plague ten or plague eight, but opened with a request for a favor on behalf of the Lord. It was only when this was turned down that the negotiation moved from cooperative to competitive, gradually increasing the negative consequences with each rejection.

To exemplify this concept, imagine opening a discussion by saying, "Look, I'm going to give it to you straight. If I don't get A, B, and C right now, I'll have your job and ruin your damn life." Can you see going from that to, "Perhaps I came on a bit strong? Would you be good enough, at your leisure, of course, to consider . . . ?" Put it this way: You can't reverse yourself in this manner and maintain any semblance of credibility.

Illustrating further: A number of years ago when I lived on the North Shore of Chicago, a neighbor came to see me one Sunday afternoon. She was a physician married to an architect and they had two young children. During the day she worked at Northwestern Hospital and they had a full-time nanny who had been with them for six years.

It turned out her problem was that on Friday evening, she noticed a pair of her diamond earrings were missing. According to her, the only suspect was the nanny. Her husband wanted to immediately call the police and fire the nanny. She was not comfortable with that solution, so they arrived at a compromise: They would fire the nanny and then retain an attorney to sue her for the return of the jewelry.

After I asked, "What for you would be an ideal outcome?," she expressed concerns about the welfare of her children, feelings about this employee, and other factors—ranging from justice to personal beliefs. During this conversation the husband arrived. Surely, my approach was nondirective, trying to help them arrive at an alternative strategy that would satisfy both of their needs.

As I recall, my only direct contribution to the discussion was in recounting how the Almighty proceeded in the negotiations with Pharaoh. Undoubtedly, this reinforced the physician's instinctive feel for the problem, that the place to start was with a sit-down friendly discussion with the nanny. If that was unsatisfactory, they could always move to the threat of discharge, the issue of references, actual discharge, and finally the plagues of civil litigation and prosecution.

The next day I learned that they never got past step one. Apparently, after the nanny was asked to help them solve their problem, the missing item was located. It had fallen behind a dresser.

Hearing that, what came to mind was a comment Abraham Maslow made years ago that especially applies to our contesting society: "If you see all problems as a nail your only solution is a hammer."

To cap it all, I am suggesting that you approach virtually all negotiations as an opportunity for mutual problem solving. At the outset emphasize the commonality of interests that brought you together. Quite often I turn to the other side and ask, "How can we come up with a solution that will meet both of our needs?" By all means you want them to understand that it is your intention that this be a joint problem-solving process that will be enjoyable and energizing.

In this chapter I have tried to focus upon style, the unique pattern that gives unity and distinctiveness to your behavior. Despite our cultural bias toward the tangible, measurable, and rational explanation, *it's your manner that speaks louder than anything else.* So if you set a positive, pleasant, and cooperative tone there's a good chance the other party will respond in kind. At the same time, regardless how big the stakes, cultivate a detached attitude of caring, but not t-h-a-t much.

Examine, for instance, a negotiation with a would-be suicide, a life-and-death situation. To be sure, those who attempt this solution to their problems are probably depressed, dejected, and feel at the time a sense of despair. For them, the suicide option is the sincerest form of self-criticism.

Let me set the scene, the person considering this choice is standing on a ledge at the sixth floor of an office building in a major city. As a crowd gathers below, he is threatening to jump.

Such a situation was dealt with by Bob Newhart in a comedic monologue that I saw him do decades ago on *The Ed Sullivan Show.* The fact that I remember this soliloquy after all these years is a tribute to both his quick-witted performance and his wise insights into human nature.

Setting the scene, the negotiator climbs through the window and is standing next to the man who is threatening to take his own life. Albeit with a couple of edits it went something like this:

"Hi there. By the way, pal, have you got a match?

"Hey, is this the first time for you? . . .

"You don't happen to be with Enron do you? . . .

"You know, in the last few years, jumping has fallen off quite a bit . . .

"From what I hear in 1929, you couldn't even get a space on this ledge . . . it was packed.

"Hey, there's a street vendor down there looking up . . .

"Why it's Stan the hot dog man . . .

"Are you hungry by any chance? . . . Gee I am.

"Maybe we can get something to eat . . .

"Hey, Stan . . . up here . . .

"Yeah we'll take two hot dogs and two Diet Cokes.

"No, it's to go, Stan!"

While humorous, it is also true to life. What Newhart did in his own casual, matter-of-fact style was to capture the best way of influencing the behavior of someone in a stressful predicament.

Earlier, I implied that negotiating involved decision making under conditions of uncertainty. Ambiguity exists because even when both sides ultimately say "yes" there are always other options but their costs are unknown. This applies to momentous matters as well as everyday decisions. Very often, what influences our resolve to go with one alternative rather than another is the *process* or the *how*.

Consider the simple decision that virtually all of us make occasionally: Where do we go for dinner? The well-known *Zagat Surveys* of restaurants, which are published annually, rate three major criteria in their evaluations: food, decor, and service. Evidently, they believe that two thirds of customer satisfaction is not about the caliber of the meal but the process of dining. In their opinion, style is twice as important as substance.

Allow me to elaborate further on this idea by asking, What do you believe is the most popular ethnic restaurant in the world? This may or may not come as a surprise, but the answer is—Chinese. Even if you were to exclude the People's Republic of China and Taiwan, Chinese dining establishments still come out ahead. Why this popularity? What makes us decide to dine there?

To try and answer these questions let me share with you my own experience.

Last fall my wife, Ellen, and I were in the Far East on business. Initially, we traveled to the People's Republic of China where quite naturally we ate Chinese food. Next stop was Hong Kong and each evening we dined on Chinese cuisine. Then came Singapore and more of the same. Finally, we arrived in Sydney, Australia. Although tired, we threw on some clothes and went out to get a bite to eat. Sitting across the table from Ellen I suddenly looked around at the decor and asked, "Why are we at a Chinese restaurant?"

"You like Chinese food," she remarked.

Pondering the exchange, I began to reflect, "Do I really like this food? No, not really. I don't think anybody likes Chinese chow, least of all the people in mainland China. They're eating it for sustenance. Further, they don't have another choice. But what am I doing here?"

Yet, if you look at my habitual behavior, you could easily say that I'm a Chinese food junkie. The question is what gets me and so many others into these restaurants? Maybe it's nutritional value? Are you kidding! No, the substance or content of the food has little to do with my decision making.

Why do I say this? Well, number 1, in Chinese restaurants anywhere you never know what you're eating. You may have ordered Moo Pao Cheng and your companion Da-Cheng Ping, but when it comes it all looks like the same stuff. Number 2, I don't care what they say: Chinese food contains MSG (monosodium glutamate), which means it is quite likely that afterward you will swell up like a banana fish and wonder whether you can even make it back out to sea. And number 3, the old cliché may well be true:

Two hours after consuming a Chinese meal you're inclined to get famished. This seems to be borne out by the fact that 20 percent of all pizza deliveries in North America go to people who have just eaten Chinese meals.

Don't get me wrong; it is not my intention to slight Chinese restaurants or those who frequent them. To the contrary, as I said earlier, I myself am an addict. But what attracts me is not the food; rather it's the atmosphere and the way the experience makes me feel.

Reflect for a moment, have you ever been denied admission to a Chinese restaurant? It doesn't matter how you're dressed. Last summer I was walking about wearing shorts in Vancouver's Chinatown. Deciding to get some dim sum I approached a Chinese tea room. My wife was shaking her head as she proclaimed, "They'll never let you in. Look at the way you're dressed." It goes without saying, we were seated without any difficulty.

Contrast this with New York's Lespinasse, where to gain admittance to this temple of gastronomy I had to go back to my room for a tie. In Los Angeles in Matsuhisa they loaned me a jacket. Now in Chicago's Spiaggia the situation was more complex. Although suitably attired in a jacket, dress shirt, and tie, the maître d' was about to turn me away because I was wearing jeans. Would you believe I actually was forced to negotiate to have the opportunity to spend lotsa lira?

Years ago, while strolling on K Street in our nation's capital, I was overcome with hunger. Consequently I decided to stop at Mr. K's, a classy Chinese eatery with two stone lions out front. Dressed in shorts and a T-shirt, I was taken aback by the fashionable furnishings and tony decor inside. It looked like Versailles at the time of Louis XV. The clientele matched the surroundings: women and men bedecked in formal attire.

Even I felt intimidated under these circumstances. I was about to leave when the headwaiter approached. "May I help you?" he asked. Hesitant at first, I eventually responded, "Gee I was just wondering whether I could get something to eat? . . . Am I dressed okay?"

"No problem," he declared. "You fine. We have a table for you in kitchen. It's better . . . is closer to the food."

You always feel valued, accepted, and attended to in Chinese restaurants. All of them seem to have the same style—a customer-friendly attitude that makes you feel good.

Many years ago, when our children were young and unruly, we would all go for lunch or dinner at a different Chinese restaurant on the weekend. The place didn't matter, but the dining process was very similar. Once seated, the busboy would place the menus on the table and bring glasses of water—always spilling a few drops. Maybe this is part of the ritual. Then the waiter comes over, bows slightly out of respect, and does something that you don't see elsewhere. He audibly counts the number of people in your party.

"Hello, one, two, three, four, five," he observes. "You gotta five. That's good." Not only have I learned that I'm a five guy, he makes me feel that five is the best number. Presumably, if the count would have been four I might be somewhat impotent. Six, on the other hand, would make me a sexual pervert. But I'm a five guy and that sounds just right. Moreover, he tells me that this number qualifies us for "the columns."

Ironically, driving to the restaurant I announced to the family, "You know, I make the same mistake every week. This time I'm not going to overeat and bloat up on this stuff. I'll just have a little chow mein and some green tea."

But whenever I hear that I qualify for the columns, forget the resolution I made in the car. The hell with the chow mein, I'm going with the columns, because that's the best deal.

Now with the columns you always start with a choice. You can select spring roll or egg roll. Honestly, I have been eating in Chinese restaurants for well over four decades and still haven't figured out the difference. Certainly my family doesn't know either. Yet, we actually discuss this. But this social exchange and decision making gives us the illusion of choice, options, participation, and a sense of mastery of our lives.

When the waiter returns, he re-counts our party. "One, two,

three, four, five," to make sure we still qualify. Or maybe he thought we had multiplied while he was gone.

"Good," he says, "you still have five. That means you can have two from Column A, two from B, and one from C." Having given us the guidelines, the waiter excuses himself while our family studies the menu, debates preferences, and ultimately engages in consensus decision making.

After fifteen or twenty minutes we have agreed on our selections for Columns C and B but are deadlocked on A. We have only been able to agree on one item. With some trepidation we call over our waiter. Chinese people, however, are wonderfully understanding and patient.

"I'm sorry," I say, "we only have one in Column A." "Ah, good," he says. Whatever you tell him it's good. "The kids are having a food fight." Same reply, "Ah, good."

"Oh you only have one in A. That's good," he declares. "So you take one in A and you trade it for two in B or three in Column C. But if you want you can do one in A, two in B, and four in C."

Despite our impasse, we have now earned extra currency so we can refashion, redesign, restructure, and retailor the meal to meet our special needs. There is a sense of exhilaration that somehow we've been involved in the creative process.

When I arrived at the restaurant that day I brought with me the baggage of concerns and regrets that we all carry. Certainly, there are qualms about the past, the decisions I made and those I didn't make. The things I *should* have done. If only I *would* have . . . And those chances missed, where I *could* have . . . What we call the shoulda, woulda, coulda of life. The what-might-have-beens.

In a world where the population is exploding at an exponential rate, where resources are diminishing, and where the average family in North America has 1.6 children, what the hell am I doing with three kids? Is it pure selfishness on my part? But then I realize, no, it's enabling me to qualify for the columns. So, in reality, I'm glad we've got them.

Having alleviated some of the burdens of the past, how does the process of Chinese dining help with the present? Well as you're chomping away the food doesn't taste all that bad. In fact, it fills you up pretty well. Later on you may retain water, but right now you're feeling satisfied and content.

The only thing left is the uncertain future, but the Chinese dining experience tries to take care of that. Unanticipated, unexpected, and unadvertised they bring you a plate of fortune cookies. Almost without exception diners want to know what life has in store for them. These are the very same people who ridicule astrology, the occult, and even the New Age movement; still they are dying to learn their fortune. Do you know anyone who ever became depressed after reading the words on those little pieces of paper? Typically, they provide some hope. For example, "You will achieve a place in the sun, but you will have to put up with a few blisters."

Thus, by virtue of style or interpersonal process, people have been able to satisfy their needs. All of which should tell us that *how* we negotiate will influence outcomes more than most of us realize. For you are not really selling products or proposals, but you're selling yourself. The conclusion is inescapable: Your style will supersede the substance of any transaction.

PROMINENT POINTS

- *How* you interact (your demeanor or approach) registers more than *what* you are discussing (terms or content).
- People are more influenced by the manner of the messenger than the message itself.
- Effective negotiators have a style that those whom they are trying to influence, relate to and admire.

- Successful persuaders within the United States, whether politicians, managers, or salespeople, are distinguished by certain style characteristics:

  - The ability to express ideas in simple terms, framing issues so that choices are clear-cut.
  - An optimism and hopefulness about the future.
  - Coming across as the embodiment of ordinary folk—regular guys or gals.
  - A congenial, humble, and unaffected way.
  - The use of self-deprecating humor to humanize and make fun of themselves.

- Start all dealings in a cooperative fashion, conveying empathy, along with a low-key pose of calculated incompetence.
- The negotiating world often contains some razzle-dazzle and hocus-pocus, so lighten up and enjoy the game. Since we can't do much about birth and death, have some fun in the time between.

CHAPTER IV

A MIXED-MOTIVE GAME

We're all in this together
But sometimes by ourselves.

LILY TOMLIN

Remember the climactic moment in the motion picture *High Noon* where Gary Cooper, the heroic sheriff, is alone as he confronts the ruthless villain? In the background are the anxious and terrified townspeople who don't want to get involved. Yet, they're glancing at the scene through partially opened shutters wondering which one will be left standing after the shoot-out.

In the movie we know what happened: a quick draw, a one-shot kill, and the triumph of right over wrong. In sum, the antagonist got his comeuppance and the protagonist, after throwing his badge to the ground, got Grace Kelly. More significantly, however, is that the townspeople—by the ignominy of their inaction—will also get their just desserts. Ignoring Burke's formulation that "evil triumphs when good people do nothing," they unknowingly choose a lawless and chaotic future for themselves. What the director, Fred Zinnemann, seemed to be saying was that almost every gross injustice has its accomplices and that consequences ensue even from inaction.

1

LABELING IS DISABLING

In everyday life, of course, things are not so sharply defined. Yet, in spite of our knowledge that gradations and shadings always exist, we still have a tendency to perceive the world in terms of entities—grouping and categorizing. For example, she's a liberal or a conservative, pro-life or pro-choice, a household engineer or a career woman. In short, it's either fish or fowl, but it can't be both. While this kind of thinking affords time-saving shortcuts in a complex world, it's always harmful to pigeonhole people and make unfounded assumptions about them. Each person is elaborate, diverse, complicated, and forever changing.

2

DIAL M FOR MONEY

About ten years ago, late Friday evening, just before Christmas, I received a phone call from a friend, Pete O'Hara, who was a longtime executive at an owned and operated television station in Chicago. Though distraught, he recounted what happened to him that day. While working in his office at 6:30 P.M. he received a phone call from the station's new general manager, Tom Johnson, asking that he come upstairs for a meeting. When Pete arrived he was informed that he was fired, effective immediately, and to clean out his desk. From what was said, the discharge was not based upon poor performance. Advised not to take it personally, he was told that his slot was needed for a member of the GM's Miami team.

The next week, when O'Hara went to see the Human Resources people, I tagged along. Surprisingly, what they offered him in a severance package was less than their personnel manual required. (Incidentally, one of my axioms is to always make the other side live by their own rules and words.)

Using this as a pretext, I went upstairs to see general manager Johnson. As I walked into his office, he stood up and came out from behind the desk. My first thought was that he looked more like a professional football linebacker than a TV executive. He was a helluva big guy. From all indications, however, he seemed pleas-

antly surprised to tower over me. Perhaps he expected that I
would be taller, better dressed, and more impressive.

"Hello, my name is Herb Cohen," I said in my New York-
accented speech, "it's a pleasure to meet you." Looking me up and
down, he smiled broadly, extending his hand. Now came his top
executive handshake—controlling and firm. Then he responded
in a deep, resonant voice. "Hi there, I'm the new general manger.
By any chance, do you know I used to be a Green Beret?"

"Used to be a Green Beret?" I say, while I'm thinking, "Why
the hell is he telling me this? Is this normal? Do I go around greeting people with, 'Hi there, I'm Herb Cohen, Korean War veteran
under Public Law 550—saved all you people from the commies.
Why if not for me, they'd be all over Chicago.'?"

Why is he doing this? Is this supposed to frighten or intimidate
me? Now if we were doing hand-to-hand combat or dueling with
bayonets I'd be scared. But we're just negotiating. So, of course,
I'm concerned, but not t-h-a-t much!

Starting with my low-key pose of calculated incompetence, I let
him do most of the talking while I took notes. And boy, did he like
to talk, expounding on his management philosophy and values.

For whatever reason, he assumed that I was an agent who represented media talent. Consequently, his approach was to use this
as leverage over me. In other words, he implied that if I wasn't ac-
commodating in this instance, it might cost me in the future. Presumably, he thought I would be coming to see him on behalf of
clients. As you no doubt suspect, this tag was inaccurate and his
assumptions were mistaken.

In hindsight, I have come to believe that Johnson didn't see me
as much of a challenge. He assumed that I was vulnerable and
could be easily manipulated. As a result, we spent the rest of that
day trying to come to an agreement. Without realizing it, he was
investing time and energy in our relationship. If he knew at the
beginning that I would not be susceptible to his pressure tactics, I
suspect he would have turned this matter over to someone else.
But fortunately, he didn't.

Thereafter other meetings ensued, in which the general manager offered to increase O'Hara's severance package beyond what was called for. In addition, he would throw in extras, from paying for a year's hospitalization insurance to allowing O'Hara to write his own recommendation, which he would sign. Accepting all of this, we still wanted more, claiming that the timing and manner of the firing constituted virtually "cruel and unusual punishment."

Throughout these discussions Johnson showed little interest in O'Hara's predicament. He tried to dominate every exchange, making statements that were coercive or outright bluffs. Eventually, becoming exasperated with the amount of time he was spending and what he termed my "attitude problem," he stated, "I don't have the authority to give you what you want."

Alas, this led to the concluding negotiating session, which was attended by two corporate Human Resources people and a network attorney from New York City. Besides Pete and myself, we also brought along a Chicago lawyer, who we optimistically hoped would draft the agreement.

When the meeting began, it was apparent that GM Johnson was fully aware of his new audience. Playing to the corporate crowd, he backtracked on his last proposal and presented it to us as an implicit ultimatum. Growing annoyed and impatient, I eventually said, "If you maintain this attitude and position, what do you think we'll do?"

Much to my amazement, Johnson suddenly became quite creative. "You will undoubtedly sue us," he said.

My response was, "Okay, what else?"

Thinking for a moment he continued, "Probably you'll go to the National Association of Broadcasters."

"And then?" I inquired.

"Knowing you, you'll complain to the FCC or even Congress."

"Do you think we'll stop there?" I asked.

"No, not you, I know your type," Johnson said. "You'll get on talk shows to gripe, to promote yourself and get more clients."

At this juncture, our new team member, the Chicago attorney, asked if we could take a break. When we were outside he turned to me, "What the hell are you doing threatening the network?"

Before I could even respond he said, "That's unethical and you're getting close to extortion." O'Hara, who was laughing, turned to his counselor and said, "What are you talking about—Herb never said a word—he just encouraged Johnson in a brainstorming session."

After the caucus, Johnson increased his offer and eventually we moved into the settlement range. It took some additional dialogue and a couple of nifty ideas from the New York outsiders but we came to an agreement. The outcome was that Peter O'Hara doubled his termination compensation and, with the excellent reference provided by the general manager, was able to get an equivalent position within the industry in a month. As for Johnson, he was elated to get rid of us, so he could direct all his energies to revitalizing the station. When I last saw him his parting words were, "Next time when you bring a client around, it'll be different." Needless to say, there was never a next time.

Looking back on this episode, there are two things that stick in my mind. First, that this GM in three weeks never learned anything about me, least of all what I did for a living. So, what he thought was his coercive power had no effect whatsoever. Second, his statement, "Knowing you . . . I know your type," was the kind of mindless stereotyping that impairs one's vision. How can anyone possibly think they know me? Truth be told, we are all largely fictitious, even to ourselves.

3

IT AIN'T NECESSARILY SO

In December 2001, the University of Notre Dame, amidst considerable fanfare, introduced George O'Leary to the public as their new football coach. Incredibly, only five days later, he resigned when reports surfaced that he had fudged his résumé. Then two weeks later, athletic director Kevin White held another press conference to announce that Tyrone Willingham, an African-American from Stanford University, would coach the Fighting Irish.

Oddly enough, when asked by the media why O'Leary was selected over Willingham in the first place, the athletic director's reply was illuminating: "We just felt that George kind of brought us something out of central casting. Second-generation Irish Catholic, a great passion to be at Notre Dame. He espoused it, he gushed at us and we loved him."

Such uncharacteristic candor is enlightening and noteworthy for at least three reasons. First of all, it's a blatant example of stereotyping. Though in this case the profile of those of Irish Catholic ancestry may seem favorable to some, it represents an oversimplified picture. Problem is, to be a creative negotiator you need to see beyond givens and categories to recognize individual complexity and often unstated needs.

Second, the athletic director in this case appeared to have forgotten that his primary objective was to hire a football coach who could restore the Fighting Irish to prominence. By emphasizing aspects of a candidate's personality and ethnicity he engaged in goal displacement. Had this been practiced in earlier times, Notre Dame would never have hired two of their legendary coaches, Knute Rockne and Ara Parseghian.

4

WHEN YOU'RE UP TO YOUR NECK IN ALLIGATORS, IT'S EASY TO FORGET THAT YOUR ORIGINAL OBJECTIVE WAS TO DRAIN THE SWAMP

Before going further, in the interest of full disclosure, let me admit that I am especially frustrated with organizations or people who focus upon activity (means) at the expense of accomplishment (goals). For as long as I can remember, I have been an advocate of hiring and rewarding people not because of looks, personality, gender, race, or background but based on performance.

Undeniably, these views were reinforced while I was attending college and obtained a summer job working for the Ford Motor Company. Reporting for work, I was given an orientation, signed some documents, and then sent to see a Technicolor short about the history of the company. At the time, I recall being impressed by the high quality of the film and the business savvy of its founder, Henry Ford.

Next, I met my foreman, who welcomed me to the Ford team. He handed me a white shirt and said, "Put this on, 'cause you're an assistant foreman—part of management and we all wear white shirts."

While I was changing, he hooked a pedometer onto my belt.

You know what this is. About the size of a pocket watch, it responds to body motion and thus measures the distance a person walks.

"Your job," he said, "is to move around among the workers so whenever they look up they'll see you and know that management cares. Then at the end of your shift," he went on, "I collect the pedometers from all the summer assistants and that's how I determine the kind of day they had.

"Any questions?" he asked.

"No sir," I replied. I needed the job!

Following these instructions, I spent the next five hours strolling about making myself visible to the workers. Simply out of curiosity, about 3:00 P.M. I glanced down at my pedometer and noticed it read 3.1 miles. Then I observed another guy with a similar job description. He was easy to spot because of the white shirt and pedometer. As we approached each other I inquired, "What have you got? What's your mileage?"

"Oh, I'm over four miles," he beamed.

"Wow," I thought, "I've got to pick up the pace." Extending my stride and moving faster, I soon saw another colleague. "Hey what's your pedometer read?" I shouted across the assembly line.

He held up two fingers, like he was giving me a V for victory sign. "Does that mean two miles?" I hollered over the noise. He nodded yes. Now I had a problem. I didn't know whether to slow down or speed up.

Getting these conflicting signals I began to feel tense, like I was stressed. So I went to the place where people go under these circumstances. I headed for the men's room where I had my first contact with "the informal organization."

Standing at the urinal next to me was an older guy. He must have been about twenty-three years old. His voice was hoarse and rasping. "Hey kid, you new here?"

"Yes sir, I am."

"It figured," he growled. "Let me give you the scoop. You do less than two miles a day you'll be fired. Two to four, you'll make it through the summer but don't figure on comin' back next year.

Four to six, you'll be here every summer and when you get out of college you could have a real job in this place. Now, six to seven you'll stick around and one day you might even be runnin' the plant. But anything more than that, fuhgeddaboudit, 'cause you'll make everybody else look bad. Capisce? You understand?"

"Yup," I said. I certainly did. So I picked up the pace slightly and that day turned in my pedometer with a reading of 3.8 miles. Clearly, that was an indication of my own social needs and career aspirations at the time.

For about two weeks everything went well. Then, something eventful occurred. There was an assistant foreman in our group who had an "enriched job." He not only "walked the walk" with us, but also ran a punch press in the morning. Through trial and error, he discovered that if he placed his pedometer on the machine, which went 120 revolutions per minute, in no time he could get his mileage. Being entrepreneurial, he spread the word and turned this discovery into the moneymaking concession of selling time on his machine. In simple terms, give him your pedometer at 9:00 A.M. and it's out by 11:00 A.M. with the desired mileage. Sure it cost a few bucks, but you could spend the rest of the day in the can engaged in self-development.

Thus, I was enjoying the capitalist system until one morning the guy with the punch press was called away to take a phone call. He left a pedometer on the machine and when he returned, it registered sixty-seven miles. This was my first exposure to the art of crisis management.

All of us gathered around the machine in an attempt to solve the problem. My personal suggestion was that we give it to the skinny white shirter and say he was hyperactive. But this idea was rejected when someone who we thought was studying engineering said in an authoritative manner, "No problem. Just look at the number of digits here. Put it back on the press and let it run. It'll go to 97, 98, 99 and then swing back to zero, 1, 2, 3, 4. Then we'll stop it at whatever number we want." (By the way, later on we learned that our expert wasn't exactly an engineering student, but he knew someone who was.)

To this day, I still recall us all gathered around watching the numbers change. It went to 97, 98, 99 . . . and then 100, 101, 102. When we stopped the machine it was at 111 miles.

Anyway, we decided to turn it into the foreman as it was, figuring that he'd never even notice. Boy were we wrong. It didn't take long for him to figure out the scheme and so ended the employment of my cohorts and myself that summer.

Who benefited from all these machinations? Certainly not Ford, which immediately thereafter changed their procedures. As for me, I had to scramble around looking for another job and ended up working in a sweatshop, cutting ribbons, silks, and velvets.

There you have it: Whenever a person or a system focuses upon personality or activity you are implicitly encouraging people to perfect the craft of gamesmanship. Becoming emotionally attached to irrelevancies, we do a disservice to ourselves, our organizations, and even what America is supposed to be all about.

What I have been discussing in this seeming digression is the importance of evaluating people based upon performance or what they actually achieve, not whether they look good, arrive on time, or keep their office space tidy. These latter items are only significant insofar as they relate to the success of the enterprise— achieving profitability in business, winning games in sports, or obtaining one's objectives in negotiations. Of course, the activities or means we use should always be appropriate and ethical, but are merely the ways to attain desired outcomes.

Having said all this, let's go to the third point in my analysis of the Notre Dame athletic director's revealing comments.

5

SAY CHEESE

Lastly, based upon the statement, "He gushed at us and we loved him," it's apparent that Mr. O'Leary, unknowingly perhaps, made use of the *liking norm* to get what he wanted.

Twenty years ago, when I returned home from the West Coast leg of my book tour, I remember saying to my daughter, Sharon, "You know I really liked the people who interviewed me on radio and TV." At the time, she was a college student majoring in psychology and her retort surprised me. "Sure you like them, 'cause they like you!"

Reflecting upon her revelation, my first reaction was denial: "That's not true, there are many people who like me but who I can't stand."

"Okay, name one," she said. Well, for the next year I consciously tried to find this person without success.

What she and professional persuaders, from Harvey Mackay (*Swim with the Sharks Without Being Eaten Alive*) to Joe Girard (the "greatest car salesman"), know is that we are more prone to say yes to someone we know, like, or identify with. Consequently, these pros have extensive mailing lists and networks, which they use to keep in touch with prospects all year round.

As human beings we are amenable to flattery, to people whose backgrounds and interests are similar to ours, and to those who are willing to go to bat for us. When a salesperson examines your trade-in prior to negotiating the purchase of a new car, he or she is not looking only at its condition. No indeed, they are gathering information as to your hobbies, habits, and the nature of your livelihood.

Of course, they will note the type of CDs you have in your glove compartment and notice whether there's a tennis racket, Roller Blades, or golf balls on the back seat. Invariably, this will be used later on when they casually remark, "I can't wait till the weather warms up so I can get out on the course." Moreover, we are all too familiar with the new car salesperson who is willing to confront his manager and put his career at risk to ensure that you get "a good deal."

Probably the most familiar example of the *liking norm* and the power of identification is the good guy–bad guy technique. Frequently displayed on TV crime shows, you may have actually experienced this approach in your own negotiations.

Let me set the scene: In a major American city an eighteen-year-old suspected of a mugging has been arrested and taken to the police station. After being advised of his rights, he's removed to the interrogation room where he proclaims his innocence to a pair of police officers.

Suddenly, one of them, who plays the role of bad cop, flies off the handle. He grabs the suspect by the shirt and hurls verbal abuse and threats at him. Whether the teenager talks back or doesn't respond, the bad cop flies into a rage, threatening to put him away for ten years of "hard time."

During this performance, his partner, the good cop, has been sitting quietly in the rear. Just when it appears that the bad cop is about to lose control and physically assault the suspect, the good cop intervenes. Grabbing his partner and pulling him away he says, "Nick, what are you doing? Get control of yourself. Cool it." But bad cop, who looks like he was trained in the Actors Studio, shouts back, "Don't tell me to cool it. I'm going to kill this lying SOB."

At this point the good cop physically pushes his partner out the door telling him, "You've got to get control of yourself, Nick. Please go for a walk around the block and then come back."

Having removed the threat of the menacing partner, the good cop pulls up a chair and speaks calmly to the suspect, using his first name. "Gee, Billy, I want to apologize for my partner. He has a terrible temper. In fact, he maimed a prisoner who was about your age in that very seat last month.

"Look, we already got enough evidence to convict you and Nick wants to put you away for ten years," he continues softly. "But this is your first offense. I have a kid your age, so I feel for you. If you admit that you did it, right now, before he gets back, I'll take charge of the case and put in a good word for you.

"Do us both a favor, Billy. Just tell me the truth and we can work together to get you through this." About half the time a complete confession follows.

Why does this commonplace technique work so often? By way of explanation, there seem to be three factors that affect the suspect's decision making.

Number one, the stark contrast between the available alternatives: the rational good cop or the irrational and crazed bad cop.

Number two, the opportunity to have a sympathetic insider working on his behalf.

Number three, the fact that the good cop has protected him from the potential of physical harm at the expense of jeopardizing his relationship with his partner. So the *reciprocity norm* comes into play.

6

BELIEVING IS SEEING

Up to this point, I have shared examples with you of individuals who were at a disadvantage in negotiations because of their tendency to categorize, stereotype, and rely upon erroneous assumptions. All of us, of course, are subject to bias, prejudice, and a tendency to see what we want or expect to see, rather than what is really there.

To escape from this liability, it is necessary that we become more skeptical about what we think we know. This is especially true in negotiating, where participants make calculations and tactical decisions in accordance with their perceptions about the other side.

7

A DYNAMIC OF DUAL DESIRES

Recall that negotiating is a process involving parties with both common and conflicting interests who come together voluntarily in an attempt to arrange or adjust their future relationship. It occurs when two or more players without the same preferences try to make a joint decision. If successful, both sides prefer the agreed outcome to the status quo or for that matter any other alternatives. But this social interaction would not come about unless both common interests and conflicting interests exist.

Years ago, after I gave a speech in Mexico City, one of the people in the audience came up to me. Thinking he had a question, I was taken aback when he asked if I remembered a friend of his, one Alfredo Santiago. As it turned out, this person was involved in a negotiation with me ten years earlier when I represented a client in Ecuador. Apparently, Mr. Santiago had some complaints about the way the agreement was implemented by my then client. The emissary wanted to know if I would be willing to discuss this matter, gratis, with Santiago.

Although this all happened a decade before and I barely remembered it, I said, "Okay, what about breakfast tomorrow morning?" Shaking his head, he said, "No, it's not possible to do that here. Alfredo is in prison in Guayaquil. He beat up his in-laws. But he has visiting privileges for one hour every Sunday."

Now, do you believe I took the next plane to Ecuador? Are you

116

kidding? I went home. While sympathetic with Alfredo's current situation and even recognizing that some conflict may exist, I didn't see any commonality. In other words, if there's nothing in common, there's no reason to resolve or even clarify differences.

So, when negotiating takes place, the parties have mixed motives or dual desires: the individual's wish to maximize his or her gain and the cooperative need to arrive at a fair solution. Cynics might even say that some competitive negotiators use the veneer of cooperation as a smoke screen to conceal their real intent: prevailing over their counterpart. But whatever your view, I believe you will agree that this game is not akin to solitaire. You and I are not like Robinson Crusoe or Tom Hanks in the movie *Cast Away*, alone in what we want. While seeking our own satisfaction we must be able to come to terms with the contrary preferences and desires of others. In negotiation there's always at least one other participant, and rules or at least etiquette of play. Moreover, there are also interdependent moves where signals are sent and interpreted, and adjusting and learning takes place.

8

A PROBLEM-SOLVING PROCESS

Negotiating should be seen as a problem-solving process where both sides interact to share their preferences and needs so that beneficial exchanges can be made and agreements that give added value to the relationship can be achieved. Certainly if the relationship is continuing, this game is only a means toward an end.

At the outset, the parties have an imperfect understanding of each other's concerns. Thus, they should begin by exploring issues that reflect feelings and interests. Then engage in a search for novel alternatives or at least identify concessions that can profitably be exchanged.

Keep in mind that initially the stakes or acceptable minimums of the parties are not known or, if they are, they're not set in cement. So, that in revealing information or by eliminating, combining, or changing any of the elements, you, in effect, affect the expectations of the other side.

This brings to mind an experience I had many years ago. When I was in Boston on a TV show plugging my book, I had met the show's producer, Leslie James, a very capable and professional person.

Lo and behold, she phoned a few months later asking if I would represent her. She had received a call from Embassy Productions in Los Angeles offering her the job of assistant producer on a new situation comedy that they were developing. From all indications, Leslie was their first choice because the creator of the sitcom concept and now the executive producer wanted her. And she was eager to get started.

Since I prefer not being a talent agent, I recommended that she use Bob Woolf. Besides being a good friend who lived in the Boston area, he was someone I trusted and respected. His clients at the time ranged from basketball's Larry Bird to NBC's Gene Shalit. Because she seemed anxious, at the conclusion of our phone conversation, I said, "Look, if he can't or won't do it, I will."

The next day Leslie called. "He's overseas," she said. "He won't be back for two weeks." Because this matter had a sense of urgency, after chatting with my new client about her situation, desires, and concerns, I was off to the West Coast.

Arriving at the corporate suite on Avenue of the Stars in Century City, I was ushered into the office of the firm's attorney. Now, I suspect that the typical show biz agent whom he has dealt with would start the conversation with, "Look my client doesn't need the job. She's got other big offers pending. Unless you're prepared to put big dollars on the table forget it."

My approach was a little different: "Leslie really wants this job. Maybe I shouldn't be saying this, but she's dying to come out here to work on this show." With this, the attorney came out from behind his desk and pulled up a chair next to me.

"I hope I didn't say anything wrong," I said.

"No, no, not at all," he responded.

"She wants this job so bad, her last words to me were, 'Herb don't screw this up.' So she wants to come here and I guess you want her?" I said.

He was grinning as he commented, "Well, that could be."

"Now, I have to ask you. I don't know this area well, would she need a car out here? See, right now, she doesn't own a car. Leslie lives right next to the MTA in Boston and uses it to go back and forth to work. How's your public transportation?"

"Not that good," he said. "She probably would need a car."

"By the way, when would you want her to start? Could she have about two or three months to look for housing?"

Looking startled he said, "No we need her now. We already sold the pilot and want to start shooting in two weeks."

"Gee," I said. "So, you think she needs a car and she has to move right away?" Pausing for a second, I went on, "Oh, I almost forgot, Leslie lives in a rent-stabilized apartment in Boston. She pays $540 a month for two bedrooms and two baths. Do you think she can get something comparable at that price around here?"

"No, you must be joking. This is L.A."

After sharing my client's concerns and issues with him, the attorney for Embassy reciprocated. He told me that his company had many projects going and a plethora of assistant producers. As he put it, "They are a dime a dozen in Southern California and they all start at the same salary."

There you have it: They want her and she wants them. It's no longer us versus them but both of us versus the problem to be solved. Succinctly put, what forms of compensation can the company give Leslie that would not raise objections from those in comparable jobs?

Since she was the only person they ever hired for this position who was not local, Leslie obtained a car allowance, a rent subsidy, generous moving expenses, and other one-time extras. Even if word of this compensation package got out, it was deemed that her peers would not object, as this was a special case, differentiated from the routine. In the end, my client almost tripled the compensation she was previously making. Not so fast. This was not all gravy because her living costs also increased substantially. In summary, though, both sides got what they wanted.

The point of this story—confirmed by a lifetime of experience—is that it is not necessary to go into a negotiation with a no-holds-barred approach as though it were a form of warfare. The two may have a few similarities, but we must never forget that the ultimate goal of negotiating is convergence—not unconditional surrender. For the agreement is usually the beginning of a new relationship not the end of one.

ITEM: Last year, a woman in the midst of a particularly bitter divorce contacted me. Her husband of twelve years had found himself a young trophy wife as a substitute for his ancient spouse, who was all of thirty-six years. Although claiming that he loved their three children, he and his attorney were pursing this matter as if they were engaged in combat. It took me considerable time and effort to get them to understand that their extreme tactics were not only doing irreparable harm to the wife but to his children as well. Even if she were to capitulate, it would be a Pyrrhic victory at the cost of his own self-interest.

Nowadays, even in the competitive world of business, thriving companies join former adversaries in partnering and forming strategic alliances. There is a growing recognition that our success does not require that others fail. Using a warmed-over metaphor, savvy executives don't spend all their time fighting for more slices of a circumscribed pastry dessert, but search for ways to expand the pie.

9

CAN'T ANYBODY HERE PLAY THIS GAME

Like Dracula, some myths refuse to die. Much as the fiction that the best defense against a vampire is to show him a cross, many believe that life is a zero-sum struggle. By channeling all their efforts into winning at all costs it's possible for these gladiators to sometimes achieve fast victories. But the result often brings only things without wisdom, leaving the "winner" enslaved to a world of objects in a pointless existence.

We all know, at least intellectually, that people are unique and that relationships involve interdependence and mutuality. Given this, the question is, How can we transform seemingly zero-sum (win-lose) contests into positive-sum (win-win) outcomes?

The key is to alter attitudes—our own and then the other side's—to believe that this is possible. Such a paradigm shift can occur by sharing information in order to develop mutual trust. Then, rearrange the components that constitute the interests involved, while also working to increase the available benefits for both sides.

Bear in mind as you read further that I'm talking about the vast majority of negotiations, which combine elements of both cooperation and competition. Admittedly, there are some instances where there are long-term close relationships and high levels of trust. Understandably, one can be more open and forthcoming in these situations.

In summary, I have been saying that negotiating contains a mixture of discord and concurrence. It's a mixed-motive game where there must always be commonality and conflict. By the same token, engaging in the process involves a strategic blend of style and substance. Let me remind you that *how* you interact will often trump *what* you are discussing. Thus, I am recommending that you exhibit flexibility with respect to means (*how*), but determination, akin to rigidity, concerning your goals and interests (*what*).

PROMINENT POINTS

- It's always a mistake to stereotype or pigeonhole people and make unfounded assumptions about them.
- To be a creative negotiator, go beyond what's stated publicly to discover underlying interests and needs.
- Always stay focused upon your goal. Never get sidetracked and become emotionally attached to irrelevancies.
- If two alternatives appear close together in time or space, the contrast makes one of them more appealing.
- We are disposed to say "yes" to a person we know, like, or identify with.
- When someone does you a favor or gives you something of value, there is a tendency to reciprocate.
- Negotiating is best seen as a problem-solving process, where both sides interact to share their preferences, so that mutually beneficial exchanges can be made.
- While displaying flexibility of style (the *how*), always keep your interests or goal in mind (the *what*).

CHAPTER V

A BARGAINING FORMULA

Fessin' up to messin' up, if done without qualification, can transform a big mistake into a little error.

Up to this point, I have tried to provide a backdrop that will deepen your understanding of the persuasive phenomenon of our time—negotiating. As I made the point in a previous book, "Your real world is a giant negotiating table, and like it or not, you're a participant."

In playing this game of everyday living, you should always do so with some aim in mind. Certainly, it's purpose that gives meaning to life. For even the most strenuous activity without direction only produces movement without progress. By the same token, following the trite counsel of keeping your nose to the grindstone merely guarantees a short bloody nose.

So, a basic precursor of effective action is the ability to envision in one's mind an image of a desired outcome. Having this vision or goal enables you not to become enslaved by details. Thus, you want to keep your eyes on the prize and have a sense of fun along the way. To help you do this, I've put in order the ten essential steps to successful negotiating.

1

SETTING OBJECTIVES

Before you even contact the other side, think about your interests and concerns and what's really important to you. This is necessary so you can formulate a content goal, which should be specific, precise, and measurable. It's the *what* (substance) that you wish to attain in the final agreement.

Should the negotiation be more complex, multiple objectives are probably needed. When this occurs, it is wise to obtain input from those who might be affected by any outcome. Also, you may want to prioritize among your goals, while contemplating fallback positions and potential trade-offs.

In this case, your objectives might fall into three categories:

First and foremost, are the *must haves*. This primary group consists of items that are the raison d'être for the deal. Those things that have substantial economic impact on the bottom line.

The second category is the *would likes*, which are of importance but on these matters there is more room to maneuver since they are not deal breakers. Indeed, often a concession can be made here, in order to obtain a more profitable edge on a primary objective.

Finally, there are the *tradeables*, items that have relatively small economic impact to you, but may have value to the other side. Invoking the *reciprocity norm*, these can be swapped grudgingly for a concession in a category that has a higher priority.

When you establish your goals prior to negotiating, make sure they are challenging. In short, stretch your thinking. Considerable research and empirical evidence indicate that a determinant of success is the aspiration level of a negotiator. Yup, kids have it right: "If you expect more, you get more." So, we ultimately achieve what we think we can achieve.

Earlier I said that an objective must be precise and measurable. Preferably, it should be written down as a number. That means that statements like "I'll do the best I can here" or, "My goal is to get everything that's possible" would fail the test of specificity and quantification.

Instead, a proper objective would be, "To purchase this home for not more than $239,000" or, "For me to change jobs and feel gratified would require a compensation package of at least $115,000."

Very much related to goal setting is *strategy*, an overall plan of action that involves a coordinated and synchronized use of all available means to attain the objective. If the goal is *What* you want to achieve, then the strategy is *How* you will get there.

Once the objective is set, you should think strategically to formulate this game plan (a pattern of actions and behaviors), which provides a vision of the direction you will go to hit your target.

2

MAKING *HOW* CONCESSIONS

Early on, look for issues where you allow the other side to have their way in matters that don't involve content. That is, in many social interactions differences arise as to where the meeting should take place, who should attend, and when it should occur.

Let's take the matter of where—their place, yours, or a neutral site. There are, of course, obvious advantages to be in familiar surroundings where you have quick access to data and supporting evidence. But there are disadvantages as well. You can hardly claim limited authority—that you need time to check with your boss—if he's sitting in the office down the hall.

Meanwhile, let's say the other side has a strong preference where the meeting should be held and you care but not t-h-a-t much, here's what you might do. Instead of immediately saying, "No problem, whatever you want is fine," your reaction could be, "Mmm, let me think it over, I'll get back to you tomorrow on this."

The next day when you call, fuss a bit, whine about being away from your family, but ultimately concede. The point is this: You have just made a concession.

Another kindred example: You are enmeshed in bargaining with the other side, yet after investing days or weeks in trying to come to an agreement, there's an impasse. Nothing seems to work and so negotiations break off.

Typically, so-called experts or mavens tell you that if you contact the other party during this hiatus, it's a sign of weakness. Presumably, it means that you want the deal more than they do. I've even heard people say things like, "The one who speaks first loses." Baloney, not true.

When I was a child, my mother told me, "If you lie still, they throw dirt on you." Accordingly, you should call your counterpart, apologize for your contribution to the stalemate, and offer to return to the bargaining table. When you do, bring a proposal with you that represents a very minor content change on what they previously rejected. However, the wording should be slightly altered and the proposal refashioned so it looks a lot different. Although the other side may understand that the apparent substantive concession was in fact negligible, they appreciate that it took some courage for you to swallow your pride, make the phone call, and be the first to yield. From their vantage point, you made a concession and now they'll feel obligated to reciprocate.

Matter of fact, you have invoked the *reciprocity norm*.

The French sociologist Tocqueville observed that Americans adhere to a doctrine of enlightened self-interest: When he asked one of our ancestors why he risked his life running into a burning house to save the children of a stranger, he got this reply: "Well, by doing it, I expect someone would do the same for me someday."

In any social exchange you can improve the state of affairs by offering concessions in psychological coin. This subtle indebtedness can come in many ways. Allowing your counterpart or boss to take credit for your idea, or something you have done, not only helps the relationship, but often brings a tangible content payback.

3

OPEN WITH COMMONALITY

I've been married to a Communist and a Fascist and neither of them took out the garbage.
LEE GRANT, ACTOR AND DIRECTOR

If negotiating has a mix of commonality and conflict, you are always faced with this question: How do I start?

The answer categorically is with *commonality*. Always begin in a cooperative manner, discussing mundane items like the weather, sports, health, and the breaking news. Such small talk at the outset and throughout is necessary because humans, like automobiles, need maintenance, and that comes from the interpersonal process. If the other side's approach is purely intellectual and lacking in feelings it makes it more difficult to establish the proper climate for creative problem solving. This occurs with so-called busy people, who say at the very beginning: "Let's cut to the chase" or, "What's the bottom line here?" or, "Okay, forget all this other stuff—what's your best price?"

Upon hearing these expressions, I'm always reminded of something that playwright Arthur Miller once said: "A worship of fact is always an obstruction if one is looking for truth." Even Freud taught that the meaning of a dream must be derived from its form (*how*), not just content (*what*) alone.

Notwithstanding this wisdom, all of us have been involved with people who distort the means in pursuit of their ends. In what seems like a prior life, when I was a young claims adjuster, I recall more than once being brought into an attorney's office where there were attempts to make me feel diminished. My chair was always lower to the ground than theirs, as if the legs were sawed off. One time I was seated on a plush couch where my knees went up to my ears making me feel like I was deformed. Over the years, I have heard stories of people who were strategically positioned so that the sun was in their eyes. If you are uncomfortable with the seating arrangements, tell the other side and offer to switch places.

Basically, start negotiating with congruence—the things you have in common. During the process, be natural, unaffected, affable, and respectful of the other person's point of view. Engage in active listening, note taking, and displays of empathy. When the other side has a complaint or objection don't be quick to respond directly. Rather, first repeat what was said to let them know you are listening. Then, after reflecting their feelings, come back with another question to try to elicit their underlying interests and concerns.

In short, you want to have a *how* or a demeanor that communicates consideration and warmth, while you yourself have a cool detachment about the *what*—your objectives and interests.

Always embark upon the least troublesome issue first, those where a consensus can be readily attained. There is value in getting both sides in the right mood by achieving success early. Not only are you establishing a positive problem-solving climate, but also you're getting investment in the process.

Once in a while, you may hear the other side say "no." But as you know, "no" does not mean never, only not now. It's temporary, a reflex reaction to the unexpected. After asking, "Why do you say that?" to gain more information, you can always move on to another issue. Remember, it takes time to get used to a new idea. So you can shelve this item and come back to it later on.

Implicit in what I have said so far is that *you should save the most knotty issue for last*. This is usually an item that is highly emotional or is verbalized as a fixed sum. It is the zero-sum nut where one person's loss appears to be the other person's gain. Simply stated: One party is taking something from the other.

Examples of zero-sum issues would be matters that deal with price, rate, term, duration, salary, delivery date, and so on. These are things that are quantifiable and can be stated numerically.

For instance, let's say I decide to remodel the kitchen and baths in my home and have an estimate of $135,000, which the contractor tells me is his "rock-bottom price." My budget and expectations are $125,000. How do I proceed? Naturally, the first option is to try another vendor. But for the sake of argument, assume that I will not or cannot do that. How do I negotiate the price?

Using the modus operandi that I have laid out, the contractor and I have already come to agreement on the following: when the job will begin and end, the quality and delivery specifications, working days and hours, noise levels, warranties, special discounts, colors and texture, cleanup, penalties for missing deadlines. All that is left is the zero-sum issue of price: I'm at $125,000, and he's at $135,000.

To avoid a win-lose slugfest, consider the *concept of fractioning*, which holds that sometimes agreement can be reached on a contentious issue if you break it down into its components.

Instead of viewing something as an indivisible one, you look at it as if it were four quarters. Using a piecemeal strategy, I now deal with various elements that make up, or relate, to the price. Specifically, when will the money be paid? What form of payment? What if a payment is missed? Will money be held in escrow? And so on.

Because contractors have had frustrating past experiences with receiving payment for services performed, they know that less can sometimes be more, so this approach may satisfy their needs.

Ultimately, our differences were resolved when I agreed to a $75,000 down payment, with the remaining $50,000 placed in escrow, to be paid upon satisfactory completion of the work.

4

THE *TITANIC* PRINCIPLE

Until now, we have seen illustrations of how what people think they want are not what they ultimately settle for. One of the biggest mistakes that we make is to believe that the initial demand of the contending party correlates with their true interest. Perhaps that is why when people sometimes get what they asked for, they're still not happy. George Bernard Shaw in *Man and Superman* recognized this dilemma when he wrote, "There are two tragedies in life. One is not getting what you desire. The other is to gain it."

A friend of mine, Buddy Soll, who would later become a respected Dallas psychiatrist, once told me that "the human mind is like an iceberg whose surface movements are determined by unseen forces below the waterline." At the time, I'm not sure I fully understood what he meant. But, as years passed, this analogy shed light on a great deal of what I observed and experienced during interpersonal dealings.

In essence, in negotiating what's visible to us is the tip of the iceberg, that which is expressed as demands or positions taken. Below the surface, though, is a multitude of unseen complex concerns, interests, values, intentions, and preferences. Interestingly, the party who tells you what he or she wants may not even be consciously aware of these forces that will ultimately determine their satisfaction.

As a result, I formulated what I termed the *Titanic* principle, named after the "unsinkable" cruise ship that had only one voyage. You, of course, recall that the *Titanic* sailed forth on its maiden journey and struck an iceberg. Unfortunately, the vessel went down, but there were survivors. I imagined what would happen if that tragedy occurred nowadays. Given the competitive nature of today's media, there would be a rush to get the first interview with a survivor.

In my mind's eye I saw a group of those who outlived this catastrophe sitting in a TV studio being interviewed by a network anchor. It's been only hours since they were plucked from the frigid Atlantic. Sitting around the table, still suffering from the effects of hypothermia, they are wrapped in blankets and still shivering slightly as they drink hot coffee from mugs with the network's logo.

When the green light goes on and the interview kicks off, the anchor person asks, "What happened?"

"Well, we hit an iceberg!" says a survivor.

"Didn't you see it?" is the follow-up.

"I guess we did, but there didn't seem to be that much on top."

Aha, the metaphor of our time! What's apparent may not count that much. But what's underneath does.

This is true in negotiating, where my expressed opening demand is what is above sea level. Below the surface are a myriad of submerged factors that influenced my choice of this opener, which I believe will eventually satisfy my underlying concerns, interests, and needs.

What I'm saying is the initial position someone expressed is only shadow not substance. It is the effect of things, not the things themselves. Therefore, if you immediately counter an opening high demand with a low offer (tit for tat), you will be engaging in positional or share bargaining, which will put you in a competitive (win-lose) contest.

On the other hand, suppose you don't fall into this narrow rut. Instead, you say: "How did you come up with that? I don't understand. Please explain the thinking behind that asking price."

Reacting to these questions, he or she will furnish information by way of justification. This will reveal facts and feelings that were not apparent to you previously. It's information about their motives, preferences, intentions, and interests. Yes, this is the real stuff or substance that affects their decision making.

More significantly, by obtaining this additional data you will expand the playing field and be able to move from distributive (zero-sum) haggling to cooperative (positive-sum) negotiations.

Having burdened you with all this verbiage, let me offer what I trust will be a clarifying example. Its venue is the criminal justice system, a place where you would not expect to find much cooperative problem-solving behavior. I learned of this case in the course of giving a speech at a retreat of a major U.S. attorney's office in the summer of 2001.

The federal government had indicted four individuals as conspirators in a white-collar Ponzi scheme that bilked the public out of several hundred thousand dollars. The evidence against one of the four defendants, let's call him George Marshall, was overwhelming. As for the remaining three, the assistant U.S. attorney felt that he needed help to ensure convictions.

For this reason, the prosecutor offered Marshall a deal. Instead of a fifteen-year sentence when found guilty, if he agreed to cooperate and testify against his co-conspirators, his sentence would be reduced to ten years. Marshall's reaction was "Fuhgeddaboudit, I'm not a rat!"

The negotiations were stalemated until Marshall's attorney asked his client, who was out on bail, why he was so adamant in taking this stance. It turned out that he and his wife had one child, a daughter, who was pregnant. Her due date was December 1. Although he knew he would be found guilty, his trial was not to start until January 7. This meant that he would be present for the birth of his first grandchild and get to spend the Christmas holidays with his family. Furthermore, Marshall said that when he was indicted he promised his wife that he would not cop a plea that would put him away for ten or more years. As he put it, "Sure I took money, but only from those who had a surplus. Nonetheless, I always keep my word." Ignoring this ethical dissonance, the assistant United States attorney saw an opportunity to make a deal where both sides could satisfy their underlying concerns and interests.

This outcome was an agreement whereby Marshall testified against his former associates, who were convicted. In return, on January 15, he received a sentence of ten years. With time off for good behavior he could be released in eight and a half years. Conceivably, it's possible he might be out even earlier in a work release program.

A concluding note: The prosecutor told me he was so pleased by the trial testimony of Marshall that he recommended to the sentencing judge that he serve his time in a federal prison close to his home.

5

THE PING-PONG TABLE THEORY OF LIFE

By now, I trust you have accepted that negotiating is a paradoxical game. It's akin to the spirit of our era, which is both pragmatic and transcendental. At the same time, we seem to value individualism and interdependence, power and humility, competition and cooperation. We like people who sacrifice, but we also admire those with material wealth. Is this not true? Mother Teresa and Donald Trump—hmm, an interesting pairing.

Moreover, such contradictions exist within each of us as well, between word and deed, reality and theory, personal pleasure and obligations. There are even two contradictory aspects of the way we think: the linear or regimented left side of our brain and the emotional, intuitive right side.

In my case, the left is personified by a guy dressed in a black leather outfit and spit-polished boots with chains and a whip. Speaking with a German accent he tells me, "You vill vin now. Dis is de only way. Accept not excuses or delays. Take hostages if necessary, but *vin*." In contrast, there's a melodious voice coming from the right side of my brain, which is lyrical and relaxed. It's a barefoot lad from Barbados, wearing shorts and a psychedelic flowered shirt, who says, "Cool it, mahn, dere's always another day and another way."

Balancing these antithetical messages to achieve equilibrium enables you not to push too hard to make things happen—but let the process unfold on its own. It's caring, but not t-h-a-t much.

At the heart of all strategic interactions is a similar paradox: We're never really negotiating for what we're talking about. Rather, we're using this discussion to satisfy our needs. This is what I refer to as the *Ping-Pong table theory of life.*

Let me explain. After Ellen and I were married we lived in various apartments in metropolitan areas. Even after having children, we still resisted the lure of suburbia.

Actually, I enjoyed the hustle and bustle of big cities, walking about on concrete, cement or asphalt, amidst a heterogeneous mix of people. I liked the feel of macadam under my feet, the smell of burning tar and the sound of honking car horns. More pointedly, an atmosphere that was visible—air you could really see—comforted me.

One day I was startled when Ellen said to me, "It's too bad, but we have to move."

"What?" I said. "Why?"

"We have to buy a home in the suburbs. If we don't our family will fall apart."

"What are you talking about?" I said.

"Well, in the city we don't do anything together. There's nothing that we share."

"What are you saying? We share the same apartment and the same weather. We see each other every morning and evening. That's a lot in common."

She said, "No, no that's not together. Each of us has separate lives."

"Well, they're kids," I replied. "They do kid stuff and we do adult stuff. What do you want us to do together?"

"We could play Ping-Pong together. Yes, Ping-Pong."

"You're putting me on," I said. "People of my persuasion—though I have no memory of being persuaded—don't play Ping-Pong. Pinochle maybe—but not Ping-Pong."

"I'm not joking," Ellen said. "We need something that we can partake of as a family."

"Okay, I'll give you that," I responded. "But if we want to play table tennis we can do it right in this place. We don't have to move."

"No, we can't put a Ping-Pong table in this small apartment. It's crowded already. A bigger apartment is too expensive, so the only option is to buy a home out on Long Island."

Apparently, she had thought this through and was not amenable to even discussing the matter. This solution, however, was very threatening to me. As someone who was born and raised in the city, this was an alien idea. I didn't know whether grass could support my weight or how all that greenery would affect my eyesight.

In any event, Ellen and our excited children jumping up and down talked me into buying a home in Syosset, Long Island. The major criterion was that it have a finished basement where we could set up the family Ping-Pong table.

By the time the move occurred we had exhausted all of our savings. Nothing was left with which to buy furniture, so the living room and dining room were barren. Except, we did make one purchase: a brand-new Ping-Pong table for the basement.

The day we moved in, before we even unpacked, the games began. We were playing Ping-Pong—first singles, then doubles. Tournaments were taking place day and night and standings were posted. For an entire week we were obsessed with the game. The woman was right, the family was pulling together.

Kids were coming over from other families to watch the play. We were breaking up other families, but we didn't care. We were possessed and preoccupied with Ping-Pong.

This fixation lasted for two weeks. Then, the third week we damaged the ball. It slowed the game but we carried on. The fourth week a paddle got broken; still, play persisted. The fifth week the net went down. We put it back up, holding it in place with string and tape. But then it drooped and finally collapsed a few days later.

From that sixth week to this day we have never played Ping-Pong again. Certainly not as a family. We have moved eight times since then, leaving behind books, giving away furniture, and throwing away toys, but that large green rectangular table always comes with us. Today, it sits in our basement, where from that sixth week on, no matter its domicile, it's been used to sort laundry.

What I am suggesting to you is the history of the Ping-Pong table in America. Nobody really wants the table per se, but they see it as a means of satisfying their needs.

Since those six golden weeks of family sharing and togetherness, I spent twenty-five years living in Illinois. While there, I learned that approximately thirty thousand convertible cars are sold in Chicagoland annually. Yes that's right, I'm talking about the Windy City—that toddlin' town. Even if you haven't lived there or visited, you know what the year round weather is like.

One day, while looking through the almanac, I learned that there are only fifty-seven days of sunshine in Chicago. More intriguing perhaps is that for forty-two of those days the windchill factor is below zero. That leaves you with only fifteen days where you can put the top down. Now, subtract the very hot or muggy days where you need the auto's air-conditioning system. What about the days you might be ill, working, or out of town? That leaves about three days. Not a helluva lot!

Regardless of this logic and reality, people still buy convertibles, because it's a means of satisfying their underlying needs. But it's not just the convertible sports car, it's the boat, the ski chalet, or the expensive piece of technology that gathers dust. As far as I'm concerned, all of these things are Ping-Pong tables, and life seems to be filled with them.

What I'm saying, of course, is that human beings do not always operate rationally in pursuit of their interests and goals.

6

BROADENING THE GAUGE

Although you and I believe we are acting rationally to satisfy our needs, each of us brings our own unique experiences into any social interaction. We are each weighed down by the luggage of living. In my case, the baggage is Samsonite and American Tourister—in yours it maybe Gucci, Pucci, or Fiorucci. Nevertheless, such different experiences affect how each of us view and evaluate the same reality, because we only register what is meaningful to us. In brief, we often don't look for or see what might be there, but only what we expect to find.

Having said this, let's come back to one of the impediments that often confront negotiators: the zero-sum or fixed-sum issue. Earlier we discussed *fractioning* but there is another way to deal with this situation.

Supposing two automobiles are traveling on a rural dirt road that measures eight feet across. Coming from opposite directions, each car is about five and a half feet wide and moving along at forty miles per hour. Surely if they do not stop or one of them pull off the road a collision will ensue.

Now, taking a similar scenario, let's assume that the vehicles are not on a narrow path but a major artery, a highway or thruway—the Champs-Elysées, Constitution Avenue, Ocean Parkway, Wilshire Boulevard, or Lake Shore Drive—there's no problem. With the expanded dimension, passage is made easier.

Accordingly, the more information that can be discovered and discussed in a negotiation, the easier it is to achieve convergence. Remember, you and I do not assess things the same way. What may be essential to me is rather insignificant to you and vice versa. Thus, you need to learn as much as you can about your counterpart, so that trade-offs or exchanges can be made on issues of differing importance.

Logrolling, heavily used in the political arena, is based on this reality—that values vary among people. Behavioral scientist George Homans showed more than fifty years ago how to take various items at stake and divide them into goods that are worth more to one party than they cost the other.

ITEM: A number of years ago, I was involved in a management-labor dispute in the printing industry. It appeared that collective bargaining had ceased and both sides were resorting to threats and filing unfair labor practices charges against the other.

Upon arriving on the scene, I met with each side separately in an attempt to find out the real importance that they placed on the issues they were contending over. Labor had two demands. The first was an increase in overtime pay of 15 percent and the other was an additional ten-minute rest break per day.

Management's major concern was increasing productivity, which would enable them to compete in the marketplace. Though vehement that they could not afford another worker coffee break, they felt that the extent of overtime was a matter within their control.

In two days an agreement was reached whereby the union leadership was able to obtain a 12 percent overtime hike at the price of giving up their other demands—at least for now.

7

THE VAIL CONDO

To further illuminate this point, allow me to share with you a story from my own life. Just a few years after the Vail resort opened in Colorado, I went there, accompanied by Ellen, to give a speech. It was a beautiful day with the sun glistening off the snow and we decided to try and buy a place. One of my goals had always been to own a piece of the Rockies.

A real estate agent took us around and eventually we found something that we both liked. It was a condominium listed at $80,000.

When we returned to the real estate agent's office I was already formulating my plan, saying to my partner, "Look, they want $80,000 for the condo. I'll open with $73,000, see what they come back with and then make the necessary adjustments."

As I'm doing this strategic thinking, I looked over and noticed that Ellen had her eyes closed. Her head was moving sideways and words came forth. "Listen Herbert," she said. "I don't think people here will appreciate your little games. I don't think haggling and chiseling have come this far west yet. If you want to make a fool of yourself go right ahead, but don't involve me. In fact, when you were giving your speech, I walked through the village and didn't see even one pushcart."

"What are you talking about?" I responded. "These people here love negotiating. Your problem is that you don't know about the history of Colorado. Actually, negotiating started for America in this very state. Two guys outside Leadville were panning for gold. Down on their luck, they decided to swap pans. The prospector with the older pan had to throw in a glove to make the deal. Right after that, they both struck it rich. When word spread, all over Colorado people were wheeling and dealing."

Ellen, familiar with my exaggerated banter, knew that it was not necessary to respond to this made-to-order story. The real estate agent, Fran Burns, on the other hand, decided to intervene on her behalf—like she might need help. Oh really!

"Your wife is absolutely right, Mr. Cohen," she said. "*We* of Vail feel, that when *we* of Vail ask for $80,000, *we* of Vail expect that . . ."

Before she even finished I found myself getting irritated by her hoi polloi approach. Definitely, I don't like people that indiscriminately use the royal *we*. As far as I'm concerned, there are only two categories of people who have the right to use the royal *we*. First would be genuine members of royalty. That would include Queen Elizabeth, Prince Charles, Philip, Andrew, and maybe even Fergie. The second group would be those people who within their bodies have active tapeworms. Other than these two, I suspect using *we* in this fashion is inappropriate, if not elitist.

Unaware of my annoyance, Fran Burns went on: "Here in Vail, *we* feel that when *we* ask for $80,000, *we* expect to get $80,000."

"Is that right?" I said. "That's too bad, 'cause *we* here in America—and the last time I looked Vail was in America—if *we* wanted $80,000 *we* would ask for $90,000. That's the American way."

Neither of them were convinced by my argument. Supporting each other, they hung tough.

To prove I was a flexible person, I decided to open with a $76,000 offer. The real estate agent, at first, attempted embarrassment or guilt to get me to raise the offer. "Mr. Cohen, surely a man in your position—"

But Ellen interjected, "What position? He's of peasant stock."

Next, Fran Burns pretended to take it personally. "Mr. Cohen, I'm a professional and I would be insulted to convey such a low offer."

"Is there possibly another real estate agent in Eagle County who is less sensitive than you are?" was my response.

Finally, with great reluctance the real estate agent agreed to transmit our $76,000 offer to the seller. At the same time, she assured us that there was no way it would be accepted because many others were interested in this condominium.

Later that day, we met Fran in the lobby of our hotel. Approaching us, she looked upbeat. For just a few seconds, I thought, "Hey maybe they accepted our offer."

No such luck. Fran was smiling because she felt vindicated. "Mr. Cohen, your offer was rejected. And as I told you, there were two other offers for the asking price of $80,000. Like I said, this is Vail."

At first I was incredulous. "I can't believe it," I said. "What's the matter with these people? Don't they understand it's called the '*asking* price' for a reason? The seller is only inviting a bid. If he really wanted that, it would be called the '*wanting* price.'"

Recognizing that I was still skeptical, Fran reached into her briefcase and pulled out the two offer sheets. In those days, all the condo owners were given the first right of refusal on all new sales, so this information was readily available.

After showing me that both prospective contracts contained offers of $80,000, Fran said, "Let me leave these with you."

"Why?" I thought. "To remind me of this negotiating disappointment?"

PASSING FAILURE ON THE WAY TO SUCCESS

Success benefits the body, but failure develops the mind.

In 1979, Andrew Tobias wrote an article about me that appeared in *Playboy* magazine. It was entitled "The World's Best Negotiator." The following year, when I was on a book tour, the question that I was asked most frequently was: "Have you ever failed in a negotiation?" The answer, of course, was: "Yes, many times."

Having made this admission, the media understandably wanted me to recount these failures in detail. Though it was clearly in my interest to do so, as the audience would better relate to what I had to say, I had difficulty recalling these setbacks. Why? In order to maintain self-esteem, human beings block things out, rationalize, or attribute lack of success to factors beyond their control.

So it was in the Vail debacle. At the time, I remember saying to Ellen, "Do you know why we didn't get this place? Probably because the Lord intervened. He knows that snow slides or mud slides are coming in the future and he didn't want his boy Herbie to get hurt."

Not stopping there, I went on. "Anyway, I never really liked this place. If they had accepted our offer we would have had to spend a week or two here every year. Imagine hanging around with dummies that offer what is asked for. These are the kind of people who, when they read about the evils of drinking, they give up reading.

"Furthermore," I said, "I can get something just as good as this, better maybe, for less, near Columbus, Ohio." In essence, I was withdrawing my ego from the encounter.

"Once again, Herbert, you have ruined the quality of our life," Ellen said. "That has always been your problem. You never take advice. We live in a capitalist system but we have no investments. That's why you're not home, and always working. If we bought this place we could rent it out at least twenty weeks a year. Then, waking up in the morning back east and watching the weather report in the Rockies, every time it snowed we'd earn money from skiers renting our condo. While we slept our capital invested would be producing income. That's the American way. But no, not you, Mr. Stubborn."

Having to endure this feedback, especially in front of Fran Burns, I found myself getting agitated and annoyed. Actually, I was thinking that every time I watched a weather forecast in the future I would be reminded of this fiasco. Concerned that I would never hear the end of this, I was determined to prove I was right in the first place.

Somewhat emotional, I blurted out, "Ellen, this isn't over yet. I'll definitely get this condo for $76,000, proving to you and your '*we* friend' here that I know what I'm doing."

In the ensuing years, I have been asked by many, "How could you have been so positive? What was your strategy?" Truly, I had none. I just reacted fervently in order to save face.

To avoid further humiliation, I was forced to start thinking. Up to this point, I had been doing exactly what I have told you not to do. I had been looking at only the tip of the iceberg, seeing the seller in only one dimension. He or she is a "money coveter," so the party who offers the most makes the deal.

To overcome this stereotypical mind-set, I needed information that would enable me to learn what's below the surface in order to expand the gauge. So I asked Fran, "Who is the seller? Why is he selling? How long has he had the place?" and other similar matters. She didn't have the answers to my questions, but referred me to the listing broker.

This real estate agent had a wealth of information. She knew the sellers: a husband and wife who worked for an energy company in Denver. They had just received a big promotion and would be moving to Zurich, Switzerland, where they would be opening an office on the Bahnhoffstrasse in the city. They were given a fifteen-year contract to relocate and told that this would be virtually a permanent move.

Therefore, they had already sold their main residence in Denver and put this weekend condo up for sale. In the process of closing bank accounts, they didn't expect to be returning stateside in the near future.

Although Fran, the real estate agent, had given me copies of the two prospective contracts, I never actually read the provisions. But now I more than just glanced at the $80,000 offers. In doing so, I realized that both of them were contingent upon the buyers' obtaining a mortgage at a certain rate within a specified period of time. In other words, there was a condition precedent to each of these deals coming into being.

Aha! I'm sure you know of situations where people thought they had something finalized only to learn that they didn't, when an activating requirement didn't occur.

Were you to ask me, "How often does this happen?," I would say, "How the heck do I know? Maybe only sixteen times in a decade." But that's not what's important. What is important is our perception that this is a common occurrence.

Upon reflection, I knew what to do. These sellers should have another concern beyond price and I was going to surface it so it would come to their attention. This was, of course, the need for certainty.

Obviously, they'd feel a lot better knowing that after leaving these shores there was no chance of receiving a cablegram or phone call at an ungodly hour saying in effect, "Buyer unable to get financing. Your place in Vail back on market."

So, I now knew what to do. I went to see their real estate agent and offered $76,000 unconditionally—no mortgage, no conditions. That's right—all cash. A clean deal.

Would you believe they took it? Yup, I got the condo for my price. The next day, however, I ran around like crazy trying to get a mortgage. You see, I really didn't have that kind of money.

This anecdote is true. To this day, I still own that condominium, which has appreciated nicely over the years. The point of the story, though, is that even an experienced negotiator in the heat of a strategic interaction can forget that he or she is dealing with people who are complex and multifaceted. Discovering their other concerns will enable you to broaden the gauge and increase your chance of success.

8

MAKE 'EM WORK

There is a mythical story about a Wall Street investment banker who after ascending from the subway each morning would pass a pretzel vendor. Though never taking a pretzel, he would always hand the seller a crisp dollar bill. This ritual went on for years. Then one day, after handing over the dollar, the vendor shouted after him, "Hey wait! You owe me twenty-five cents. Pretzel prices have gone up. They're now a buck and a quarter!"

What is the import of this tale? First, people value what they acquire as a result of their labor. Second, when the recipient of a concession has not expended energy, what's given tends to be devalued. Lastly, when something comes too easy, it often raises expectations that more will be forthcoming.

Moses Maimonides, one of the foremost intellectuals of medieval times, understood this aspect of human nature. In writing how the moral requirement to help the poor ("tsedakah") should be performed, he actually rated the different means of fulfilling this obligation. The best way, he said, is to help someone help himself. What this physician and philosopher knew over eight hundred years ago was that people prize those things that they have expended effort to achieve. Moreover, in doing so, they maintain their dignity.

Likewise, in the game of negotiating, what happens when a party spends considerable time and energy pursuing an objective?

When attained, it is cherished and savored. Thus, the more re-sources expended and the more aggravation endured in pursuit of a goal only enhances its desirability.

Taking this one step further, there are instances where people become so enmeshed in the game, that the return on their invest-ment can never be adequate. When I'm in Las Vegas or Atlantic City, I see unlucky gamblers putting quarters or dollars in the same slot machine. They refuse to call it quits or even change ma-chines because "this one is due" or "the percentages are now with me."

Whatever the rationale, we are dealing with the *investment prin-ciple*, which as a practical matter can cause negotiators to adjust their expectations and distort reality as they become more in-volved.

Take the case of Humpty Dumpty, who sat on a wall and had a great fall. In the aftermath, we might imagine what happened. The King appeared before his council to update them on devel-opments.

"Using all of my horses and all of my men, I tried to put Humpty Dumpty back together again," he said, "but to no avail. So the solution is obvious: We are going to get more horses and more men."

By the look of things, the monarch was not walking away from his investment but intended to do *more of the same*.

Perhaps this even sheds some light on why President Johnson and Nixon had such difficulty extricating the United States from the war in Vietnam.

Similarly, President Clinton invested considerable political cap-ital in an attempt to establish peace between Israel and its neigh-bors. Yet, all of his efforts, from July 2000 to January 2001, could not produce an agreement. (If you are interested in how I applied the concepts we have been discussing to the abortive Camp David negotiations, please refer to my memorandum of February 1, 2001, written to Secretary of State Colin Powell at the start of the new administration, in Appendix 3).

Leon Festinger, the social psychologist, studied this paradoxical behavior in humans and animals for years, concluding that, "Rats and people come to love those things for which they have suffered."

All this means is that if you are negotiating in a climate where there is less than total trust, you must make the other side work for the concessions you give them. No doubt about it, the way in which you concede in time and increments sends a message. Indeed, if the relationship is adversarial, the contending party may see a concession that came too easy as a sign of weakness, which can engender suspicion.

In summary, concessions will be valued and appreciated commensurate to the extent that the recipient labors for them. So, in an environment that lacks mutual trust here's the rule: Make 'em work!

9

YOU OWE ME AN APOLOGY

Want to make God laugh, an old saying has it, just tell him your plans. Of course, this relates to negotiating as well. No matter how much time you have spent formulating a strategy, or even rehearsing, the unexpected always occurs. Moreover, since any protracted social exchange cannot be scripted, participants spontaneously react or say things that, upon reflection, they wish they hadn't.

During heated multiparty negotiations, I have been present when one person called another a liar. Undeniably, the target of this slur had been exaggerating and bluffing, but using the L word is a breach of negotiating etiquette. It can only offend face and poison a relationship.

Should such impromptu invective ever pass your lips, the antidote is, of course, to immediately apologize. Better yet, if you see negotiating as a game, where you're caring, but not t-h-a-t much, you will be less likely to have this problem. Having this attitude means that, even when dealing with a con man, you will view him not as a liar, but as someone who is "augmenting reality."

Of all the run-ins with the truth, my favorite occurred a few years ago in a four-sided negotiation that took place in Washington, D.C. We were supposed to begin at 10:00 A.M. and three of us were present at that time. While waiting for the fourth person to arrive, those already present kept glancing at their watches. Finally, twenty-five minutes after the hour, Mr. Tardy walks in.

"Ahem, I'd like to apologize somewhat for being a bit late," he said. Hearing this, I initially thought, what's this "somewhat" and "a bit" late?

He didn't stop there. "Although it looks like I'm twenty minutes late," he said, "I'm really not. When I first got to the building it was 9:55 A.M., but the parking lot was filled. So, I had to drive around looking for a space. Then, when I finally got to this floor, no one was at the reception desk. I waited for nine minutes before someone came to show me to this conference room. Actually then, I may not even be late."

Listening to this recitation, what did Mr. Somewhat Tardy expect us to say? "Oh you poor boy, you're having a bad day. Let me give you a hug."

Truly, the result was that after his recountal of woe, we realized we were dealing with a person who was immature and unreliable. Unintentionally, he had affected the level of trust.

What should he have done? If you are twenty-five minutes late, you ought to say, "Please forgive me. I'm terribly sorry for keeping you waiting. I'm almost an hour late."

If this had occurred how would we have reacted? One of us would have probably said, "What are you talking about, you're only twenty-five minutes late: no big deal."

Then, there's usually the guy who chimes in with, "Well on my Rolex, it's twenty-three minutes and forty-eight seconds."

The point is, if you're fessin' up to messin' up, do it without qualification and people will identify with you. You have admitted that you are not perfect and have humanized yourself. In fact, it may even be regarded as a *how* concession that requires reciprocation.

This is also true in politics, where the attempted cover-up is always worse than the initial transgression. From the Watergate scandal to the Enron bankruptcy, the rules of damage control are rather simple:

1. Be the first to release all the bad news, so there's nothing left for someone to uncover.
2. Your revelations should be honest and accurate.
3. Accept total responsibility for your misdeeds without blaming others or circumstances.

During the last years of his presidency, Bill Clinton put himself and the nation through the ordeal of impeachment by violating these principles. Finally, in August 1999, he got on television where he acknowledged his relationship with Ms. Lewinsky. He admitted that his grand jury testimony contained unusual responses and offered an apology to the American people.

Although coming late, Mr. Clinton was doing well in fessin' up to messin' up. But after fifteen minutes, he switched gears. Starting with the word "however," he then spent almost equal time attacking the special prosecutor, Ken Starr.

Not surprisingly, the electorate did not regard this speech as a heartfelt apology. As a result, President Clinton had to spend the next two months meeting with religious leaders, expressing his regrets, and asking for forgiveness.

Of course, this concept applies to all of our relationships—not just political and business, but personal as well.

For over four decades I have been married to the same woman. Apparently this is so rare nowadays that they run bus tours past my home.

This longevity, though, has not been without occasional disagreement, differences of opinion, and arguments. In my younger days, I was more analytical and precise. Thus, when it came time to resolve a dispute where I was mostly at fault, I would say something like: "Well, I guess I'm about 72 percent wrong, so I apologize for that, which leaves 28 percent of the blame with you."

Would you believe that never worked? It only caused the discord to become more prolonged and bitter.

But now I know that if I intend to apologize because I'm the major cause of an argument, to do so without any qualification.

In essence, I say, "I'm sorry I was totally wrong." Whenever you accept full responsibility in this manner, observe that you will stun your significant other, who is waiting for you to add "however" or "but." And we all know that these words are interpreted as, "I don't mean what I just said and now comes the real message."

ITEM: Heinrich Heine, the renowned poet, on his deathbed asked his family if God would forgive him for his sins. Before they could respond, he said, "Of course he will—from this he makes his living."

10

CLOSING THE DEAL

We now come to the benchmarks necessary to successfully conclude a negotiation. There are four major criteria:

First, *gain sufficient investment in the process.* It is this expenditure of time and energy that affects expectations and calculations and minimizes the potential for buyer's or seller's remorse.

Second, *furnish a basis for comparison.* If a party can view some seemingly objective data (a standard price list or published policy), it helps him or her evaluate the terms offered.

Third, *use the concession rate to signal the best deal.* Move from the opening position in decreasing steps, beginning with the largest concession and then gradually diminishing the amount conceded. This signals the other side that the bottom line is being approached.

Fourth, *after obtaining involvement, provide options or choices.* Keeping in mind that people support that which they help create, you always want the other side participating in the process. Further, to avoid any semblance of an ultimatum, you must be flexible with elements that will comprise the final agreement.

Let us take these four criteria and show how they come alive in an all too familiar experience: the purchase of a new automobile.

A number of years ago, I returned home on a Friday evening, after spending the week involved in a business transaction. When I walked through the door, Ellen said, "Welcome back, Mr. Negotiator." By the way, this is not a term of endearment in my household.

"Why don't you do something for your family?" she said. "You know that we have needed a new car for months. Instead of helping others, help your family for once. Tomorrow, no later, go out and make this purchase. It will be easy for you, because you'll be dealing with *your* people."

According to Ellen, "my people" are apparently used car dealers.

Initially, I tried to avoid this responsibility, claiming that I didn't have the requisite information and needed to do some research.

Unfortunately, she was prepared. "That's no problem," she said. "Our neighbor John, who is a good husband, just bought his wife, Mary, the very automobile I want. He spent hours negotiating a very good price. Here's the salesman's business card and what they paid written on the back. All you have to do is walk into the dealership, show them the card, sign some papers, and drive the car home."

Knowing this is an oversimplification, I was nevertheless trapped. So, the next morning I embarked upon this adventure.

Arriving at the dealership, I met the salesman and showed him his card. "Yes, it's mine," he said, "but who wrote the numbers on the back?" Naturally, I mentioned John and Mary, but he remarked, "The only John and Mary I know are from the Bible."

Notwithstanding this problem, he was anxious to sell me the car I wanted. Taking me into the showroom, he showed me the coveted new car, which was so highly polished it sparkled.

As we got close, the first thing I noticed was the "sticker price," which was literally stuck to the car. Truly, this form of legitimacy always intimidates me because I remember the trouble I had scraping it off the window of my last vehicle. Ergo, this appears as a permanent marker that is not to be tampered with.

Now, the "sticker price" doesn't round out the numbers. It never says, "This could be yours for approximately $30,000." Absolutely not. Rather, everything is itemized with the unequivocal final cost stated at $32,387.16. They've got it down to the penny.

Interestingly, the last two items are the state and local taxes. Thus, you have the feeling that if you get it for less, the revenue people will be tracking you forever.

Not knowing what to do, I walked around the car, kicked the tire, rubbed the hood, and opened and closed the door. The salesman said, "You look like you're in sticker shock, so I'll give it to you for $3,000 less."

Upon hearing this, what do you think I did? Yup, I again kicked the tire and opened and closed the door. Sure enough, he dropped the price another thousand dollars.

When I said only, "No, not enough," the salesman responded, "Look, I like you, so I'll take $350 out of my commission—the bread from my children's mouths—and give it to you."

"I'm sorry," I said. "I'll be humiliated if I don't get at least the same price as my neighbor."

"When did he buy the car?" he asked.

"About five days ago," was my reply.

"That explains it," he said. "It's inflation. But I'll tell you what I'm going to do, I'll throw in floor mats and undercoating. That's about another $150, so do we have a deal?"

"No," I replied, "it's not enough. But I'll tell you what I'm gonna do. Out of respect for your children and their nourishment, I'll kick in $75 out of my personal allowance, which puts us only $100 apart."

Abruptly, the salesman shifted gears and began his acting performance. Heretofore, he had been conversing with me in a routine manner. But now, he started moving about, looking up at the ceiling, as if checking for overhead surveillance. Indeed, he even lowered his voice, so I found myself moving closer to hear what he was saying.

Then his face became twisted and his lips moved toward his ear. And suddenly he started whispering out of the side of his mouth.

Shocked at first, I remember thinking, "The man looks like he's having a stroke." Accordingly, I even said, "Please sit down. Can I get you a glass of water?"

What was really happening? This experienced salesman was merely playing the game. He knew that offers that come from the side of the mouth in soft tones have 37 percent more credibility than those made in a normal fashion.

Certainly, people tend to believe almost anything if you take them aside and whisper to them through the corner of your mouth.

At this point, the salesman continued his playacting. He took me behind his desk and removed a key from his wallet.

"Mr. Cohen," he said, "because you cared about my children, I'm going to show you something no customer has ever seen."

Unlocking the desk drawer, he removed a printed document. "This is for your eyes alone," he said. "It is the actual invoice cost of the car. As you can plainly see, according to this document, every vehicle sold at this price, the dealer loses $11 a car."

Somewhat bewildered, I asked, "How can he do that and stay in business?"

"He makes it up in volume!" was his reply.

Still perplexed by this revelation, I maintained my composure. "Look," I said, "I still need the other hundred dollars to match what my neighbor got."

"I'm sorry, Mr. Cohen," he said, "but I don't have the authority to do that."

When hearing this, all of us react the same way: "Okay, who does have the authority?"

The salesman always points to an upstairs corner office or beyond the building and says, "Only the sales manager, or in this case, the dealer who lives in a shack."

"What do you mean in a shack? This dealership is four city blocks, why would he live in a shack?"

"He lives there with his dogs, two Doberman pinschers and two German shepherds that are ferocious."

"Listen," I said, "I don't care who he lives with. You go back there and tell him you've got a customer who's walking unless he gets that $100."

After telling me about his fear of these carnivorous canines and lack of sufficient life insurance, the salesman reluctantly departed to plead my case.

Ten minutes passed and I thought about leaving. But then, I believed I heard the sound of barking dogs. No, it can't be.

Finally, my emissary to the guy in the shack returned. Limping into the showroom, he looked like he'd been on a roller-coaster ride. His face was ashen and haggard; his tie was off, and water or saliva was on his shirt.

"I begged the guy in the shack and I fought for you but the best he'll do is $33."

At that point, I was overcome with déjà vu, realizing I had been a pawn in the game. Obviously, I felt annoyed and angry. My initial reaction was to get out of there and go across the street where they were selling similar cars.

What do you think I did? First off, I thought if I go to the dealer across the way, I've got to start all over again. I'll have to go back to square one. Aha! once again it's the *investment principle* that affects my calculations.

Then, contemplating further, I realized that if I leave this dealership, I would be going from the certain to the uncertain. So, the old maxim applies, "The devil known is better than the devil unknown." Alas, this is the essence of the *certainty principle*. In the end, as bad as these guys are, I know what they are. Who knows what the dealer across the street has in his shack? Maybe snakes or other reptiles.

There was, however, another alternative. I might have gone home and discussed this with Ellen. She and I could have formed a taskforce, bought some Puppy Chow or Alpo, gone over the head of the salesman, and dealt directly with the dealer and his dogs. As the old cliché goes, "Why waste your time with the monkey when you can deal directly with the organ grinder?"

As it turned out, I weighed the amount of time and energy that would have to be expended against the potential monetary gain, and reluctantly said, "I'll take it."

Clearly, the four closing criteria that I mentioned are evident in this negotiating experience.

First, consuming so much time and effort engaged in this process made it more difficult to relinquish this investment.

Second, being exposed to the clearly visible "sticker price," and learning of the concealed or secret "factory invoice," afforded a touchstone to measure the deal.

ITEM: Years ago I did an award-winning commercial for the General Motors Corporation, which was shown repeatedly in the state of California. This made me a quasi-celebrity for several weeks. During this time, I was approached in elevators, restaurants, and on the street by people who had just purchased new automobiles.

In each instance, they wanted to tell me how well they did in their negotiations. Virtually in every case, success was measured by the printed standard of the "sticker price."

Third, the use of the amount and interval of concession making sent the message that the window of opportunity was closing.

Consider: The salesman's first price drop was $3,000, followed by $1,000. Then came $350 from his commission and the floor mats and undercoating valued at $150. At last, the $33 from "the guy in the back" for which he seemingly put his life in jeopardy to attain.

Lastly, by drawing the customer into the process, it makes him or her more willing to endorse the final outcome.

PROMINENT POINTS

- Before the strategic interaction occurs, establish a specific and measurable goal that gives direction to your activities.
- Being flexible on *style* enables you to grudgingly yield on some *how* items to gain substance (*what*) concessions in return.
- Open all discussions with commonality and a demeanor that communicates consideration and warmth.
- Save the most knotty or zero-sum issue for last.
- Since human beings are complex and multifaceted, probe below the surface so you can broaden the discussion. This enables you to make trade-offs and exchanges to facilitate agreement.
- Concessions are not appreciated unless effort is expended to obtain them.
- If you say or do something inappropriate, immediately offer an unqualified and unconditional apology.
- There are four major criteria that will finally induce your counterpart to say yes:

1. Sufficient investment.
2. Having a basis for comparison.
3. A concession rate that signals the approach of your bottom line.
4. The feeling that they were involved in producing this outcome.

CHAPTER VI

THE PERCEPTUAL TIP

"I ought therefore I can."

IMMANUEL KANT

Decades ago, early in my career, I received a phone call from the Million Dollar Roundtable, asking about my availability for a speaking engagement in Hawaii. Everything sounded terrific, until I heard the details. Apparently, my talk was to last fifteen minutes and the topic was "The Three Keys to Negotiating Success." But there were additional specifications. My presentation was to contain motivational illustrations and also be uplifting.

When I called back, in an effort to negotiate for more time, I felt I was dealing with a very rigid person, who thought he was ordering a standard widget. Although refusing to budge, he was certain that I would accept this proposal as stated. After all, as he put it, "this exposure could mean over $100,000 in future bookings."

Displaying considerable enthusiasm and a positive mental attitude, he was certain that he would be greeting me personally at the group luau. Back then, I had a favorite saying, "Don't compromise yourself, because that's all you've got." With this principle in mind, I told him, "From your mouth to God's ear."

By the way, this is an ancient expression that is uttered to someone who has just described a scrumptious but unlikely future happening—like winning the lottery. That is, may the Lord make it happen, but don't hold your breath. Basically, I somehow reconciled myself to a life without this booking, the accompanying luau, and all the money that was to follow.

But as you know, every setback can produce progress. Just as every disadvantage, with perspective, may become an advantage. For example, while egotistical people tend to be self-absorbed and tedious, the good thing is that they never gossip about other people.

Consequently, this reversal of fortune caused me to think about distilling a handful of factors that could bring about more satisfying negotiations. Were there, in fact, a few operational components in this process, which crossed many fields and disciplines, from claim settlements to selling to child rearing?

Coincidentally, I ultimately settled on three variables that were common in most of all negotiating situations: *time, information,* and *power,* or the TIP acronym.

1

PERCEPTION IS REALITY

Perception is like Krazy Glue—it quickly hardens into reality.

ANON

Before going further, let me remind you that human beings respond to events as they *perceive* them, not necessarily to objective reality. That means that my negotiating leverage depends on someone else's perception of my situation. So what matters is not reality but what others think. Indeed, the three crucial variables that form the nucleus or core of negotiations—time, information, and power—are magnified or minimized based upon perception.

The bottom line: If they think you've got savvy and potency (even if you don't), then you have it.

Therefore, you must always believe that you have leverage and options, for to think otherwise makes you vulnerable to manipulation. If you allow self-doubt and lack of confidence to dominate your state of mind, you will have to rely upon the kindness of strangers. And in a competitive culture, this is not a promising thought. All evidence seems to indicate that people underrate their own strengths, while overrating those of the other side. We judge others by what they have accomplished, whereas we judge ourselves based upon how far we have fallen short of our potential capability.

It's a shame, because we then focus on our flaws, foibles, and faults. Even executives and administrators manage by exception, spending most of their time and energy fixated upon defects and subpar performance. Naturally, this causes them to depreciate and devalue what they have and even themselves.

This fascination with our own imperfections is what I call the *personal pimple principle.*

2

THE PERSONAL PIMPLE PRINCIPLE

When I was teaching at the Graduate School of Business at the University of Michigan from 1969 to 1980, I had an experience that reinforced this notion. During this time, I would use felt tip markers to write on white flipcharts. Occasionally, my hands would become stained and if I touched my face some of the color might rub off.

After one session, a student approached me and politely said, "I think you've got some of the black marker on your face." Before I could even react, he said, "No my mistake, you don't. It was just a shadow from the lighting."

Despite this retraction, I wasn't convinced. So I asked the program coordinator, Michael Fortuna, if he noticed anything. Looking me over, he remarked, categorically, "No."

Then I went to the men's room, where I checked my reflection in the mirror. Still, I couldn't find a discoloration.

But I didn't stop there. Flying from Detroit Metro Airport to Chicago O'Hare, I visited the unisex toilet on the plane, with the same result.

Arriving home in Chicagoland, I went to the final arbiter of blemishes. You guessed it—the Magnifying Mirror that seems to be found in most residences. While I don't know who bought it, I was glad that it was there.

Gazing at my reflection, every pore looked like a fist-sized carbuncle that was distorting my features.

Continuing to stare at the glass, I noticed a pimple, so enlarged that it seemed to have taken over my entire face. No longer did I have a normal visage, but one ugly puss. In my mind, if I walked into a room and people turned my way, they would be looking at arms and legs that were merely appendages to this thing. My whole being seemed to be enveloped by this simple pimple. At that moment, it was the hub of my life.

The truth, however, is that others, coming from a different place or perspective, would never notice my so-called problem. Why? Because perception is a complex notion. It's not just what we grasp through our senses but also involves some process of interpretation, selectivity, or judgment. Thus, we are instinctively blind to what is not relevant to us.

It's a fact of life that your negotiating muscle will depend upon how you are seen by the party you are trying to influence. If you think you've got brawn, you will subtly convey this to others and this will become the perceived reality. So all personal achievement begins in your mind. Conversely, if you believe you can't do something, it will be impossible for you to do it.

All this means is that the process culminating in negotiating success begins with you. It's *your* apprehension of *time, information,* and *power.*

PROMINENT POINTS

- Every regress contains the seeds of potential progress.
- The TIP acronym—*time, information, power*—is present in most all negotiating situations.
- Don't underestimate yourself. You always have more potency and options than you at first believe.

CHAPTER VII

TIME AND TIMING

Time is the longest distance between two points.

TENNESSEE WILLIAMS, *THE GLASS MENAGERIE*

In this turbulent world, we never seem to have enough time, yet everyone has all there is. Hence, while all of us deal with the tyranny of this commodity, it's our perception that matters. For time, as a psychological concept, is relative or subjective.

Americans tend to view time in linear-spatial terms in the sense that there is a past, a present, and a future. In this young, future-oriented culture, it's easy to ignore the past, to grab the brass ring on the carousel and go for the ride of your life.

Contrast this with other societies, which see the future as pre-determined by factors beyond an individual's control. For example, Zen (an offshoot of Buddhism), which has influenced Japanese thinking, treats time as a limitless pool in which certain things occur and then recede.

Yet even in the United States, time consciousness varies. Consider when a seven-year-old is given a time-out and asked to remain quiet and tranquil for ten minutes. It's an agonizing ordeal for him or her to fulfill this parental request. By the same token, the child's seventy-year-old grandparent can remain motionless for hours without any discomfort.

While children are, by and large, present-oriented, they are living with parents who are future-oriented, concerned with schedules, obligations, and deadlines. So when a kid doesn't start his homework when he said he would, he's not just being contrary or reneging. Rather, he is affected by a present stimulus (TV, Internet, video game) far more compelling than the memory of his past verbal commitment.

Certainly, how we view the time horizon changes as we get older. Speaking personally, when I celebrated my fiftieth birthday, I realized—in basketball parlance—that I no longer had a full shot clock. Then at sixty years, it struck me that in the game of life I was probably in overtime.

Recognizing that time is a prominent cause of stress and forces decision making, let's review some general concepts as they relate to negotiating:

First, because parties often start negotiating with faulty assumptions and fanciful goals, time is needed for them to adjust to reality.

Second, since a novel proposal is usually greeted with resistance, ranging from scorn to skepticism, it takes a while for the recipient of the offer to get accustomed to it.

Third, train yourself to be composed and imperturbable as you play the game.

Fourth, when torn between the efficacy of striking while the iron's hot and the virtue of patience, remember that he who hesitates is sometimes saved.

Fifth, regardless of how much time you have allocated to wrapping up the deal, it almost always takes longer than you expected.

Keep in mind that negotiating is a mixed-motive pluralistic game. It is played on a continuum that ranges from partnering (creative problem solving) to ersatz combat (competition and conflict). Although lamentable, empirical evidence indicates that the vast majority of negotiations involve some adversarial components.

What follows are some timing tidbits and insights that will help you better anticipate and understand this reality.

1

THE DEADLINE RULE

In most negotiations, parties wait until the eleventh hour to alter their expectations, soften their demands, and attempt to arrive at a settlement. Only then does the concession-convergence ritual occur in proximity to the deadline.

During the Cuban Missile Crisis in 1962, an agreement was reached for the Soviets to remove their missiles only a few hours before the bases were to become operational. Years later, we learned that when the threat first came to his attention, Robert Kennedy is reported to have said, "We will have to make a deal at the end, but we must stand absolutely firm now. Concessions come at the end of negotiations, not at the beginning."

ITEM: Political scientist Lloyd Jensen spent years studying the Soviet Union's bargaining behavior. As it happened, over seven decades they had virtually perfected the competitive (adversarial) approach to negotiations.

His findings were that in pursuit of win-lose outcomes, they made 80 percent of their concessions in the final quarter of the bargaining time frame, as the deadline approached.

2

DEADLINES PRECIPITATE ACTION

If there is no perception of a deadline there's little inducement for taking action, much less for accommodation and compromise.

Unfailingly, all of us know that legislative bodies from Parliament to Congress enact most of their bills and appropriations just prior to recess.

Where a manager or secretary is asked to complete a report at his or her leisure, when will it get done? Even the most conscientious person will put it off, to work on matters that have a more immediate due date.

Still not convinced? Ask your child to clean his or her room when they have time. Just see when it gets done.

Previously, I mentioned the Soviet negotiating style and the timing of their concessions. They had another salient characteristic though: It was their practice of "bladder bargaining"—which involved stalls and delays. Not surprisingly, political negotiations with them, from the 1963 Nuclear Test Ban Treaty to the SALT agreements, lasted for four and a half years to over a decade.

Yet, economic negotiations with the U.S.S.R. (e.g., wheat purchases) often involving the same players were concluded in months. The difference, of course, is that when there's potential starvation looming, you have a built-in deadline.

THE PRODUCERS

Implicit but often neglected in these tenets is how deadlines delicately work to bring about concession making. For this purpose, I offer the following case study, which makes several points about negotiating leverage.

About two years ago, while walking on Rodeo Drive in Beverly Hills, I encountered a former student of mine. Matt Blake, an attorney with the Justice Department when we first met, was now in private practice in Los Angeles.

We went for coffee at Nate n' Al's restaurant, where he told me about a case that was troubling him. Apparently, his client, twenty-eight-year-old Emma Davis, had complained about sexual harassment and was immediately fired. A graduate of the UCLA film school, she had been working as a development person for a major independent film production company. One evening, after working late, she went to the ladies' room. While there, she was startled when one of the producers, Oren Jones, a sixty-three-year-old married man, walked in and without warning proceeded to grope and fondle her. She resisted the assault but was traumatized by what happened.

The next morning, Emma, still in a state of shock, confronted her assailant. Denying that the episode occurred, Jones claimed she was delusional.

That day, when a female co-worker inquired about her trembling hands, Ms. Davis recounted what had transpired. The fellow employee did not seem surprised, remarking, "That's the way it is in this town. You're not the first and you won't be the last. In this place alone, there have been at least three cases that I know of where Jones and even his boss, Mr. Talbott, have done things like that. That's why women hardly ever wear skirts to work."

Appalled by what she had just heard, Emma went to see Greg Talbott, the CEO of the company. After she had recounted her experience, he said, in a matter-of-fact manner, "What's your problem? Are you a team player or a loose cannon?"

Shocked by his attitude, she replied, "All I want is an apology and your assurance that this behavior won't be condoned."

"Don't give me any damn ultimatum," he said. "We don't need any femi-nazis working here. You're terminated as of now."

Subsequently, in attempting to obtain comparable employment, Emma Davis found it difficult going. All indications were that in this close-knit industry she had been labeled as an "undesirable aggressive feminist"—a troublemaker.

Thereupon, she retained Matt Blake to represent her claim against Oren Jones, Greg Talbott, and the production company.

At first, Blake tried to settle this case out of court but the company's general counsel, Tom Walker, under orders from Talbott, refused to meet with him. This caused him to file suit and the case was now progressing through the legal system.

At this point, Matt Blake had taken the deposition of two current and two past employees of the company. This testimony unequivocally supported the view that Oren Jones had made a practice of harassing female employees and Talbott tolerated this behavior.

Furthermore, a routine investigation turned up several instances where over the past decade the alliance of Jones and Talbott had paid off other complaining women from $10,000 to $40,000. These payments did not come from insurance policies, but were concealed as "expenses" from films in production.

Although both defendants, Talbott and Jones, had been served notices for depositions, they had successfully stalled for over a year. By comparison, the plaintiff, Emma Davis, had been deposed, an experience that was both humiliating and dehumanizing.

If you will indulge me a personal aside, I am offended and incensed when our legal system and even the media defame "victims." It happened in the so-called Preppie Murder case of Jennifer Levin and the brutal facial slashing of model Marla Hanson. Here again, the same thing was occurring.

Truth be told, it was probably my gut reaction to this attempt to blame the victim that got me involved. Joining the plaintiff's team as an unpaid consultant, it struck me that we needed to change the other side's perception of this case by emphasizing three strategic issues:

First, the *concept of value.* Up to this point, Matt Blake had thought that the settlement range should be between $300,000 and $400,000. He made this estimate because research showed that comparable sexual harassment settlements in California ranged from $400,000 to $500,000.

However, as I explained to him, these are mere guides to worth, *the real value of anything is what the buyer is willing to pay.* In this instance, the buyers are Jones and Talbott, who are purchasing Ms. Davis's cause of action.

So we had to do more to convey to them that this was not just a routine business expense, but also a matter that had the potential to place their livelihoods and reputations in jeopardy.

In short, we needed to raise their concerns and, in turn, their expectations.

Second, the *correlation of forces.* Used by the Soviet Union during the Cold War, their thinking measured power not just by calculating military might alone. More significantly, it included economic strength, political will, endurance, willingness to sustain loss, diplomatic voltage, and the employment of propaganda.

Applying this theory, we should contemplate the worst-case scenario from the standpoint of the defendants. In other words, what damage might ensue from this litigation that would prove personally embarrassing and prevent them from continuing as successful film producers?

Obviously, if their pattern of sexual harassment were exposed by the media, this would be a problem for them. When the lawsuit was initially filed, the local print media had run small stories containing the charges in the complaint and the vehement denials of the defendants. Since Ms. Davis had declined all interviews, the requisite drama was lacking and there was no follow-up.

Moreover, the producers' use of creative accounting, whereby they paid operating funds to buy silence, if known, would surprise investors and major studios with whom they had joint ventures. What's more, what if these payoffs were scrutinized by the Internal Revenue Service? Do you think that the payment of hush money qualifies as a legitimate business expense?

All this is not to say that such threats should be made to the defendant's attorney. Rather, by indirection and attitude, you want them to recognize this potential reality by themselves.

Lastly, the *imposition of a deadline.* To this point, despite the overwhelming testimony to support Emma Davis's contentions, no settlement offer had been made. Why? Clearly, the defendants had not been sufficiently inconvenienced or placed in jeopardy by the leisurely flow of events.

In my opinion, the producers mistook attorney Blake's gentlemanly demeanor and professional courtesy as his reluctance to take on the Hollywood establishment. Hence, it would be necessary to convey more resolve, determination, and assertiveness to our adversaries. This had to be done by both word and deed, so they could fully understand that they would soon be facing the negative consequences of their actions. Only if they came to realize that the threat to their careers and reputations was imminent would they place a deadline on themselves and make concessions.

Accordingly, we settled upon a threefold plan for moving our adversary from intransigence to yielding.

Number 1 was to use the pending litigation to insist that Jones and Talbott appear for their depositions on a day certain within the next month. There would be no more delays. Also, a discovery motion was made to obtain detailed financial records of all films produced by Talbott and Jones over the past decade.

Number 2 was to agree to cooperate with the media as much as possible. Early on, Blake had received a phone call from a producer of a highly rated TV network magazine program. They were formulating plans to do a half-hour segment tentatively titled, "Why Don't High-Grossing Hollywood Films Have Net Profits?"

Previously, he had given them the standard "no comment." But now we would assist them in this endeavor, as professional ethics permitted, provided that they also interviewed Talbott and Jones to get their viewpoint on this story.

Number 3 was to arrange a settlement conference three weeks hence. This meant that by that time the TV producer would have contacted them they'd be in the midst of scheduling depositions and gathering financial documents.

Obviously, giving sworn testimony and providing data of this type could portend danger, because this information might easily be leaked to the media.

LET'S DO LUNCH

People all wrapped up in themselves make for smelly packages.

Lo and behold, general counsel Walker beat Blake to the punch. Ahead of our timetable by a week, he called to arrange a noontime settlement conference at a Japanese restaurant in Beverly Hills. He said that he and the chief financial officer of the film production company, Eric Neilson, would attend. Participating on our behalf would be Matt Blake and myself.

Upon entering the restaurant, Blake and I were taken to a private room upstairs to meet our counterparts. After the customary introductions and small talk, general counsel Walker took the opportunity to tell us about the virtues of his clients.

According to him, these men were pillars of the community— respected in the movie business and philanthropic as well. Their films had received Golden Globe Awards and even Oscar nominations. But even more noteworthy as he put it, "Every year they are invited to Oscar's A party—the *Vanity Fair* bash."

Both Blake and I were furiously taking notes. Perhaps this served to encourage him, because he went on and on detailing Talbott's and Jones's accomplishments. He even said, "They have climbed to the top of Hollywood's ladder of success." Indeed, he contrasted their position to that of Ms. Davis, who "hadn't yet gotten her foot on the first rung of the ladder."

To put the icing on the cake, he let slip that, "Only a few days ago, a major network TV producer called to do the story of their lives."

Walker went on like this for about twenty minutes, only interrupting his spiel for us to order food and drinks.

Toward the end of this pitch, the general counsel pulled a piece of paper from his pocket. Looking down at what was written (or maybe averting eye contact from embarrassment), he said, "Because my clients are charitable, they are prepared to offer Miss Davis $40,000 to avoid the hassle of this baseless lawsuit."

Neither Blake nor I were surprised by this ornery offer. Between ourselves we had discussed how we would respond if this happened.

"Mr. Walker, *I* empathize with what must be for you an uncomfortable position," I said. "From what *I* know of this case and your experience, *I* think you may even feel personally distressed in having to deliver what *I* consider such a pitiful and pathetic offer."

(Please note, that although this is clearly an adversarial relationship, still, I had tried to soften this message by using "I." "I" is less judgmental than "you," communicating that these were my personal feelings and reactions.)

"But before I tell you what it will take to settle this lawsuit, permit me to make two comments.

"For one thing, you mentioned that your clients are at the top rung of the ladder of success. Not only do I agree with that assessment, but also I think they're at an even higher altitude. Piggybacking on your apt analogy, I see your clients on the terrace, in a penthouse residence on the twenty-second floor of an exclusive high rise. Our client, on the other hand, would not even be able to get past the doorman to gain admittance. And if she did, she would at best be on the second floor."

Walker was nodding and smiling while CFO Neilson sat there not reacting in any way, cold as marble.

"Let me remind you, though," I continued, "when you fall from the second floor of a building, you get bruised, maybe even sprain or break your ankle, but you are able to walk or limp away. However, falling from the twenty-second floor leaves an enormous impact upon the human body as it hits the ground."

Walker had stopped smiling, but Neilson remained stony and detached.

"And now for the second point," I said. "The flow of events has currently put us in an asymmetrical situation. Instead of attempting to solve this problem creatively in its early stages, someone on your side, and I *know* it wasn't either of you, selected a strategy of intimidation.

"Unfortunately, there was an effort to further psychologically bludgeon and demean our client via excessively broad and invasive discovery and then a deposition that attempted to humiliate her even more.

"In essence, your attorney, metaphorically speaking, struck her repeatedly with a club. Though bleeding profusely, she's still standing tall. What can you possibly do now? Shout at her?

"Contra wise, Messrs. Talbott and Jones have, to this point, remained unscathed in their tuxedos watching from the sidelines. Although I personally find all of this abhorrent, in America there's a strong *norm of reciprocity.*

"Tom, because I think I understand your difficult predicament, I'll share some unsolicited advice with you. Go back to your philanthropic and charitable clients and tell them that you met a religious scholar today. He recommended that they should read their Bible, particularly the Book of Exodus, and notice the way God tried to negotiate for the release of the Hebrews. Unlike the defendants, the Almighty didn't start off with plague ten."

Tom cynically remarked, "Thanks for your help, but we're here to talk about money for this inconvenience to go away."

"All right," I said, "but before getting to that, let me give you the basis for our appraisal."

At this juncture, I went into a detailed analysis of why this case had the potential to produce record-setting general and punitive damages.

From all indications, Walker was growing impatient with my

lengthy exposition. Even Neilson, for the first time, was starting to fidget.

As I was building suspense, Walker was growing more perturbed. About then our meal arrived.

"Let's eat first," I said.

"Oh no you don't," Walker said. "Just tell us how much you want and then we'll eat."

"Okay, if you insist," I replied. "First, I'll furnish our record demand and then what it would take to settle this right now."

Holding up my hand and pausing as I swallowed a piece of sushi, I said, "For the record, our asking price is $1.6 million. But off the record for you alone, right now, if you want to conclude this matter, I'll give you a one-time-only number."

Walker picked up his pen and was poised to write.

"Whaddya doing?" I said.

"I'm going to write it down."

"No you're not," I said. "This is off the record. Commit it to memory."

"Okay, I understand," Walker said. "What is it?"

Lowering my voice slightly, I said, "Are you ready?"

Walker had moved his chair closer to mine and even Neilson was leaning toward me.

"Off the record, on special, here's the sale price for a limited time only . . . $1.2 million."

Walker shifted uncomfortably in his chair and frowned. Neilson pushed back from the table. No longer emotionless, his face became flushed and his eyes narrowed to snakelike slits. He looked at me with loathing.

"So do we have a deal?" I optimistically said. Neilson's face had become ruddy. He dipped his napkin in a glass of water and put it to his brow, then picked up his glass of water and gulped.

"Obviously, I'm surprised by your asking price," Walker said. "We thought we could settle this in the low six figures. That's all the authority I have. But—"

Suddenly, Neilson shakily got to his feet, his wet napkin still pressed to his face.

"I'm going," he said, throwing his napkin on the table as he headed for the door in a wobbly gait. Apparently, Mr. Stoneface had cracked.

"He's going to report what happened," Walker said. "He's Talbott's tough guy."

"Gee, he seemed nice and particularly friendly toward me," I deadpanned.

"Let's get back to this case," Walker said. "By Neilson's reaction, you can tell what you're looking for caught us by surprise."

"You may think we're a *little* high," I said, "but offering low six figures or $400,000 is *very* low."

"No not $400,000, we meant $300,000," Walker responded.

"Who cares," I said. "Three, four, five, or even six hundred thousand are insulting offers."

"Go back to Talbott and tell him to get ready for his deposition, 'cause we're not bidding against any $600,000 offer."

Blake and I were eating our meal and Walker was drinking his, as our conversation was winding down. Looking over at Neilson's vacant spot, I noticed his large untouched bowl of soup.

"Gee. What he ordered looks good," I said to Walker.

"Yeah, Eric picked this place," he said. "They know him and make a special U Don Noodle Soup for his gourmet palate."

Of course, Walker paid the check and we walked out together. As we shook hands, he turned to Matt Blake and said, "I'll call you about this tomorrow."

Returning to Matt Blake's law office we discussed with each other what had transpired.

"Wow," Matt said. "I was surprised they went from $40,000 to $300,000 in one session."

"Look, they're running scared now," I said. "They've got an ominous cloud of doom hanging over their heads. It's not just the financial records and their impending depositions, but who knows what pressure they're under from the major studios. Further, we all know that the network TV producer didn't call them to do a 'This Is Your Life' show."

"So our strategy is working," he said. "They are imposing a deadline on themselves."

Nodding in agreement, I said, "Yes, the balance has shifted in our favor."

"By the way, Herb, do you think we should have done anything differently?"

Reflecting for a moment, I replied, "Yeah, I should have eaten that U Don Soup that Neilson never touched."

What happened next? The general counsel phoned as promised and gave "the defendant's *final* offer of $620,000."

Matt Blake felt that, all things considered, this was at least in the ballpark. Moreover, since it was more than $600,000 they were entitled to a counteroffer. As a result, he reduced the demand to $900,000, which still left the two sides far apart.

Two days later, prior to the start of Oren Jones's deposition, Walker took Matt Blake aside and said, "We'll go to $750,000, but not a penny more."

Blake's response was to call his client, Ms. Davis, and after the conversation, he dropped to $850,000. Still there was no deal.

With the start of Oren Jones's questioning, it was evident that he was edgy and snappish in his replies. Clearly, Mr. Jones was not enjoying this first-time experience. And his ordeal had just begun.

At noon, when they recessed for lunch, the general counsel came over to Blake and offered to "split the difference." In the end, before they reconvened, the lawsuit was settled for $825,000.

The conclusion: While you will never know what constructs motivate behavior, all indications are that our threefold strategy helped alter the perception of the other side.

3

INDUCING CONCESSION MAKING

The previous case study provides an example of how it's possible to affect events to influence decision making.

As a negotiator, you will often be confronted with this question: How do I get obstinate, self-willed, or intractable people to impose a deadline on themselves and move to convergence?

What you want to do is create incentives for them to concede and close. Here's how:

First, try to have them understand that further delay on their part could prove dangerous to their interests.

Second, facilitate their realization that continuing their recalcitrant behavior will not cause you to soften your terms. In effect, maintaining such willful conduct will prove a poor return on their investment.

Third, structure the situation so they come to believe that a continued impasse might cause you to up the negative ante. In other words, as time passes, there is potential for escalation— which means that what you have already conceded could be taken off the table.

Finally, if you want your opponent to impose a deadline on themselves, they must accept the fact that your last offer is preferable to no agreement.

ITEM: In mid-March of 2000, I was negotiating a line of credit with a bank lending officer. In this process, we had arrived at crunch time. Their best offer to me was an interest rate of prime. My position was that I needed and expected to pay prime minus one eighth. We were close but not yet there.

Suddenly, the lending officer advised me that the rate they had offered was a special rate for only their "best customers." It had been approved by the loan committee and authorized by his boss.

Moreover, if I didn't accept these terms by the end of the month, it could not be recorded in the first quarter of the year. That meant it would have to be resubmitted to the loan committee, which met periodically.

To further complicate things his boss was being transferred to another position in the bank. The indication was that a recent audit turned up some laxity in the unit's lending policy. And here's the kicker: His new supervisor would be one of the auditors.

So here I was being given incentives to concede. They had "sweetened the pot" to induce me to accept the deal now.

What did "Mr. Negotiator" do? I waited two days to save face and then called to say, "I accept."

4

DEADLINES ARE NOT ALWAYS DRACONIAN

As you may recall, in the book *You Can Negotiate Anything,* I tried to make the point that anything that has been established as a result of some interpersonal or intrapersonal communication process is negotiable.

What this means is that those things which are nonnegotiable are very few in number. They would include, of course, ethical or moral principles, scientific laws (the speed of light, for instance), and, if you're a believer, religious rules and precepts.

Putting aside what Mel Brooks has told us, the Ten Commandments did not come into being as the upshot of a negotiation. Although a spurious story once circulated that when Moses read over the Commandments that God etched in stone, Moses commented, "Mostly they look good, except Number 7—Adultery. Maybe we can talk about this one?"

In effect, deadlines, which are set arbitrarily, unilaterally, or stem from an interactive or exchange process, are not as firm or unbending as some would assume.

The point is, don't blindly follow a deadline that exists for convenience sake. It is probably not as uncompromising as it initially appears. Rather, analyze the deadline and calculate the risks and benefits that might ensue in going beyond the established concluding point.

Reminder: "It ain't over till the deacon says amen."

5

THE OTHER SIDE ALWAYS
HAS A DEADLINE

Regardless of how placid, untroubled, and becalmed he or she seems, *the party dealing with you always has a deadline*. If this were not the case, they wouldn't meet with you or respond to your e-mails and phone calls.

ITEM: In 1992, while sitting in my office in Northbrook, Illinois, I received a phone call from a Stan Smith. He and I were involved in an ongoing negotiation that had drifted along for months. You might say we were "stalemated" in our deliberations.

When I got on the line, I learned that Smith "just happened to be in the area" and wanted "to visit for a little chat."

Once we sat down together I inquired, "What brings you to Northbrook?"

He replied in an offhanded manner, "Well, I was heading for Boston and you were on the way."

"Aren't you in Palm Beach, Florida, this time of the year?"

"Sure," he said, "so it was easy for me to stop off."

Knowing a little geography, I thought he needed either a new travel agent or a map of the United States. Actually, the only place Northbrook is on the way to is Buffalo Grove.

6

WHERE DEADLINES ARE
NOT EQUIVALENT

The side with the tighter time frame is at a disadvantage if this is known by an opponent. All evidence shows that the one that feels most constrained by time limits will make more substantial concessions.

7

WHERE DEADLINES APPEAR IDENTICAL

Should both sides have similar time constraints, how one perceives "the end" is all important.

Were I to find myself negotiating with a tough competitive opponent, I would try to have him or her see the concluding moment literally. Clearly, an attitude of caring, but not t-h-a-t much would enable me to remain composed.

From my experience, I know that deadlines can be renegotiated and clocks can be stopped if there is mutual desire to avoid a breakdown in negotiations.

Suffice to say, a negotiator is not in the position of Cinderella, who, at the stroke of midnight, would be transformed back to a serving wench. In fact, I guarantee that you won't find a large pumpkin in the space where you left your car.

8

PATIENCE GENERALLY PAYS

In negotiating, quick is risky—especially if you are less prepared and cannot evaluate the fairness of a proposal. Thus, if caught by surprise or confronted by an unanticipated offer, stall, delay, and use time to your advantage.

In most instances, the general rule for negotiators is to slow down and thrive amidst silence and ambiguity and be prepared to recess in order to think things over.

Thus, effective negotiators most often display forbearance and a capacity to endure. Helping them with maintaining this composure is often a sense of humor and recognition that, after all, "it's just a game."

But as we know, negotiating takes place over a range of time, where leverage can easily shift. The passage of days or months imposes costs, produces psychic wear and tear, and affects positions, expectations, and perceptions.

Think of it: Right now you may be sitting on top of the world. But then again, the earth rotates every twenty-four hours. So, what is up may be down and vice versa.

Reflecting on this potential volatility, we should always analyze and contemplate how the passage of time affects bargaining leverage.

Consider the axiom that "anticipation is often greater than reality." Extrapolating from this, we might surmise that once a service is performed its value may diminish.

Therefore, if your basement has three feet of water or your toilets won't flush, when will the plumber want to negotiate for the cost of his services? The answer, of course, is before he alleviates the distress.

A kindred example comes to us from the so-called oldest profession, where prostitutes, reportedly, "get it up front." This has been labeled the *hooker principle*, where the seller finds it beneficial to establish the price when the need is at its peak.

Imagine what would happen if the hooker waited to negotiate the fee until after her services were completed and the john satisfied? At that point, he might well say, "Are you kidding? You mean that was it? Hey, I could have done a better job myself!"

ITEM: Recently, a woman who was a systems analyst in the field of information technology contacted me. She expected that her firm would soon be offering her a promotion to the position of project manager.

She explained that as a project leader she would be operating in an environment of enormous pressure because of the ever-changing demands and constricting deadlines. What concerned her was that in the past there had been a high failure rate in that position. Indeed, after being in the job for six months, her predecessor could not secure the appropriate budget, staff, and authority necessary to achieve his objectives.

After discussing the issue of timing, we agreed upon the point where she would have the greatest negotiating leverage to secure the requisite people and funding to succeed. It was, as you might suspect, just *after* she was offered the promotion—but *before* she agreed to accept it.

Employing this timing, she was able to negotiate for all the resources needed to achieve her goals.

9

REMAIN CALM AND COOL
UNDER FIRE

By this time, I believe you understand the value of perspective and detachment in the occasional stormy sessions and turbulent times that occur in negotiating.

Having this gaming spirit and the outlook of an outsider will enable you to stay calm and cool and not overreact—even when provoked. If nothing else, it will reduce your anxiety and stress, while giving you a psychological shield between your self-esteem and the potential aggressiveness of others.

Throughout these pages, I have counseled you to care but not t-h-a-t much as you confront pompous and overbearing people or magisterial institutions. While conveying persistence, still, don't push too hard to make it happen. Instead, let the process unfold on its own.

Therein lies the challenge: How should you react to low or high-handed tactics in the course of negotiating?

THE CHEVYMOBILE MATTER

It was about eighteen years ago when General Motors decided to put Chevrolet engines in Oldsmobile cars. Many of the purchasers of these vehicles thought they were getting the "Rocket

Olds engine." When they learned the truth, a class action lawsuit was initiated by these consumers against GM.

Years later, a trial took place in federal court in Chicago, where the plaintiffs prevailed. However, on appeal, the verdict was set aside and the case sent back for retrial.

Considerable antagonism existed between both sides and no serious negotiations had ever taken place. In fact, the defendant had never even made an offer.

At this point, I was contacted by the federal judge, who once again would soon be presiding over this trial. He asked if I would work on behalf of the plaintiffs in an attempt to settle this litigation. According to him, all parties were amenable to having me involved.

The first negotiating session was held at my Northbrook office. Attending were three plaintiffs' attorneys and the GM team, which consisted of two corporate counsels and three members of a very prominent law firm (I know because upon their arrival that morning, they told me—"We're from a very prominent law firm").

Sitting across the traditional rectangular table from each other, here's how the outside counsel's lead negotiator opened:

"Before we even get into the substance of this matter, let me clear the air. It's been almost three years since you filed suit and we have yet to offer one dime. Do you want to know why?"

As best I could tell, no one on my side of the table nodded or said anything, but he continued. "We regard this lawsuit as a frivolous shakedown. It's an attempt by you damn trial lawyers to enrich yourselves at the expense of the American people and our economy. We're in the midst of the Cold War and you're undermining the free world. What you're doing is un-American and it's giving aid and comfort to the commies. The auto industry is the engine that powers our prosperity and you're trying to destroy it. Yeah, because of lawsuits like this, we incur extra costs, making it harder to compete with the Germans and Japanese."

As if this broad tongue-lashing wasn't enough, he then went on a personal rant. "What you're doing is disloyal. It's selling out your country—all for greed. Because of your despicable behavior we don't feel we can trust you. No matter what we offer, you'll want to extort more. It'll never be enough."

Softening his tirade somewhat, and by way of explanation of why they were there, he said, "The judge though is a softie and he wants us to offer you something. So, we might have to do that. But you guys are *greedy*. Whatever we give you won't be enough. You'll want more. So, we have decided after all this time, against our better instincts, to try and settle this case.

"There is, however, one nonnegotiable condition—that is, that you agree to accept our offer without any further dickering. In other words, we're not gonna make any offer unless you agree beforehand to accept it."

Upon hearing this, our side of the table sat in stunned silence. Never had any of us heard anything comparable under such circumstances. Not knowing what to do, we called for a caucus.

Meeting outside in the hallway, our team could not agree on how to respond. Although there was commonality in that they all represented car buyers who were shortchanged, there was conflict over personal needs.

One attorney said, "We've been at this long enough. I'm overinvested in this case. My wife is divorcing me and they're threatening to foreclose on my home. Let's take the money and run."

Another plaintiff's attorney had an opposite view. "The hell with them. Who do they think they are? As far as I'm concerned, I'm willing to fight this out in the courts for the next decade. This is a matter of principle."

At last, it was agreed that I would respond for our team and reject their condition.

Returning to the meeting room, we all took our seats around the table. Then I rose to speak. This was unusual, because we only had nine participants and no one had previously stood.

"I'm a half-century old," I said, "and when I look back on my life, I have had some setbacks, disappointments, and despair. At the same time, however, I have also experienced joy, moments of elation, and happiness."

The General Motors negotiating team appeared bewildered by this personal and seemingly irrelevant recitation.

"Sure, I lost loved ones, encountered difficulties, and faced intermittent lows. But there was also delight and good fortune along the way. So on balance, I probably got better than I deserved. Looking back on these fifty years, with all these ups and downs, I think that overall I've been blessed. To paraphrase Frank Capra, 'It's been a good life.'"

"What's the point of all this?" the GM lead negotiator said. "Do you accept our condition?"

By now, even my associates were looking puzzled about my peculiar ramblings.

"Would you believe," I said, "that in these five decades, I never got a single offer from GM? Yet, even without this occurrence, it's still been a good life.

"So, I have decided that I can go another twenty or thirty years without an offer and would you believe that my team concurs in that decision? Putting it bluntly, we don't want your offer, 'cause no *normal* person would accept such a condition."

Almost immediately the GM top negotiator said, "Okay, forget it, we'll give you our offer."

"Maybe you don't understand, we do not accept your condition," I responded.

"I know," he said. "We are removing the condition and are offering you $6.2 million to settle all the class action litigation."

Naturally, there was no agreement on this day. It took a few more bargaining sessions to bring both sides close. Not surprisingly, the day before the case was to be retried, we met at the Federal Courthouse and settled this matter.

Actually, in the final give-and-take, the defendants had become reasonable. Accordingly, in the end stages, I served more as a mediator than a partisan for the plaintiffs' position.

Thus, in the game of negotiating, expect inventive maneuvers designed to throw you off stride.

The rule of thumb: Even in the face of provocations, don't get ruffled or riled but remain placid and untroubled.

Having discussed the subject of *time* and *time consciousness,* let's move to the next component: *information.*

PROMINENT POINTS

- Time adds pressure, producing stress and forcing decision making.
- Most concessions and agreements occur in proximity to the deadline.
- As the deadline approaches, remain confident and composed. Fretting and fussing is like a rocking chair: It gives you something to do but gets you nowhere.
- Virtually everything, including deadlines, has some give, making them negotiable. So, "It ain't over till the deacon says amen."

CHAPTER VIII

INFORMATION

Spontaneity is too good to be left to chance.

Almost everybody knows that input can change output. Our appraisal of a situation and the decisions that we make can be no better than the information that we have. Simply put, if you don't know the score, the chances are you've lost.

We live by information and it can be the great equalizer. Just like the sun, it can illuminate and affect mood and behavior.

If this is true, or as Francis Bacon said, "Knowledge is power," why do we fail to obtain information about our negotiating counterpart?

1

DON'T WAIT FOR THE STARTER'S GUN

The primary reason is that too many of us tarry until a critical incident occurs before we prepare for the inevitable strategic interaction.

Living in a complex culture, storm clouds are always gathering even though the rain has not begun to fall. In short, whether we like it or not, the prospect of negotiating is always in our future.

By that I mean: You have been asked to take some medical tests which may or may not be covered by your HMO, the car you have had for ten years is on its last legs, your daughter has just obtained her driver's license, another child is about to apply for college, there is a rumor that your organization will be offering employees up to $50,000 in cash if they take early retirement, you have obtained a long-sought-after meeting with a Fortune 500 company with the possibility of a financially lucrative relationship, and, finally, the lease on your apartment is coming to an end.

There you have it: In short order the winds of negotiating will blow your way. Indeed, as you read this, you are in the introductory stage of many negotiations that won't take place for some time yet.

Unfortunately, we often wait for the downpour before we start to gather information. By then, we are across the bargaining table from our opposite number where information is more difficult to obtain. Suffice to say, the only option at that point is to improvise or just plain wing it.

All the same, our culture is filled with aphorisms that caution us to contrive and *not* improvise in these situations—from Benjamin Franklin's dictum "If you fail to plan you're planning to fail" to the former football coach George Allen's truism that "The definition of success is total preparation." We should know by now that it is important to make use of your lead time.

Consequently, if you can foresee a potential negotiation in the offing or an opportunity to shape future events, start planning *now*.

If the matter is of great importance, you may want to research SEC filings, check *Who's Who*, obtain annual reports, and use the Internet to find related Web sites and news reports. You will be surprised by how much published material is out there.

Less time-consuming and often more productive is your network of friends, associates, and acquaintances who may have had personal experiences in this situation or can refer you to someone who has.

Whenever I am about to go into a negotiation, I remind myself of the Chinese proverb "If you want to know what to expect on the road ahead, ask someone who has just come back." Applying this, I always try to contact those who have been in a similar situation or dealt with these people previously. After all, the best predictor of future behavior is past behavior!

2

MAPPING PRIOR TO THE
FORMAL EVENT

Professional negotiators understand that they are involved in a continuous process. They know that prior to the formal give-and-take of bargaining, information can be obtained about the other side's interests, deadlines, and concerns.

It is commonplace in labor relations that future negotiations over the next contract begin the day this one is signed. Major defense contractors who sell their products and services to governments start working on a potential deal years before they expect an award will be made. In this interval, they try to determine who the key decision makers are and who can influence them.

The art of diplomacy, with its long history, has always used ambassadors as honorable spies. Gathering intelligence all year round, they also try to identify and win favor with the key players in foreign governments.

In the field of purchasing, it is a matter of course for procurers to visit supplier plants where, in a congenial manner, they ask questions, listen, and probe for information. What they are looking for is data about the vendor's inventory, reliability, deadlines, quality, and interests. Experience has shown that plant managers, foremen, engineers, or staff personnel may inadvertently let slip information that can affect future bargaining leverage.

In fact, years ago a purchasing agent told me that on one of these routine trips to a manufacturing plant, he was asked by a personnel manager, "How long do you think next month's negotiation will take?" Before he had a chance to respond, the questioner said, "If it drags on, we may have to lay off 25 percent of our people."

Therefore, before the starter's gun goes off (during the lead time stage), collect as much intelligence as possible. As we have seen, this information may be available from research, informal contacts, and from others who have negotiated with the other side previously.

What I have been saying is that *communication is at the heart of the negotiating game.* And it is not passive or static, but active and continuous without beginning or end. So, potential negotiators must view their initial contact with the other side as the start of the process. During this prepatory stage—prior to the formal bargaining event—all interactions should be anticipated and planned.

To sum up: A raft of information can ferry even the inexperienced negotiator to a successful crossing.

3

THE BLESSING OF GIVING

At the same time, however, communication is a two-way process that involves not just getting, but giving as well. Affording your counterpart the chance to obtain information complies with the *norm of reciprocity*, and can affect their attitude, trust level, and, most of all, expectations. Hence, care must be taken early on to send consistent, coherent, and timely messages that are in accordance with your ultimate bargaining objective.

So, what is said and done—or not said and left undone—prior to the bargaining event will have an enormous impact on the final outcome.

This is especially significant when you recognize that the person or group you'll be trying to influence has erroneous assumptions and unrealistic expectations. As soon as you realize this, you must give them reality-based information in order to alter their thinking. Otherwise, proposed changes when introduced during the formal strategic interaction will be seen as unexpected and unreasonable. Predictably, they will react by saying "no."

Reminder: It takes a while to digest and get comfortable with anything that's different. This is the *principle of acceptance time,* that people need the opportunity to get used to a new idea, concept, or approach.

To illustrate, let's look at a simple scenario:

Three years ago, you gave a valuable employee a 7 percent

salary increase. The next year, this increment was repeated. Again, last year, this person got the same raise in pay.

Since then, however, your business has had reverses and cash flow problems. Let us further stipulate, as lawyers would say, that you cannot increase expenses in the coming fiscal period and that the employee is unaware of these circumstances.

If this is the case, what does he or she expect when the two of you meet to discuss compensation?

Definitely 7 percent. Truly, this person may be counting on these funds to pay for an expenditure that was already made. If you, in a magnanimous gesture, offered a 5 percent raise out of your own pocket, I suspect the employee would still feel short-changed by 2 percent.

The way to avoid such a dilemma is to share this negative information with the employee as early as possible, months before the formal compensation get-together. Of course, these revelations will cause him or her to revise what might be expected to conform to the new reality. More significantly, if you get people involved at the outset by soliciting their input, they tend to be more understanding and supportive of the outcomes.

> ITEM: Years ago, I asked a congressman why he had not come to the aid of the President of the United States, a member of his own party, who was in a great deal of political difficulty. His reply was illuminating: "If I wasn't present during the plane's takeoff, how can I be there when it crash-landed?"

Consider another example of how lead time can be used to affect expectations and change behavior.

When I last lived in an apartment building, a neighbor approached me in the elevator and asked, "Does all that racket and merrymaking in 11E keep you up at night?"

"Actually, I don't know what you're talking about," I said. "Remember, I live in apartment 11B at the other end of the hall."

"Well, unfortunately, I'm in 11F, right next door to 11E," he said. "These thirty-year-old kids party and play that rock 'n' roll music till 2:00 A.M. I've banged on the wall, rung their phone, and complained but nothing helps."

From all indications, he was upset or, as kids would say, "ticked to the max."

Trying to lighten things up, I said, "Maybe you should try to relax and relate to the hullabaloo. It's rather unique you know, it's the only music where the melody is played by the drummer."

He didn't appreciate my attempt at humor, but I was saved when the elevator doors opened at the lobby.

A month later, at the same place I met him again.

"I've got good news and very bad news," he said. "The thirty-year-olds moved out, but they are being replaced by an even younger and wilder-looking couple.

"The new ones are musicians. I watched them move in. They have amplifiers and the biggest stereo and speakers I've ever seen."

Feeling compassion for his situation, I decided to give him some unsolicited advice: "Obviously, your past strategy of wall banging and phoning in the midst of a party didn't work. So why don't you try something different?

"If I were you, I would use the current lead time to try to influence their behavior, instead of reacting during the event when you're upset and emotional.

"What I would do is buy or bake a pie for the new neighbors. Delivering it in person, I'm sure you'll get invited into their residence. Once inside, you'll be able to answer all their questions about local restaurants, shops, transportation, and so on.

"Then, you might discreetly tell them how happy you are to have them as neighbors, because their predecessors played their music so loud."

Actually, this counsel comes from my own experience, which has shown me that if desired behaviors are communicated early in the developmental stages of a relationship they have a good chance of taking hold.

Two months later, I received a visit from the beaming occupants of 11F. They indicated that my plan had worked. Not only were they friends of the people next door, but they had attended two of their parties.

Most surprising of all was that they had become big fans of Bruce Springsteen and had tickets for his next concert. As Linda Ellerbee has said, "And so it goes."

4

THE SATISFACTION PRESCRIPTION

All empirical evidence seems to indicate that satisfaction or dissatisfaction at the conclusion of negotiation is related to expectations. That's right, it's not the outcome per se, but the gap between *what you anticipated and the actual result that will gratify or dismay.*

More to the point, if you ignore the unrealistic expectations of the other side during the introductory stage, you are risking a deadlock when this chasm between expectations and reality surfaces during the face-to-face bargaining period.

For example, let's say you're attempting to purchase the XYZ Company. Based upon your financial data, you believe that a fair price would be $5 million. Yet, during early contacts with the seller, it is apparent that they are anticipating twice that amount. If you wait until the give-and-take get-together to disabuse them of their inflated value, you'll be courting disaster.

As we saw in a prior illustration (the employee who foresees a 7 percent salary increase), the way to deal with this problem is to furnish relevant information as soon as possible. This can be done directly or indirectly via third parties. The purpose, of course, is to adjust the other side's mind-set to conform to the reality of the particular situation.

What happens when we allow someone to arrive at the bargaining event with inflated notions? Too often, negotiators will then resort to lowballing in an effort to alter or rectify the problem that they allowed to develop.

The tactic of lowballing can be used in one of two ways. In the XYZ example, the buyer, realizing that he or she is dealing with an excessive expectancy, could make an initial lowball offer of $2.2 million. Most often, this will put the seller in a state of shock and rupture the relationship.

But what if the seller stays, under the mistaken belief that there are no other options or because they have already invested so much? In this case, their notion of value has been lowered and the buyer still has $2.8 million that can be given in concessions.

Let's be clear here: I am not an advocate of this tactic. While I concede that an excessively low offer or a high demand can favorably affect the other side's expectation level, it can also tarnish trust. You can, however, gain the benefit of this advantageous opener without ruining a relationship if you offer factual support as justification.

The other way lowballing is used is clearly unethical. It occurs when a retailer puts an ad in the paper advertising a product at an incredibly low price. Arriving at the store, you're virtually salivating at the thought of this bargain, as the salesman takes the imprint of your credit card. At this point, he casually says, "By the way, for this to work you'll need to also get—."

What then follows is a recitation of indispensable accessories— all at a cost. By the time you add up the total tab, you'll end up paying more than you would have had you gone to a competitor whose advertised price was much higher.

5

EXPECTING LITTLE DIMINISHES DISAPPOINTMENT

Nothing is so good as it seems beforehand.
GEORGE ELIOT, *SILAS MARNER*

There is an oft-repeated adage that "If you've got to borrow money, make sure it's from a pessimist, 'cause he never expects it back." By the same token, we know that dissatisfaction comes from the difference between what we expect to occur and what actually happens.

Recently, my travel agent booked a flight for me on American Airlines from Dulles to LAX. Purchasing a full-fare business class ticket on my behalf, she advised that I was on the waiting list for an upgrade to first class.

It should be noted that I hold an AAdvantage Platinum Card (having flown over two million miles with this carrier) and had a number of unrestricted upgrade certificates.

Arriving at Dulles to pick up my electronic ticket, I was informed that I was upgraded to first class and could obtain the boarding pass at the gate.

Following these instructions, I again stood in line and was given a first class ticket and seat number. About thirty-five minutes before the flight time, I was summoned to the desk, where I was told that my upgrade was a mistake.

As they put it, the seat was vacant, but it would cost me an additional $426 to be among the privileged few.

Truth be told, up to this point, I didn't really care whether I went business class or first. However, having raised my expectations, I found myself Really Caring—maybe too much. Actually, I was incensed by American Airlines's greedy and duplicitous behavior. Moreover, they were arrogant and not at all apologetic.

During the next twenty-five minutes before the door closed I was told to visit the pricing expert at the Admirals Club, the gate supervisor, and an unidentified gentleman in a shirt and tie. None of these individuals were able to give me a plausible explanation of their policy and behavior.

Not wishing to miss the flight, I ran out of time. Traveling to Los Angeles business class, I noticed that my first class seat 3J was not occupied.

Ordinarily, I would inform you of the outcome of this matter. However, all this happened last week, so to paraphrase John Paul Jones, "I've just yet begun to negotiate."

From my perspective, this is now a matter of principle, where I see myself representing all consumers.

What I have already done is write directly to the CEO and marketing director of the airline. In this letter, I expressed my wish to continue doing business with them—if they understand and rectify this problem. Also, I suggested it would be a display of good faith on their part if one of them or a member of their staff call me.

During this phone conversation, if their solution doesn't meet my needs, I will ask this person for advice, along these lines:

- If you were me, what would you do now?
- Do you think I should write my congressperson or contact the FAA directly?
- I've been advised that the chair of the Senate Aviation Subcommittee and House Transportation Subcommittee are interested in these matters. Should I go that route?

• What about the secretary of the Department of Transportation? Would he be able to help me?

Of course, the purpose of this conversation is to convey to my negotiating partner that I have options and will not just fold my tent and move on. Notice, though, my demeanor will be friendly and there's no direct threat, which only produces rigidity and defensiveness.

Candidly, with the passage of time my annoyance has subsided. Right now, I'm caring but not t-h-a-t much, which as you know, is the best attitude to affect the behavior of the doctrinaire and disdainful.

Hopefully, this tale of how a weary passive traveler was transformed into an energized activist makes the point that once prospects are raised, realization is expected.

Further afield perhaps, but applying the same concept, is the plight of African-Americans in the United States. With the passage of civil rights legislation and the use of affirmative action programs they rightfully anticipated that their social and economic circumstances would improve. And things did get better.

Be that as it may, because expectations were raised and actuality lagged behind, disappointment ensued. Arguably, many African-Americans seemed less content, or at least more vocal about inequality, than they had been prior to the start of the civil rights movement.

The nub of the problem is that all human beings measure gratification by the gap between expectation and reality. In sum: You cannot placate people with a recitation of what has been achieved when they expected more.

Truth be told, this principle doesn't only apply to minorities, but even to our "better majority" as well. In my lifetime, women have appropriately attained considerably more opportunities and options than their grandmothers. Yet, despite this progress, a great number are still disheartened and vexed by the inequities that remain.

Revealingly, a popular commercial attempted to have women

identify with their product by giving vent to this frustration: "You've come a long way, baby"—the implication being that "You *still have a long way to go.*"

Now, I do not want to be misunderstood: What I'm saying is that those who play the game of negotiating measure their satisfaction by two primary criteria:

1. Was the process fair and just? Did the other side listen to what I had to say and respect my point of view?

2. How close did the final agreement come to satisfying my needs, interests, and especially expectations?

Thus, you must always be cognizant of the expectations of the other side and give him or her information as soon as practicable to help adjust their aspiration level.

6

DELUSIONS ABOUT DISSATISFACTION

Frustration is greater when we have much and want more than when we have nothing and want some.

ERIC HOFFER

Because there has been so much misinformation on television in the wake of the September 11 atrocity, allow me to elaborate further on this notion of dissatisfaction.

Listening to some naive reporters, who style themselves as journalists, one gets the impression that barbarous acts arise spontaneously from people who live in a state of suffering and squalor.

Accepting this premise, media mavens are then especially anxious to interview these criminals or their apologists to broadcast "the root causes" of their so-called grievances.

In truth, however, history has shown that misery alone does not produce action or rebellion. In the most repressive regimes, like Hitler's Germany, Stalin's Soviet Union, Pol Pot's Cambodia, or Idi Amin's Uganda, there were no indigenous freedom movements.

Indeed, totalitarian states know how to handle dissidents. Take for example what happened in Syria in February 1982. Haffez al-Assad, the country's secular dictator, learned of a budding Islamic movement in Hama, the country's fourth largest city.

Acting without delay, he surrounded this heavily populated area with artillery. After four days of round-the-clock shelling he transformed the city into a vast parking lot, murdering from ten thousand to twenty thousand civilians. Would you believe that, since then, there has been no opposition to the entrenched dictatorship?

More noteworthy is the fact that there were no resolutions of condemnation passed by the United Nations, the Arab League, or the European Union. Additionally, Syria replaced the United States on the U.N.'s Human Rights Commission and currently sits as a member of the Security Council.

What does all this have to do with expectations? The point is that it is not actual anguish and despondency, but the hope that things will get better that activates dissidents. "The moment of greatest danger for a tyrannical government," Tocqueville said, "is when they begin to show liberal tendencies."

Certainly, this was the case in the late 1970s when the Shah of Iran instituted reforms, which weakened the totalitarian framework of his rule. Had he been willing to crack down and slaughter thousands of Khomeini's followers, his family would still be in power today.

Related to the chasm between expectation and reality is the problem of Islamic militancy and its portending danger for the West.

From an American perspective, the two most crucial allies that we have in Arabdom are Egypt and Saudi Arabia. The former with 70 million people and its tradition of Islamic scholarship and pan-Arab leadership. The latter because of oil reserves and its control over the Muslim holy places.

Both these countries have a populous and growing class of educated and unemployed young men. Born and raised in the aftermath of the Arab oil boycott, which tripled revenues, they envisioned a prosperous future for themselves and their people.

But these expectations were not fulfilled. What happened was that the Egyptian and Saudi economies became stagnant, accompanied by widespread nepotism and corruption. Affording little opportunity for those who did not have connections, these nations were producing a multitude of educated poor.

In the case of Egypt, they were awash in youth with almost 60 percent of the population below twenty-five years. Unemployment was at 25 percent. And this would have been even higher, save for the fact that one third of the workforce is given government jobs at an average salary of $65 a month. Still, universities and law schools continue to graduate students who cannot find employment.

Saudi Arabia, on a smaller scale, is the demographic mirror image of Egypt. The revenues from oil production, which seemed unlimited, are not enough to subsidize today's youth the way it did their parents. This should be apparent when we realize that per capita income has dropped below $7,000 a year, half of what it was.

But these regimes have chosen not to deal directly with the problems that have caused internal disappointment, resentment, and anger. Instead, their strategy has been to focus their population's attention upon Israel—the common enemy. In addition, they have encouraged their state-controlled media to fan the flames of anti-Americanism as a way of diverting pressure that would otherwise be directed at their own authoritarian rule.

Although being encouraged to institute reforms, Hosni Mubarak and the Royal Saud family know that such changes may increase expectations and produce greater instability; for it's the taste of better things that stimulates the appetite for revolution.

Paradoxically, Iraq and Syria, as repressive dictatorships, are not caught in this bind.

I have spent considerable time discussing the importance of expectations in ultimately achieving agreement because I have seen too many negotiations fail when erroneous assumptions and unrealistic goals are ignored in the early stages of the process.

Accordingly, if negotiating is give-and-take, I want to reiterate the importance of giving information in a timely fashion.

The other side of this equation deals with obtaining information, which is our next topic.

7

GETTING INFORMATION

Obviously, not every negotiation requires the same research and intelligence gathering. How much time you spend in attempting to collect data will depend upon the importance and the complexity of the deal, as well as your time constraints.

Furthermore, it should be remembered that it's not the quantity of information acquired that is important but whether the information can be utilized to better understand the other side's underlying concerns and interests and the factors that affect their decision making.

Most of all, relevant information can be used to discover more options and alternatives enabling you to develop creative solutions that are beneficial for both sides.

If I had my druthers, here's a list of some of the questions that I would like to have answered:

- Why are they negotiating with me?
- What are their time constraints and deadlines?
- By whom and how will their decisions be made?
- How do they react to conflict?
- What is their negotiating style?
- What are the limits of their authority?
- What is their negotiating experience and background?
- Do they have a realistic alternative to making this deal?

- What incentives do they have to make this deal?
- What are their underlying interests and concerns?
- What's their track record for honesty and integrity?
- What are their expectations with respect to the outcome?

Additionally, if they represent a large organization:

- Who do they report to?
- Does he or she have a budget or quota?
- How are they compensated?

8

BARRIERS TO OBTAINING INFORMATION

Arriving at the negotiating event, let's discuss the kind of behavior that both inhibits and encourages the flow of information.

First, don't prematurely judge what your counterpart actually wants or needs.

Hearing their initial offer or demand, there is a tendency to equate these expressed positions with their genuine concerns. Don't make the mistake of being a literalist.

As I mentioned previously, in discussing the *Titanic* principle, when confronted by an extreme opener, stay calm and cool. Just ask questions and probe below the waterline to ascertain underlying interests and needs.

Second, recognize that trust is a fragile thing, built slowly through incremental steps that require risk and reciprocation.

When we have no experience with the other party, there is a natural hesitancy to share information, especially if one believes that such disclosure may be used against them.

Demonstrating at the outset that you understand and empathize with your counterpart's concerns and predicament can alleviate these apprehensions. Most of all, you want to convey by word, deed, and attitude that differences are natural and an opportunity exists to explore creative solutions that will result in a mutually beneficial agreement.

Third, there is a reluctance to provide feedback that might produce a disheartening reaction. After all, who wants to be the bearer of bad news that will bring on depression or even anger?

We are all familiar with the plight of the mythic Greek messenger, who presumably ran over twenty-six miles to bring news of the battle to his King.

Upon arrival he was asked, "How are we doing?"

"We're getting slaughtered," he gasped.

The King did not say, "I appreciate your effort to bring me this bad news in such a timely manner."

Instead, his reaction was, "Take this panting pantywaist out and behead him. He just ruined my day."

Imagine when word got out about the fate of this courier. Not surprisingly, the next runner with a negative report would either never arrive or alter the message to make it more acceptable.

So the question is obvious: How can we allay the anxiety of those from whom we wish to obtain accurate information?

This is the challenge that always confronts negotiators, managers, executives, medical doctors, lawyers, accountants, and certainly parents.

Let me share with you a child-rearing episode from my life that may dramatize this dilemma.

When our daughter, Sharon, was about sixteen years of age she was invited to the high school prom. Arriving at our home at 7:30 P.M., a half-hour late, her date informed us that he couldn't get his family's car. Not wishing to put a damper on their big night, we loaned him ours.

Ellen and I watched as he pulled out of the driveway. Turning to each other, we simultaneously blurted out, "Where did the time go?"

Going back inside, I listened as Ellen gave vent to her concerns: "He looks so young. Does he have a driver's license? How well does she know him? Does he look like he's on drugs?"

These questions were coming so fast, I didn't even have a chance to respond. Finally, in a knowing and authoritative manner, I said, "Hey, they'll be back in five or six hours and I'm not waiting up. You either trust your child or you don't!"

I didn't even know what that meant, but it seemed to soothe her. Feigning confidence in our daughter's upbringing, we didn't sit up to await her return, but went to sleep in our king-sized bed a little after midnight.

Since I am referring to marriage, a negotiable relationship, bear with me as I stray from this story to share with you two of my general rules of spousal behavior. When Ellen and I arrived at our tenth anniversary, I was asked by a friend, "How did you do it?"

This question caused me to write down and reflect on some practical, albeit selfish, canons of conduct that I have tried to follow in my marriage.

Number one, when you have an argument with your mate that spills over into the early morning hours, never leave the bed. No matter how contentious or emotional the dispute, stay where you are, because wherever you go it will never be as comfortable.

The result: Ellen, whose boiling point is much lower than mine, doesn't subscribe to this precept. Consequently, she has spent more than a few nights sleeping on the couch, the floor, and in the bathtub of a hotel room.

Number two, allow your spouse to sleep on the side of the bed where the phone is located. This means that the person closest to the ringing receiver is the family's communications manager. The delegation of this responsibility enables you to sleep through all the wrong number calls that come at ungodly hours.

Admittedly, these self-serving practices won't work for everyone. But as for me, I'm better at dispute resolution after a good night's rest.

Returning to the tale of our daughter's prom date, Ellen and I were sound asleep when the phone rang.

Ellen picked it up and this is what I heard: "Sharon, do you know what time it is? It's 4:00 A.M. You've got a lot of nerve. You're irresponsible! You said you would be home by the latest, 1:00 A.M. Don't give me that bull, it's a new car."

Slamming down the phone, Ellen turned toward me and said, "I couldn't help shouting. She got me so angry. Did I do the right thing?"

"Well," I said, "it's hard for me to say . . ."

"No, tell me. I want to know."

"Let me put it this way," I said. "Where is she?"

"I don't know," Ellen responded.

"When will she get home?"

"I don't know."

"Who is she with?"

"I don't know."

"What's wrong with the car?"

"Sharon said it broke down."

"When did that occur?"

"I don't know."

"Why didn't she call earlier?"

"I don't know."

"So what do you think?" I asked.

"Next time—and there better not be a next time," Ellen said, "I'm going to get more information before I hang up on that rotten kid."

Returning now to the question posed earlier: How can we interact with others in ways that help us obtain accurate and timely information?

9

THE PROCURING PRINCIPLES

As regards eliciting and extracting helpful information, experience has shown that there is a fundamental formula of five steps that can be followed:

1. LISTEN MORE AND TALK LESS

It should be evident that acquiring information demands that you engage in active listening. Your challenge is not just to hear the lyrics but to be sensitive to the background music as well. These are the hints of the feelings and attitudes that help uncover the real objections. Just like the basic black dress or charcoal gray suit, information is accompanied by accessories—emotions, values, experience, and expectations.

At the same time, you want to let the other party know you are empathizing with them. Leaning toward the speaker, making eye contact, nodding and smiling when it's appropriate, and uttering appreciative sounds like "uh-hum" can do this.

Earlier in this book, I mentioned the importance of taking notes, which serves several purposes:

• It disciplines you to focus your mind and concentrate on what is being said.

• Invariably, the speaker regards your note taking as a compliment, implying that what he or she is saying is valuable.

• You are compiling a record of what your opposite number has said. This might be used later to help influence their decision making. For example, "It seems to me you may have previously said _____. Well, wouldn't this provision be in accordance with that?"

• Having written notes of the discussions enables you to compose the memorandum of agreement. And being the scribe has its advantages.

To cap it all, the less you talk, the less likely you are to say something you'll later regret.

2. POSE NON-THREATENING QUESTIONS

At the outset, employ a natural and unaffected approach to put the other party at ease. Initially, start with a view that conflict provides an opportunity to engage in problem solving where both sides can meet their needs—the proverbial win-win outcome.

Begin with open-ended questions, ones that cannot be answered with a yes or no response. Here are some possibilities:

• "What's the basis of your position?"
• "How did you come up with that?"
• "Why do you feel that way?"
• "Can you help me understand what you're saying?"
• "Could you elaborate on that?"

These probing questions attempt to reduce defensiveness and gain critical information. Pursuing this objective requires that you never interrupt or overreact to whatever they say. Hence, you must restrain any urge that you may have to respond or correct what has been said.

3. REFLECT THEIR FEELINGS

Listening to what they are saying, try to understand their thinking and look at this situation from their point of view.

ITEM: In the Broadway musical *Cabaret*, the master of ceremonies of a bawdy Berlin nightclub dances affectionately onstage with his paramour. The audience is dumbfounded initially by the twosome, because the girlfriend is a gorilla. Then, by way of explanation, the MC sings to onlookers, "If you could see her through my eyes."

Similarly, that's what you should try to do in every strategic interaction: *Observe the situation through the mind-set of your client, customer, potential partner, opponent, or adversary.* Of course, as you display a genuine interest in what they are saying, you are transmitting empathy with their situation. Listening to the inflection and tone of his or her voice, consider the feelings being expressed.

At the conclusion of their presentation, pause to contemplate. Then, reflecting upon their attitudes and emotions, find things that you can agree with. Though it is necessary for you to deal with areas of conflict, don't forget that you are attempting to find common ground to build upon—a foundation for agreement.

Here, you can communicate that you identify with their predicament by saying something along these lines:

- "Gee, if that happened to me I'd be irate."
- "Obviously, no customer deserves to be treated that way."
- "If I were you, I'd feel the same way."

4. RESTATE THEIR OBJECTIONS

Next, before you respond to the content of their message, you want to make sure you're on the same wavelength. Hence, using your notes, you want to try to repeat what they find unacceptable. This will help narrow and clarify areas of disagreement.

Here's how:

- "Let me make sure I understand what you're saying . . ."
- "If I heard you correctly, you mean . . ."
- "So, if I'm not mistaken, your point is . . ."
- "Could you clarify this for me . . ."

What you are ultimately striving for is agreement on the nature of the problem and an understanding of the underlying reasons for the differences in your positions. If nothing else, you want to achieve a consensus as to your counterpart's objections and the factors that underlie it.

5. PRACTICE POSITIVE REINFORCEMENT

Whenever the other side is forthcoming with information and reveals underlying concerns and reasons, express your appreciation.

If nothing else, accompany these disclosures with a smile, a wink, or a nod. Be generous with praise for openness and simply ignore behavior that you don't want repeated. Finally, the appropriate attitude can be summarized as follows: You never know what you don't know. That's why, the more you learn, the less you realize you know.

To complete the TIP theory, let's examine the final component, *power.*

PROMINENT POINTS

- Use your lead time to give and get information.
- Invariably, human satisfaction or dissatisfaction is determined by the gap between anticipation and outcome.
- During the early stages of the negotiating process, give the other side timely information to bring their expectations in accord with reality.
- The fundamental formula for gathering information is to listen more and talk less, pose nonthreatening questions, and practice positive reinforcement.

CHAPTER IX

POWER

What really corrupts is not power, but a sense of powerlessness.

On September 9, 1965, while on a mission over North Vietnam, naval fighter pilot James Stockdale's jet was shot down. On the ground, with a shattered knee and a fractured clavicle, he was assaulted by a mob of peasants and then booked into the infamous "Hanoi Hilton."

Branded a war criminal, he was thrown into a cold and windowless cell that was eight feet long and four feet wide. And so began almost eight years of imprisonment that involved torment and torture.

During this time, he was kept in solitary confinement for three years, spent one month blindfolded, and was handcuffed and shackled in leg irons each night. As a senior officer he was given especially brutal treatment in order to debase and demoralize him.

Despite these inhumane conditions of captivity, he helped devise a tap code so that the hundreds of POWs could communicate clandestinely among themselves. This enabled the prisoners to maintain a semblance of solidarity, morale, and dignity under these horrendous circumstances.

Most impressive of all was that Stockdale established rules of conduct that were disseminated to all Americans in such camps— the "Four Rs": Refuse to make propaganda broadcasts, Refuse early release, Refuse to admit to war crimes, and Refuse to bow to one's captors.

When it became evident that Stockdale was the ringleader, the North Vietnamese attempted to force him to make a filmed propaganda appearance.

Their purpose was probably twofold:

Number 1: To dispel any rumors circulating in the West that American POWs were not being treated humanely.

Number 2: If they could get Stockdale to violate his own rules, the rest of the captives would all fall into line.

In this trying situation, even a courageous man might be resigned to his fate. After all, he could not prevent his captors from dragging him before the cameras. Perhaps he wouldn't bow or speak; nonetheless his image would be captured on film.

James Stockdale, however, was not only heroic but ingenious as well. Before his scheduled appearance, he used a wooden stool to maul and disfigure his face into a bloody mess. The outcome: The photo opportunity was canceled.

The point of this dramatic tale is that even under the worst circumstances, a presumably powerless person can take control of his own destiny. It's done by a willingness to risk and a belief that you always have options. This is the stuff of genuine heroes.

As a result of his attitude and behavior, Stockdale was dragged from his cell into a courtyard where he was tied up to bake in the hot sun. After days of lapsing into and out of consciousness, delirious with fever, he heard the snapping of a piece of cloth coming from one of the cells. As he tried to concentrate, he realized that it was the tap code. And the letters being communicated were G-B-Y-J-S.

He understood the message:

"God bless you, James Stockdale."

Clearly, prisoner Stockdale, even in his dire situation, thought he could control his fate. Acting upon this conviction, he brought about the result he desired. For him, power was circumscribed only by the bounds of his belief.

In this respect, the idea of power lies within each of us. It's your faculty to affect the behavior of others in accordance with your desires.

1

DEFINING POWER

Because power often decides who gets what, when, and where, it's not surprising that philosophers, political scientists, and behaviorists have been concerned with man's ability to influence others from the time of Plato's *Republic*.

Almost fifty years ago, Robert Dahl observed, "Power is the capacity to get someone to do that which they would not otherwise do." As he put it, "It's the ability of person A to get person B to take action X, minus the probability that B would do X anyway."

In a nutshell: Power is the capability—exercised or not—to produce an intended effect. Coming from the French word "to be able," it's the know-how to influence the behavior of another.

Returning to Stockdale's resolve not to be used in a propaganda campaign, it was his belief that he had the knack and resourcefulness to exert influence over his captors.

2

PERCEIVING MAY BE DECEIVING

Bargaining strength depends not so much on what power
attributes exist, but on what others believe them to be.

FRED IKLÉ

From a negotiating perspective, your leverage is how the other
side perceives it. If they think you can affect their satisfaction or
dissatisfaction, you wield the power to determine the outcome.

They view your strength according to what's going on in their
minds. Therefore, you don't actually need a strong position, as
long as the other side thinks you have one. It's all subjective.

Let's assume that you have an ardent desire to purchase a one-
of-a-kind antique ring. If the vendor cannot detect your eagerness,
he has gained no advantage.

Thus, although desperate to make the deal, if you can conceal
this ardor from the seller, you'll gain an edge. When you present
your "final offer" in a detached manner close to the deadline, the
other side will look at your caring, but not t-h-a-t much attitude
and concentrate only on their probable rejection costs—the loss of
a desired sale.

Once their one-sided calculations are done, if the probable
costs of rejection are greater than the cost of acceptance, you'll
get a yes answer.

3

POWER—NEUTRAL AND OFTEN NEGLECTED

Despite the significance of power, to some this is a word with negative connotations.

The reason for this bum rap, I suspect, comes from the exposure that too many of us have had to those who abuse power. From an autocratic parent ("Right or wrong, I'm your father, so I'm always right") to a dictatorial boss ("It's my way or the highway"), we have learned to become apprehensive about power seekers and power wielders.

Certainly, this is a valid complaint. However, it's not about power per se, but about the overbearing and coercive way in which it is employed. Another well-founded gripe is that sometimes we don't approve of the ends to which power is devoted.

But other than these two instances, power is a desirable attribute that gives you a sense of mastery over your life.

In the absence of power, you will, at best, be in a situation of dependency—existing at the whim of others. And if you think for a moment that you might be better off in a dependency relationship, just ask the Native Americans, who had the United States government looking after them for two hundred years.

Given all this, we can see that power itself is neutral—neither good nor bad. Like the wind or electricity, power is often felt but not seen. As a means to induce change and cause intended effects, it's the equivalent of a sword that can cut in any direction.

Take the example of a power source like gasoline that propels vehicles. Suppose that I used my car to transport food packages to the needy. No doubt, such use of gasoline would be approved.

On the other hand, assume that under the influence of alcohol, I filled up my auto with gasoline and went for a joyride. Due to my intoxicated condition, I crashed into a school bus injuring many children. In both instances the power used (gasoline) was the same. Yet in the latter case my conduct would be met with disapproval.

Obviously, in this simple analogy, the difference between acceptable and unacceptable behavior has nothing to do with the source of power.

Still, in spite of the importance of power in making things happen, why is power too often overlooked?

First, there is the issue of causality or the difficulty in measuring kinetic or active power. Because there are many variables that influence any action, behavioral theorists have a problem in quantifying and isolating the role of power. In fact, it was Bertrand Russell who once posed the question, "Would history have been different if Cleopatra's nose had been an inch longer?"

Second, unlike Niccolò Machiavelli, who wrote about how things are, some starry-eyed types prefer to discuss only the way things should be. Thus, they use "truth" and "love" as substitutes for power and influence. And this utopian idealism sounds good— until it comes into contact with reality.

Finally, the lingering pejorative association makes power one of America's last taboos. Like sex in Victorian England, it is something not often discussed in polite company, only appreciated under the covers.

Accordingly, those who mastered the power game, like Senate Majority Leader Lyndon Baines Johnson, went to endless lengths to mask this fact. You may recall that while engaged in arm twisting to get legislation passed, Johnson often quoted the biblical Prophet Isaiah, who said, "Come, let us reason together."

In the realm of international relations, power is constantly employed to change the behavior of sovereign states to achieve desired outcomes.

Consider NATO's exercise of coercive power (air strikes) to put a halt to Slobodan Milosevic's ethnic cleansing of Kosovo; then, the use of reward power (economic aid) to change the Serbian government's initial decision not to turn Milosevic over to The Hague War Crimes Tribunal.

What happened in this situation was that NATO was able to get Serbia to do something that they were originally disinclined to do by managing the options that they perceived were available to them. This was accomplished by using power to manipulate their expectations and preferences.

ITEM: During a recent labor relations negotiation in the picture-framing business, the union originally expected that their members would receive a 5 percent across-the-board increase in compensation. After all, this was the precedent established in the two prior negotiated contracts.

However, a month before that first bargaining session, word got out that the company was seriously considering closing the unprofitable plant and relocating elsewhere. This information did not come directly from management but a reliable third party source.

This bit of intelligence caused the union to perceive their alternatives differently. Consequently, they were more than willing to accept a 15 percent *reduction* in salaries and cooperate with management in trying to make the operation profitable.

Yet for all this, let me remind you that there is a difference between subjective or perceived power and objective or actual power. *What matters in the final analysis is not what you've got but what they think you've got.* Much like beauty, power is in the eyes of the beholder.

4

YOU GOTTA BELIEVE

The sense that we are in charge of our lives is a basic human need that is meaningful for a person's physical and psychological well-being. In this respect, the *belief* that we are not powerless—but have the capacity to influence behavior and attain desirable goals—may be as important as our actual ability to do those things.

Those who think they have some control of what happens to them can more effectively deal with setbacks and stress. Conversely, those who lack this sense of mastery often become easily frustrated, depressed, and even physically ill.

Think for a moment how a patient feels the night before he or she is about to undergo heart bypass surgery. Or, how about if your identity has been assumed by someone who has stolen your credit cards? How does a person emotionally react after a mugging or a burglary?

Now, let's take this feeling of powerlessness and put it in an organizational setting.

My own experience has shown that, when people do not feel empowered, they are unwilling to exercise initiative, take few risks, cover up their mistakes, color or falsify feedback, and become adept at writing protective (cover-your-ass) memos. These ominous symptoms indicate that the organization is no longer serving the purpose for which it was originally intended.

So, believing you have power may be indispensable for both effectiveness and mental health. Also, it will help you realize your ambitions—enabling you to gain favor with those from whom you might want things, such as security, justice, prestige, respect, recognition, money, fame, or love.

Yes, even love. Henry Kissinger, you may recall, said that, "Power is the ultimate aphrodisiac"—only to be corrected by a critic who commented, "No, it's not an aphrodisiac, only a deodorant."

Whatever your orientation, don't underestimate your capacity to make things happen the way you want them to.

Reiterating one more time:

Power begins with you.

PROMINENT POINTS

- What matters is not what power you've got, but what the other side thinks you've got.
- Don't ever underestimate your options or capacity to make things happen.

CHAPTER X

SOURCES OF POWER

You can get much further with a kind word and a gun than you can with a kind word alone.

AL CAPONE

Before the negotiating process formally begins, take an inventory of the power assets potentially available: both your own and the other side's. This will increase your confidence and help you adjust the expectations and preferences of the other side.

Always keep in mind that negotiating is an exploratory game involving discovery and learning that can lead to the rearranging of expectations and the reshuffling of behavior.

What follows is a concise summary of some, but not all, of the wellsprings of your power.

1

COMPETITION—OPTIONS

Whenever you generate competition for something you possess, that possession increases in value.

If you envision that you will be making a purchase of some furniture, a car, a residence, insurance, or software for your computer, realize that vendors abound who are salivating for your money. Mind you, they know that financial wherewithal is a volatile thing. They know that if you were to leave their premises or presence without concluding the sale, you can get the same or a similar item elsewhere. After all, who knows more about their competition than they do?

Likewise, if you are selling a product or service, whip up as many prospects or potential customers as you can through advertising, trade shows, social contacts, mailing lists, or the Internet.

While all of this appears obvious, there's one ingredient that you want to add to this recipe that will help you stand out from the crowd. Earlier I called this variation *differentiation*.

Knowing from experience that beaten paths usually lead nowhere and that only dead fish move with the current, I'll apply this variation in the examples that follow.

GETTING HIRED

When I was growing up, it was difficult for college graduates to get a decent entry-level job in a good company. Unemployment was high, so I took whatever I could get. I did everything from pushing a cart in the Garment District to working as a salesclerk at Goldsmith Brothers.

My strategy for gaining meaningful employment was about the same as everyone else's. I bought the *New York Times* on Sunday and answered want ads, enclosing my résumé.

After weeks of never even receiving a return call to arrange an interview, I phoned a company that had advertised a job opening. It was then that I learned that they had over three thousand applicants for that one position. I did not have to be a mathematical genius to realize that statistically I would have a much better chance at the Las Vegas gaming tables or the Irish Sweepstakes.

Recognizing this reality, I changed strategy to make myself distinctive and memorable—maybe even peculiar.

The next morning, I got dressed in my best suit, white shirt, and tie and went to the corporate office of a major firm in the city—which employed about two thousand people. Arriving at 8:15 A.M., I waited in the reception area for anyone in Human Resources to arrive. When someone did, I informed him that I was there to apply for a job.

Paul Peabody, the personnel manager, told me that there were no current openings. Instead of uttering a perfunctory "thanks" and leaving, I implored him to give me just a few minutes of his time.

Sure, there were no openings right now, I thought, but if they have only a 10 percent annual turnover, that's two hundred spots he'll need to fill. In fact, right now there's probably an employee who's typing out his or her letter of resignation, which Peabody won't learn of till next week.

Whether it was my forlorn look or the fact that he identified with my plight, we went into his office and spent twenty minutes together. During this time I asked questions, listened intently, took notes, and asked for help. Truly, when this interview ended, I knew more about him than he did about me.

Undoubtedly, he put my résumé in his file and thought that would be the end of it.

That evening I sent Peabody and the receptionist personal thank-you notes. Then, two days later, I again went to the corporate office at 8:15 A.M., greeted the receptionist, and waited for Peabody to arrive. When he did, I inquired about employment and got the same negative reply.

The next week, I repeated this routine three times with the same discouraging results. On one occasion, though, I brought coffee for the receptionist and Peabody's secretary. This was the least I could to do reciprocate for the courtesies extended to me.

In candor, I may have realized even then they were individuals who might indirectly influence decision making. Akin to the Queen's consort or King's mistress, these are power people who have access to those who were important to me.

About three weeks after my first encounter with Peabody, he called with the news that a position was available. When I saw him the next morning I was briefed and prepared for my meeting with the sales manager, who would decide if I got the job.

Apparently, an account executive, sensing that his boss was going to discharge him, quit without notice. Primarily, what irritated the sales manager was that the employee never got to work on time. I also learned that the sales manager wanted the slot filled right away.

Peabody said, "When I heard this, I thought of you. You don't even work here, but each morning you seem to open up the building."

Needless to say, I got the job and my first taste of life in the big corporate arena.

GAINING ADMISSION TO A
HIGHLY COMPETITIVE COLLEGE

When our daughter, Sharon, entered New Trier High School in Winnetka, Illinois, I thought she should participate in varsity sports. My rationale was as follows:

1. Believing in gender equality, I wanted her on the playing field, while on the sidelines "pom-pom boys" would be cheering for her.

2. Competitive sports are good preparation for dealing with both the ups and downs of life.

3. When she ultimately applied to college, this credential would distinguish her somewhat from her peers.

The only problem with this idea was that Sharon maintained, with some justification, that she had no natural athletic ability. Claiming impaired hand-eye coordination and no inherited speed, she ruled out volleyball, soccer, basketball, tennis, and track.

I said, "What about long-distance running?"

"I can't do that!"

"Oh yes you can. You're certainly able to walk a fast five or ten miles. Make believe I'm chasing you."

Realizing how determined her father can be when he gets one of his crazy ideas, she reluctantly worked out that summer in an attempt to make the squad.

Surprisingly, when she appeared for the tryout, there was only one other long-distance candidate. Hence, she made the team.

In those days, when they competed against another school in the ten-mile run, the entire field often consisted of three girls. Consequently, Sharon often finished in third place, picking up a bronze medal and one point for her team.

Now fast-forward to gaining admittance to a popular college. Her application contained good grades, high SAT scores, but more significantly the added value of varsity track, where she was a "medal-winning long-distance runner." Indeed, her track coach—never impressed with Sharon's athletic ability but impressed by her resolve—even offered to personally make calls on her behalf in order to differentiate Sharon's application from all the others.

In the end, she was accepted to many undergraduate schools that seemed a big stretch if they considered only her academic credentials. One even offered her an athletic scholarship. That says it all!

OBTAINING FINANCING

Of particular interest is the occasional need that we have to secure money to help us take care of our obligations.

In my case what I usually do is gather together all my personal financial records and past income tax returns and visit my bank's lending officer. Giving him or her time to review this material, I ask for their best rate and terms for a $100,000 line of credit.

Never appearing pressed for time, I have on occasion left this data with them for their consideration.

When they contact me with their proposal, no matter what they say, I regard it as an opening bargaining position. After all, I see myself as a buyer of money.

Thereupon, I take back my financials, thank the lending officer, tell them, "I'll think about it and in all likelihood return."

At this point, using the same modus operandi, I visit their competitor across the street. Giving them time to digest my financial track record, I accurately inform them where I've been and the offer received.

Usually, I quickly cut to the chase and say something like, "Can you beat that?" Invariably, this competing seller can and does.

The next step, as you might surmise, is back to the original prospective lender, where I inform them of what transpired across the street. More often than not, this lending officer goes back to the boss or loan committee and either matches or beats the competition.

Years ago when I had more time and was enjoying the gamesmanship, I sometimes said to this original lending officer, "Let me further reflect upon this."

What I did was not even go back to the second bank, but went to lunch. Then returning to the first bank, I had the audacity to say, "Do I have to tell you where I've been?"

In that single instance, the bank, caught up in what they perceived as a bidding war, dropped their rate even further.

By the way, whom were they competing against? The answer, of course, was themselves.

By this time, you understand that *the more options and alternatives they think you have, the greater your power and negotiating leverage.*

THE AUCTION GAME: BIDDING AGAINST YOUR OWN BEST INTERESTS

When I was conducting two-day seminars in negotiating in the late 1970s I used an exercise that involved bidding. The idea came from an article that I had read by researcher and theorist Martin Shubik in the *Journal of Conflict Resolution.*

My purpose at the time was to illustrate how the need to win at all costs or unbridled self-interest often produces unexpected and undesirable outcomes.

During the program, I passed out a crisp Ulysses S. Grant $50 bill among the participants, who were primarily private and public sector executives. While they examined it for authenticity, I announced the ground rules for the auction of this denomination of American currency.

They were as follows:

1. Anyone in the room could choose to participate in the auction.
2. All bids must be in increments of $5.

3. The winning bidder would receive the $50 bill, less the amount of his or her bid.
4. No collusion among the participants was allowed.

And here was the wrinkle:

5. The second highest bidder or loser would be required to forfeit the amount of his or her final offer.

Early on the offers came at breakneck speed until they reached $30 to $35. At that level, most of the participants dropped out, leaving only two competitors.

Astonishingly, these two would continue on, vying with each other past $50—a point where acquiring the bill would be unprofitable for both contestants. Most often, the auction ended in the range of $70 to $125.

Assuming that the winning tender was $60, that meant that the second-place finisher or loser would have to pony up $55. But what about the "winner"? He or she would sustain a net loss of $10—the $60 winning bid less the $50 value of the currency.

While this is a fashioned game, it reveals much about human nature and helps explain some of the illogical behavior that we see in negotiating.

First, *even the most rational decision maker is influenced to some extent by ego and face-saving needs.* What affects behavior is not only what might appear evident or logical (profitability), but a myriad of other factors that are unseen and often unknown.

Second, *once we commit to a course of action it skews our perception.* This cognitive dissonance may cause us to rationalize, justify, and do more of the same.

Third, when establishing an objective and strategy, *we all too often do not take into our calculations how our counterpart will respond.* We tend to forget that we do not act in a vacuum, but try to exert influence on others, whose choices interact with ours. In this respect, negotiating is more like chess than roulette or craps.

Fourth, because of our investment, *it becomes difficult to reverse course and cut one's losses.* The *consistency principle,* whereby we admire those who are unvarying, predictable, and constant, magnifies this problem. Indeed, one of the worst epithets is to be called a poseur or hypocrite.

Lastly, *in our society we revere and reward the victor.* Whether it's the World Series, the Super Bowl, the Olympics, political elections, or academic class standing, winner takes all. This mentality, of course, seeps into our consciousness.

This analysis may help explain some of the seemingly irrational behavior that we see exhibited by those who know better. A case in point might be the airline industry, where unprofitable carriers continually cut fares and expand costly frequent-flier programs. Likewise, we have seen zealous bidding for trophy companies or properties that bear no relationship to their market value.

SOTHEBY'S SINATRA AUCTION

For that matter, have you ever attended an auction? Well, I have.

Years ago, when Frank Sinatra disposed of his home in Palm Springs, California, much of the personal contents were offered for sale at Sotheby's, a licensed auction house in Manhattan. The day before, I visited the facility and selected two of the least costly items that I considered acquiring.

One was a sterling silver cigarette case containing the monogram "FAS," which was listed in the catalogue at a value of $950. The other was an original oil painting appraised at $650.

Before attending the public auction I established the maximum bid I would make on each item. For the cigarette case it was $975 and the painting $920.

The next day, Sotheby's had a packed house. As the auction began, I learned that I was not just competing against those in the room, but there were bids that arrived by phone and fax.

When the bidding started on the items I wanted, the offers already exceeded the objectives I set. As an observer, I watched people furiously compete, not only for Frank's personal property, but also against each other. Most revealing of all was the impression I got that, in some instances, the bidders' primary motive was not obtaining the article, but making sure that the other party didn't. What my mother used to call, "Cutting off your nose to spite your face."

In another setting, I have observed a similar phenomenon: a different drummer but the same drum. When a Hollywood movie producer purchased a script sight unseen, I asked him why. "It's not that I wanted it," he replied. "I just needed to make sure that the other son of a bitch didn't get it."

Going back to the Sinatra auction, the cigarette case was sold for $3,200 and the painting for $2,600.

So there we have it: If you can encourage enough competition for what is perceived to be a one-of-a-kind unique item, its price will soar. In this case, you become the owner of something that Francis Albert Sinatra looked at or touched.

In effect, Sinclair Lewis had it right when he said, "People will buy anything that's only one to a customer."

Assuredly, negotiating is a game, but never allow yourself to get so wrapped up in play that you lose perspective and sight of your original goal.

THE BIDDING TRAP?

Years ago, after giving a speech for an association of suppliers, I was asked about a frequently encountered dilemma:

"A prospective customer called and told me that their company is no longer happy with their current supplier. In short, they want our bid with the possibility that they will switch this business over to us. What should I do?"

Ordinarily, when asked anything, I try to obtain more information from the questioner so that they can determine the answer themselves.

The problem, however, is so common that I'll present my outlook on this situation.

From my experience, the likelihood is that the customer is using you to gain a better price from his current supplier. Yet, if you don't enter the fray, you may cause the customer to become disaffected, forfeiting any chance of future dealings. In the meantime, if you guess wrong and they do change partners, you'll be hearing about this from your boss.

What I would do in this situation is employ the *concept of differentiation, distinguishing what you have for sale from that of other competing vendors.* As you know, though we talk price, other elements of the deal may be just as important. What I'm referring to is reputation for quality, ability to supply the quantity desired, on-time delivery, the type of warranty provided, and so forth. Certainly, the customer knows that you get what you pay for and that if you lowered your standards or service provided you could easily drop the price.

Previously, I made the point that what is given away free is often not appreciated. In this instance, for you to tender a bid requires effort on your part and you should be recompensed in some fashion.

What I'm suggesting is that in return for submitting an offer you receive access to confidential information about the company and obtain a meeting with the end user—at which time you can sell the uniqueness of your products or services. Additionally, you might, answer their question with a question and say, "What specifically do you have in mind? Could you quote me the price that will result in our getting your business?"

To summarize what has been said thus far:

1. When you're a *seller* of products, services, ideas, or proposals, reach out to as many qualified prospects or potential consumers and customers as possible. If you're in selling, your job is to beget buyers.

2. As a *buyer*, generate as much competition for your money as you can. All told, the more people that want your business, the more negotiating leverage you have.

3. Realize the danger lurking in situations where you care too much about winning or making the deal. (This was one of the points of "Obtaining Financing," "The Auction Game," and this section.)

4. Differentiate yourself, your services, products, and ideas, from the norm or usual. This added value enables you not to be compared with your competition and moves bargaining from the sole criterion of price. Wasn't this why my daughter—the "medal-winning long-distance runner"—was accepted to highly competitive colleges?

OPTIONS EQUAL POWER

The belief that there are always options creates independence, whereas the perception that there are no alternatives gives rise to dependence and submission.

When you cannot see a choice or another way of satisfying your needs and interests, you're on your way to servitude. But not to worry, you always have options. In fact, I have yet to encounter a situation where this is not so.

Even when confronted with the certainty of death, you have the choice of the attitude and demeanor that you will display. History contains many examples of individuals who faced this fate with an assertion of bravery and valor. "True courage," wrote Mark Twain, "is not the absence of fear, but the mastery of fear."

Which brings me to a more mundane example: dealing with a sole source.

Periodically, I am challenged in my optimism over options by a person who tells me his business is subject to the pricing whims of a manufacturer who is the only one making what he needs. Resigned to his dependency relationship, he throws up his hands and says, "What can I do? I have no alternative!"

Doubtless, if he really looked, he could get it elsewhere, but let's assume for the sake of argument that's not possible. So here are some ways of breaking out of bondage:

1. DISCOVER A SUBSTITUTE

As crucial as this product is, there are always ways to redesign around it or obtain a replacement.

2. MAKE IT YOURSELF

If this item has such value there are many like you in a similar predicament. Hence, it may be possible for you alone, or in a joint venture with others, to go into this profitable manufacturing business.

3. USE AN INDIRECT THREAT

If the situation actually is as described, there may be a violation of antitrust laws or monopolistic practices. What I'm suggesting is that it may be possible to send a vague and indirect message to the sole source supplier that if these policies continue, they may in the future come under the embarrassing scrutiny of a governmental agency. The big advantage of this approach is that it avoids direct confrontation, permits "plausible deniability," and allows for face saving.

Accordingly, before you begin the formal give-and-take, consider what other alternatives you may have. If you can't satisfy your needs with this person or this company, what other options are available? And what acceptable choices does the other side have?

If they somehow come to believe that you can find a suitable alternative elsewhere, you will have the leverage to make the deal you want.

More important, with a viable concrete alternative, you yourself have a basis for measuring their best offer against exercising this option. This is the indifference point, where you care, but not t-h-a-t much, if the negotiation with this party is not consummated and results in a deadlock.

THE BATNA

In their widely acclaimed book, *Getting to YES*, Roger Fisher and Bill Ury coined the acronym BATNA, or *best alternative to a negotiated agreement*.

This is a useful concept, where beforehand you research and explore what you will do if you cannot achieve congruence. Having this specific option in your back pocket allows you to better assess the other party's last and final offer against the prospect of no deal.

Ultimately, your objective in this interaction is not merely closure at any price, but to achieve an agreement that is better than your BATNA.

Recapping: Since a lot of life's doings are determined by the feeling that it can be done, always believe you have power and options.

2

LEGITIMACY

All progress requires the occasional questioning of authority and its symbols used to limit human potential.

People crave stability. So over centuries symbols have developed that give structure to society. The problem is that these manifestations of control can also stifle initiative, repress the human spirit, and sometimes result in blind obedience to authority.

On April 8, 1956, at Parris Island, South Carolina, a Marine drill instructor, Sergeant Matthew McKeon, issued an order to a group of recruits who immediately marched into water over their heads. Reports of the incident revealed that none of them considered disobeying the order, even though some of them could not swim and subsequently drowned.

Conceding that this took place in a military setting and is an extreme example, still, it illustrates the inclination that exists to obey those who appear to be in charge.

Sergeant McKeon, in this case by virtue of his rank and position relative to the trainees, possessed formal authority to use power and exert influence. In fact, at his court-martial, attorney Emile Zola Berman used the defense that he was exercising "legitimate power," albeit with bad judgment and tragic consequences.

Typically, in our daily lives, we come into contact with those who have formal authority.

In the organizational world, it's a superior or boss, whose rights and prerogatives stem from his or her spot on the organizational chart. This positional power comes with the territory and vests the right to establish norms and make decisions, which can be enforced via the use of carrots or sticks. This power is on display throughout a corporate or government headquarters by meaningful symbols—from titles to the size of an office.

Another illustration of formal authority translating into power would be a uniformed traffic cop, who lays claim to obedience based upon position and status. When directing traffic or stopping motorists, they obey his instructions, believing he has the means to coerce compliance.

However, from our perspective as negotiators, we are primarily concerned with the power of legitimacy as manifested in signs, price tags, forms, and official-looking documents. These take on the aura of societal norms and precedents, which shape behavior and have an impact on our decision making. Whether it's a hotel checkout time posted on the door, or the "sticker price" stuck to the window of a car, we tend to react in knee-jerk fashion. All too often, we are obeisant to social conventions, printed forms, and traditions, whose original justification lacks current validity and certainly doesn't apply to our unique circumstances.

Yet, incredibly, we allow these pieces of paper to change our thinking and prescribe our choices.

ITEM: When I was attending law school and working as a claims adjuster we used a form that was titled, "Parents Indemnity Agreement."

Learning that our insured's vehicle struck a ten-year-old child, I was dispatched to settle the case. Arriving at their home, it appeared that the youngster was not seriously injured. He had sustained minor contusions and abrasions, seen his family's doctor, and was back at school.

This was a week after the accident and the mother and father were willing to resolve the matter with a monetary payment. After negotiating, we agreed that $320 was a fair settlement.

At this point, I wrote out a company check for this amount and presented them with a "Parents Indemnity Agreement" for their signature. Actually, I never used the grim word "sign" because people are resistant to signing anything without getting advice. Instead, I said, "Would you mind putting your name to this?"

Pausing for a moment to contemplate, I could sense them thinking, "Oh, just scribbling my name. Hey, no problem."

Rarely, if ever, would anyone read this official-looking document; they just assumed it was a receipt for the money tendered. As far as they were concerned, the case was closed.

But in reality, the form stated that if they decided to reopen this matter, because they later came to learn that the settlement was inadequate or the injuries more serious, their only obligation was to return the $320.

Based on the law of averages you would think that this would have occurred about 5 percent or 10 percent of the time. But in all my years, I never heard of it happening.

The moral: We are too often subjugated by symbols that limit our options.

This printed form was one of these symbols of legitimacy, designed to cause acquiescence and resignation.

In your life as a negotiator, when you encounter these items, recognize them for what they are. Coming into being as a result of negotiation, they are, of course, negotiable.

Here are some examples along these lines:

The Official Form

Real estate lease
Bank loan agreement

Limited warranty
Legal retainer
Standard contract

Official Procedural Manuals

Corporate pricing books
Personnel pay grades
Relocation and severance policies
Operational directives

The Professionally Printed Sign

"No Personal Checks Cashed"
"Minimum 7 Days for Alterations"
"No Exit—Alarm Will Sound"
"Not Responsible for Personal Property"
"Home Under Electronic Surveillance"
"Keep Off the Grass"
"It Is Unlawful to Remove This Tag from Mattress"
"On Sale—7 Days Only"
"No Smoking Room"

And my favorite: "So Nice to Look at, So Easy to Hold, but if You Break It, It's Sold."

Incidentally, I have a friend who frequently travels to Los Angeles on business. While there he stays at a hotel where smoking is not permitted. While checking in he advises the front desk clerk or assistant manager that he is a smoker and asks for their help. What they do is give him a room with a terrace or balcony (at the same price), where he can satisfy his need to puff away.

Don't get me wrong, I'm not advocating that you push where it says pull or spend your time trying to enter through the exit. What concerns me is that you not allow forms of legitimacy to curtail social interaction and discussion, stifle initiative, and exclude the need for explanation.

THE HERD INSTINCT

Man is a gregarious animal, and much more so in his mind than in his body. He may like to go alone for a walk, but he hates to stand alone in his opinions.

GEORGE SANTAYANA

Also intrinsic to the power of legitimacy is the unconscious impulse that we have to follow the crowd. This propensity seems to be ingrained in the very structure of our being.

Anthropologists tell us that gregariousness was necessary for the survival of our species. And this sensitivity to the reaction of others has left its residual effects. It might even be argued that this is what makes us so susceptible to conformity, peer group pressure, demagoguery, and mob passion.

"Print gives additional authority to influencing behavior," Giles St. Aubyn wrote, "because its official look bears the stamp of herd approval. Sellers of goods or opinions rely on people's pathetic faith in the printed word."

Those who violate the norms, customs, or traditions of society risk disapproval and even ostracism. Fundamentally, we have an innate hesitancy about new ideas, which threaten comfortable habits and ways of thinking.

Accordingly, *if you intend to introduce a new notion or change an accepted practice, do it gradually in small increments and support these changes with some form of legitimacy (i.e., precedent).* Otherwise, you risk a stampede by frightening the herd.

History abounds with examples of the tragic destiny of those thinkers ahead of their time. If they disregard the *concept of acceptance time* and did not proceed step by step, they ended up ridiculed, scorned, and sometimes exiled. For true originality is too often an ill-fated malady.

Society exists through the communication of symbols, which are used to shape behavior. From the standard form, which we are programmed not to question, to the red light, which causes us to halt, we have been conditioned to react without thinking.

CROSSING AGAINST THE RED

About thirty years ago, Allen Funt of *Candid Camera* fame installed an official-looking traffic signal on a sidewalk in Manhattan. Based upon my recollection, I believe it was set up on Fifth Avenue between 56th and 57th Streets near where Trump Tower stands today.

Funt had five members of his staff, acting as pedestrians, start at 57th Street and walk south on Fifth Avenue. They proceeded side by side toward the mid-block hoax traffic signal, which was green.

About thirty yards from this symbol of legitimacy, they slowed their pace so the crowd walking behind them built up.

When Funt's crew got about ten yards away, the light suddenly turned red. The crew stopped in their tracks, cooling their heels and marking time.

Surprisingly, the pedestrians behind them also paused, waiting for the light to change to green. Let me remind you, these were New Yorkers, who are known to be impatient and always in a hurry.

The cameras focused on the pedestrians standing behind Funt's bunch. Some of them were anxiously looking at their watches, obviously annoyed by the unanticipated delay.

After thirty seconds, one man toward the rear of the growing crowd took matters into his own hands. Apparently late for an appointment, he speedily jaywalked across Fifth Avenue between moving traffic to get around the waiting queue. The remaining pedestrians, though appearing edgy and irritated, didn't move.

Then, about thirty seconds later, one of the "young and restless" moved into the almost empty lane of oncoming pedestrians and headed to the front, where Funt's bunch was standing.

Once there, he stopped, looked both ways across the sidewalk and dashed through the red light. Thereafter, with this precedent established, others, using a similar head-glancing technique, followed.

There you have it: The power of legitimacy affects all of us to some degree. In your hands it can help you shape behavior in ways that you desire. But recognize that there's also a flip side as well, whereby in knee-jerk fashion we accept things that should be questioned and challenged.

3

RISKING

Why not go out on a limb? That's where all the fruit is!

MARK TWAIN

Since life is filled with uncertainty, everything that we have, including happiness, can be fleeting. Our only guaranteed permanency is—change.

No one can play it absolutely safe. Even inaction may present danger. The only time you won't encounter some risk will be the day it's "Miller Time in Hell," and those consigned there are guzzling cold beer from frosted mugs.

All negotiating progress involves some element of chance. So you cannot take a Chicken Little approach. Don't be inhibited by the fear of trying.

Of course, I'm referring to risk taking that is sensible and cautious. Always use foresight and intelligence as you calculate the odds and the timing of your moves.

For some, though, life is akin to a poker game, where they count on always drawing an inside straight. But such reckless and indiscriminate play will cause your stack of chips to dwindle rapidly.

But I'm urging you to take prudent and reasonable risks. Truly, if nothing is ever ventured something will be lost.

Picture this scene:

Take 1: I'm negotiating with Al Accommodator, a person who is renowned for his dread of "deadlocks." Arriving at the "eleventh-hour crunch time," I'm inclined to "hang tough" and not make any concessions. Why? Based upon his reputation, I know he will waiver at the end.

Take 2: The same setting and circumstances, with the exception that my counterpart across the table is different. Instead of Mr. Accommodator, I'm dealing with Will Walkaway, reputed to care but not t-h-a-t much. To be exact, he has been known to occasionally deadlock in these situations.

Now what do I do?

Unlike in the prior instance where I was steadfast, this time I'm more inclined to yield.

In January 1956, in the midst of the Cold War, Secretary of State John Foster Dulles unintentionally coined the term "brinkmanship."

At the time he remarked that the United States had to take chances in order to stay out of military conflict. "The ability to get to the verge," he said, "without getting into war is a necessary art. If you try to avoid risk, if you run away from it, if you are scared to go to the *brink*, you are lost."

Although criticized for what was seen as a reckless statement in the nuclear age, subsequent events have demonstrated the inherent geopolitical danger in being seen as disinclined to risk.

Indeed, the Islamic militant radicals who planned and organized the September 11 atrocity viewed the United States as a nation loath to suffer civilian or even military casualties.

They were familiar with our national trauma when the body bags came home from Vietnam, the "Jimmy Carter Desert Classic," when we invaded Iran with eight helicopters, the bombing of Kosovo for seventy-eight days at an altitude of fifteen thousand feet to insure that we sustained no casualties, and Bill Clinton's use of million-dollar cruise missiles in Afghanistan to destroy empty tents.

What they believed was that if they could cause America to sustain considerable loss of human life and produce sufficient fear, that, over time, they would sap our morale and our will.

From the perspective of the terrorists, who set out to murder innocent people, our lack of response to past attacks and provocations (the Beirut Marine barracks, the USS *Cole* in Yemen, and so on) caused them to see us as risk-averse—unable to endure casualties and unwilling to exercise power.

While the projection of mega-power involves the same principles, this is not the time or place for a more detailed discussion. Suffice to say, you always want the other side to see you as a nation, or as a person, disposed to take risk to uphold core values and beliefs.

Therefore, should you develop a reputation as someone who cannot bear with an impasse, you have unfortunately put yourself in a position where you can be manipulated.

Given all this, why are individuals hesitant to take a chance, even when the odds are overwhelmingly in their favor? The answer is, whatever the odds, we focus on the worst-case scenario—losing.

The way to overcome this bugaboo is to find ways to syndicate or spread the risk. Take on partners and get others involved. Such diffusion will enable your expanded group to accept greater risk for a high payoff.

For decades in the business world we have seen the "urge to merge"—whereby a smaller company voluntarily combines with a larger corporation. This affiliation enables it to take on what previously would have been prohibitive. In addition, any financial loss can be spread over a greater base.

This smaller entity knows the old truism that "money makes money." Whether in poker or business, you're in a stronger power position if your capital is considerably larger than that of your competitor.

Thus far, in analyzing power we have examined three major components. But there are other ingredients that comprise the robust recipe.

When Oliver Twist said, "Please sir, I want some more," I don't think he was talking about this particular dish of power. Nonetheless, as you turn the page, we'll continue to furnish the formulary for the *power prescription*.

4

COMMITMENT

Unlike Robinson Crusoe or *Cast Away* Tom Hanks, alone on an island, as negotiators we find ourselves tangled in a complex interpersonal web. To make a deal we must take into account the needs, concerns, and interests of ourselves and others as well.

Realize it or not, we have constraints that come at us from three directions.

First, as human beings we have our individual values, predilections, emotions, disposition, foibles, quirks, ambitions, and expectations.

We have hair-trigger wants, from a second helping of dessert, to a desire to get this over with now. And these immediate cravings often conflict with our longer-term interests and welfare. So before getting into this process, we should engage in intra-self negotiating to reconcile these internal differences.

Neglecting this step is probably what caused Walt Kelly's Pogo to remark, "We have met the enemy and he is us."

Second, improving Mark Twain's advice, when you're in pursuit of fruit, don't crawl out on a limb alone. Get others involved beforehand, so they are committed to this endeavor.

In virtually all negotiations we have a constituency, whose support can magnify the impact of our words and transmit "unity power"—"E Pluribus Unum."

Conversely, their lack of commitment to your bargaining position can prove downright subversive.

Have you ever taken your family along as you attempt to negotiate for a new car? Once, I told a Buick dealer that if he didn't lower his price further, I would have to go elsewhere. Before he had a chance to respond, Ellen came running over with a big smile on her face.

"Oh Herb," she said. "I'm so excited, we can get the car in the exact color combination I've been searching for."

While trying to signal that her expressed commitment to this particular automobile wasn't helping me finalize things, our son strolled over.

"Dad, can I have some money, I'm going across the way to buy some CDs for our new car's disc player."

Likewise, when trying to get a home seller to reduce the asking price, the same undermining behavior might occur.

Years ago, a neighbor in Glencoe told me of the negotiating strategy she employed in buying her home.

"I used two real estate agents as intermediaries to make the owner aware that I was considering another home in the area.

"Once they knew we had an acceptable alternative, my husband and I, along with the two real estate agents, went to see the seller.

"Undoubtedly, the other side believed that we could walk away because they made two quick concessions. We went from $50,000 apart to only $20,000.

"Suddenly, my husband, who seemed impatient throughout, stood up and started to draw a floor plan for the placement of his furniture in the den. If this weren't enough, he asked if he could borrow a ruler, so he could measure the windows for drapes.

"Not surprisingly, the previously anxious seller seemed to toughen his position. Finally, I had to give in on the whole $20,000—sabotaged by my own spouse."

Similar events transpire in international relations, when the President of the United States (our foreign policy CEO) tries to communicate our national intentions, resolve, and determination to opposing nations. Because in a free society communication occurs across a broad front, the President can be stripped of bargaining chips and leverage by the media, Congress, public figures, and mass demonstrations.

To sum up: Always get the commitment of every member of your team and constituency before you interact with the other side. This ensures that the message being sent is consistent and coherent.

Third, most evident of all is the pressure exerted upon us by the other side, who is occupying a different role and represents other interests.

Under this rubric, the power of commitment can operate in two ways.

A HOUSE DIVIDED

One aspect of commitment is to recognize that often the person with whom you are negotiating terms and price is not the end user. He or she is a purchasing agent, who upon concluding this transaction goes on to something else.

Of course, it means that sometimes the price and terms are excellent, but the product or services can leave much to be desired.

Experienced people who are responsible for integrating and using what has been acquired, know all too well that what comes cheap can often prove costly.

Thus, if you are able, during the lead time stage, to gain their commitment to what you're selling, they will exert leverage on your behalf with their own purchaser.

ENHANCING BELIEVABILITY

The other facet of commitment is a move made to convince an opponent that you mean business. It's a blatant power tactic used to reinforce the believability of a communication and express resolve.

For example, if I say I will not retreat, back down, or compromise, this may be seen as boastful bluster. But what if, in effect, for all to see, I burn my bridges behind me. In this case, my desire has been transformed into a necessity.

When Spaniard Hernando Cortéz's soldiers went ashore in Vera Cruz, Mexico, they set ablaze the vessels used to transport them across the Atlantic. This communicated to the indigenous people that they meant business, since retreat or return to their homeland was no longer possible. Updating this concept, isn't this what NATO did after World War II, when it stationed troops in West Germany? What about the American forces in South Korea and Japan, whose presence acts as a deterrent against aggression?

ITEM: At the height of the Cold War (1953–1955), I was a tanker in the 14th Armored Cavalry Regiment stationed at the Fulda Gap in West Germany. NATO strategists anticipated that this was the likely spot that the Soviet bloc would use in the event they invaded Western Europe.

During our briefings we were advised that we were "a mere tripwire contingent," who in the event of an attack would be behind enemy lines. Nonetheless, we were told, "Your sacrifice will not be in vain, because it kicks off World War III." Presumably, this was supposed to reassure us!

Such deployments constituted an irrevocable step that committed us to a definite course of action should one of our adversaries cross the Rubicon. In making these moves, what we tried to do was alter our opponent's expectations by limiting our own options. Isn't this what deterrence theory was all about—the accumulation of nuclear capabilities that we were prepared to use, to prevent aggression and minimize world conflict?

Hence, this type of commitment is a promise or pledge of what you will do in a contingency. It's a high-risk maneuver that may often be interpreted by the target as a threat. In essence, if he or she does not comply, negative consequences will certainly follow.

Because this is a potent and rigid tactic, converting a negotiation from positive-sum to zero-sum, one might think that its use is very limited in everyday dealings. However, this is not necessarily so.

Consider the following prosaic illustrations:

1. The chief union negotiator tells the media "If we don't get a 6 percent across-the-board increase, we'll be walking the picket line tomorrow night at midnight."

2. Professional football owners acknowledge publicly that they are taking 2 percent of their gross revenues to establish a "strike fund."

3. As the "deadline" for concluding contract negotiations nears, management in broad daylight moves cots, bedding, cooking utensils and food into the factory.

4. Israel's Likud party, while in control of the government, encourages approximately 100,000 settlers to move to the West Bank (Judea and Samaria) and Gaza, knowing that ultimately it will be more difficult to return this land to the Palestinians.

5. A popular cola soft drink bottler tells a local supermarket manager, "If we can't get a shelf display of twelve feet minimum, get your supply from our competition."

6. A Major League Baseball owner announces at a press conference that if the city and state won't pay for the building of a new stadium, he will move the franchise to another city.

7. After a hectic election among the rank and file, a new union president, running as a moderate, barely defeated a radical element within the membership. At the start of collective bargaining, he informs management that if he cannot get two more paid holidays for the workers, he will resign and they can take their chances with the extremists.

Such commitments fix a negotiator to a particular position. It's a trade-off of flexibility and possibly reputation if not followed through, for an emphasis upon resolve and determination. To some extent, these are intended as "offers that can't be refused."

COMMITMENT OR THREAT?

Having said all this, it should be evident that this attempt to enhance believability via an expressed commitment is often taken as a direct threat by the recipient. Because people resent bullying attempts, when this does happen, it sours the negotiating climate and transforms potential partners into adversaries. Moreover, most negotiators who have been targeted, tend to dig in their heels and reciprocate in kind.

Accordingly, in everyday negotiations, *I am not an advocate of direct threats, which I consider evidence of poor taste and a lack of maturity.* All too often, they come from those with frustrated ambition, shamed pride, and self-esteem problems. In fact, my life's experience has shown that cruelty and threats come from the weak, whereas decency and compassion flow from the strong.

RESPONDING TO THREATS

After a direct threat is communicated to me, I exhibit no change in demeanor and act like what was said is inconsequential. Having established the fact that I'm a slow learner, it's easy for me to say, "Gee, I don't understand" or "Whahdja say?"

Usually they have to repeat and elaborate upon the threat. But even then, I remain calm and detached. Sometimes I smile, regarding what transpired as a humorous digression. At times, I have even laughed and said, "I love the way you set that up. Could you do it again?"

By this time, most threateners move off this risky tactic and we can get back on track, attempting to solve the problem at hand. By treating their attempt at intimidation as being no big deal, it's easier for them to save face.

Assuming they remain adamant I try to probe for the reasons that underlie this uncharacteristic behavior. Then, if all else fails, I point out why I don't have the capacity to comply (lack of authority, legitimacy, precedent, whatever). Indeed, in the past, I have been known to remark, "You know, I wish I could do what you want, but regrettably I can't. I'm sorry."

STICK 'EM UP

Better still, here is a more vivid and dramatic example of a successful response to a direct threat.

In the motion picture *Take the Money and Run,* Woody Allen plays Virgil Starkwell, an inept criminal down on his luck. Determined to change his life with one bold strike, Virgil attempts a $50,000 bank holdup.

After presenting the teller with his handwritten stickup note, the dialogue went something like this.

TELLER: What does this say?
VIRGIL: Ah, uh, can't you read it?
TELLER: No, I can't understand this. This looks like GUB: G-U-B. What does it mean? Please put $50,000 in the bag and AFT natural. I'm pointing a GUB at you?
VIRGIL: No it's an N not a B.
TELLER: (Turning to another teller)
George, could you step over here for a moment. Does this look like a B or an N?
VIRGIL: It's an N.
TELLER: (Using the power of legitimacy)
Sorry, you'll have to have your note initialed by one of our VPs before we can give you any money. It's bank policy.

In the next scene, various bank employees and the VP, Mr. Miller, are in a heated discussion, arguing over whether the note says GUN or GUB. Finally, Virgil is apprehended and ends up in jail.

The moral of this vignette: It's impossible to stick up someone who doesn't know he's getting stuck up.

Of course, this is movie make-believe, coming from the comedic mind of Woody Allen. However, there have been real-life situations where either dim-witted victims or those who deliberately react in unanticipated or unwonted fashion have caused robberies to abort.

When I was at the FBI Academy in Quantico, I heard of numerous teller reactions that foiled holdups:

- "Forgive me, but I'm a trainee and not authorized."
- "Please step to the next window, this one is closed."
- "Sorry I can't help you, I'm on my lunch break."
- "I don't have a bag. Would you wait right here till I get one."
- "You've just got to be kidding!"

ITEM: Years ago, when Senator William Proxmire of Wisconsin was jogging in the Capitol area of the District of Columbia, he was accosted by an armed assailant who demanded money. The quick-thinking senator said something to this effect: "Go right ahead and carry out your threat. In fact, I want you to. I have terminal cancer and was thinking of suicide, but if I did, my wife could not collect on my life insurance. So if you kill me, you'll be helping out my family."

At this point, the mugger, who didn't see himself as a murderer, took off!

5

PERSUASIVE CAPACITY

Facts . . . Don't bother me with facts when my mind is made up.

SAMUEL GOLDWYN

Inescapably, in everyday life we find ourselves interacting with family members, vendors, customers, associates, employees, bosses, and sometimes mulish mandarins. During these exchanges, we attempt to influence their behavior using rational arguments and common sense. But in many instances, these encounters prove futile and frustrating.

Why does our use of reasoning and impeccable logic often fail to bring about the change we desire? The glib answer, of course, is that human beings by nature are not rational and reasonable. To some extent, we are all afflicted with "neophobia"—an initial aversion to anything that is novel or different. So whenever we propose a new idea, it will be met with resistance. In knee-jerk fashion, a polemic will be presented to justify the status quo. And as one sage put it, "These arguments are used in the same way that a drunk leans on a lamppost—for support not illumination."

In Eugene O'Neill's classic work *The Iceman Cometh,* the patrons of Harry Hope's saloon all cling to some pathetic self-delusion. Each is a master at rationalizing yesterday's setbacks while clinging to tomorrow's sham hopes. The play is about the human need for sustaining illusions, even as the hollowness of these illusions is cruelly exposed.

Similarly, when negotiating, we sometimes encounter people with pipe dreams (unrealistic expectations) who are reality-resistant. In such cases, we must delicately help them gain an understanding of the consequences of their behavior. While doing so, it's valuable to appreciate the existing barriers that restrain their willingness to adapt and change.

ROADBLOCKS TO CHANGE

To be certain, negotiating is about communicating to convert, so let's review some of the barriers that exist which inhibit the other party from shifting from "no" to "yes" or going from reluctance to acceptance.

1. FONDNESS FOR THE KNOWN

While the existing situation or relationship has its problems and difficulties, we have become accustomed to it, knowing its routines and proprieties. Such familiarity and investment gives us a stake in continuing things as they are. Isn't this the *certainty principle?*

A case in point: Attempting to transform a strategic interaction that has always been conducted as positional or distributive bargaining (competitive negotiation) into a creative problem-solving process could be a difficult task.

2. ANXIETY INHERENT IN RISK TAKING

Though we accept the maxim that all progress entails risk, most of us are pragmatic and innately conservative. To voluntarily move into the unfamiliar and uncertain has the ominous aura of a high-stakes hazard.

3. The Threat to Vested Interests

Because there is a presumption that "the ways things are, is the way they're supposed to be," there is a hesitancy to change. Moreover, a feeling exists that higher-ups who established, or at least maintained, these traditions might become peeved or even angry.

4. The Desire to Conform

The deeply rooted instinct to go along with the herd causes us to accept opinions and procedures that have been repeated over time. Being in harmony with customs and standard practices makes most of us comfortable.

We see this bandwagon effect manifested in peer group pressure, which I suspect may determine fashion styles and music preferences.

5. Order Is Preferable to Disorder

Because life itself is so unpredictable, in our job or career we welcome areas or times of stability and tranquillity. If we do A, we want to know that B will follow. But any change has the potential to produce the unforeseen and unanticipated. In short, doing A could also give us the undesirable side effect of X.

There can be no doubt that as negotiators we must overcome this general resistance as we attempt to use our persuasive capacity to influence behavior.

Based upon my experience in sales and as a practicing negotiator, let me share with you an interactive approach or model that will afford you *persuasive power*.

You will note that there's no emphasis on highfalutin rhetoric or slick tactics. The reason: You can only change the other side's position by altering their attitude and the way they look at things.

THE PERSUASIVE POWER PRESCRIPTION

At the outset, try to gauge the mood and expectations of the other party. Consider a change of pace, using self-deprecating humor to reduce tension. Look for something ludicrous or incongruous as it applies to you. This means that your repartee or levity should always be self-denigrating.

> ITEM: At his first press conference, the newly elected President Kennedy was asked by one of the media, "How did you become a hero during World War II?"
> "It was involuntary," he said. "They sunk my boat."

1. REDUCE DEFENSIVENESS

While displaying an interest in your counterpart, exhibit warmth and friendliness. Have them see you as authentic and sincere—warts and all. Which means if you make an error (arriving five minutes late, say), profusely apologize without qualification. Remember, fessin' up to messin' up is an endearing quality.

What you are trying to do is *construct a climate of mutual respect and trust.*

This can be achieved in a number of ways:

First—Never be confrontational, dogmatic, or abrasive. Express *your* point of view in a soft tone with some hesitation.

If you are too assertive and your proposal threatens a person or group's values, defiance will be generated along with resistance to the slightest accommodation.

Second—*Don't unnerve the other side with your demeanor or words.* An unseemly display of knowledge or experience will do this. Ogden Nash's rhyming couplet put it this way: "Here's a good rule of thumb— Too clever is dumb."

In my years as a keynote speaker, addressing high sales achievers (IBM's Golden Circle or General Electric's Incentive and Reward Cruises), the one overt characteristic that these pros had in common was a congenial and humble manner that was easy to relate to. Indeed, some had even perfected this into an art form. By using colloquial speech and the calculated fumble, they came across as regular guys or gals.

For that matter, isn't this the bearing and style of the Los Angeles Police Department's most effective detective? Clearly, I'm referring to Peter Falk's TV characterization of the clumsy and inelegant Columbo.

Third—*Show you're listening by maintaining eye contact and taking notes.* Display courtesy, empathy, respect, and understanding as you try to grasp their underlying concerns, interests, and needs.

Before reacting, always hesitate briefly. Such a pregnant pause communicates that you are giving serious thought about what was said. It also holds their attention and builds suspense.

Fourth—Realize that your response will be most effective when it's in close accord with the predispositions of the other side. *Accordingly, as you begin, tell them what they would like to hear.*

Persuasive communicators have always started this way. Indeed, recorded history and literature are filled with examples that support this approach.

MARK ANTONY'S METHOD

One of the most well-known addresses is Mark Antony's speech to a hostile crowd at the funeral of the assassinated Julius Caesar. William Shakespeare captured its essence in his historical drama.

The play opens with the return to Rome of General Julius Caesar after another military victory. As he moves through the streets, he is greeted by a cheering and doting public.

Meanwhile, Cassius, a declared political opponent, jealous of his adulation, conspires to murder him. Attempting to enlist Brutus, the general's personal friend, in the plot, Cassius argues that Caesar's acclaim poses a menace to the republic. In effect, Brutus's love for Rome must prevail over his admiration for Caesar.

The next day (the Ides of March), as Caesar is addressing the populace on the steps of the Capitol, the conspirators dagger him to death. The last assailant is Brutus and as Caesar falls he utters, "Et tu Brute?" ("You too, Brutus?").

Because the onlooking Romans were dazed and appalled, Brutus arranged for an immediate funeral, where he could mollify the masses by justifying the assassination.

At the funeral, Brutus explains to the mourners that this was a "principled murder." He had been forced to join the plot to save Rome from dictatorship ("Not that I loved Caesar less, but that I loved Rome more").

When he concluded he had won over the multitude with his eloquence and sincerity.

But then, foolishly, Brutus asked Mark Antony, Caesar's subordinate and confidant, to address the crowd.

When Antony rose to speak, the audience favored the plotters and accepted Brutus's justification. Antony's task was formidable, yet the way he used his persuasive skill transformed their initial hostility into support. At the end, the listeners were so moved that they turned their anger against Brutus, driving him and his cohorts from Rome.

Most noteworthy in Mark Antony's famous speech is how he leads off, agreeing with the predisposition of his audience. Since it's illustrative of the point I'm making, here's the beginning of his talk:

> *Friends, Romans, countrymen, lend me your ears:*
> *I've come to bury Caesar, not to praise him*
> *The evil that men do lives after them;*
> *The good is oft interred with their bones:*
> *So let it be with Caesar. The noble Brutus*
> *Hath told you Caesar was ambitious:*
> *If it were so, it was a grievous fault,*
> *And grievously hath Caesar answer'd it.*
> *Here, under leave of Brutus and the rest,—*

For Brutus is an honorable man;
So are they all, all honorable men,—

Moving from the theatrical to the practical, let's look at some things you might say to convey this agreeable bent:

- "I generally subscribe to what you're saying."
- "Thanks for your candor in sharing that with me."
- "Granted, what you're saying makes sense. In fact, if I were you I'd be saying something very similar."
- "I see your point and it's quite compatible with what I was thinking."
- "You're absolutely right, so you may want to consider this . . ."

2. EXPLORE AREAS OF AGREEMENT

While attempting to raise the level of trust, relate what you're saying to the other side's interests, problems, and concerns.

In this respect, employ illustrations, stories, analogies, and comparisons that relate to *their* background. Use these devices to make your material come alive—getting and holding attention.

Make no mistake: You should be operating on two fronts. One is the appeal to reason and logic, which should be illustrated by familiar examples. The other deals with basic human drives (self-esteem, status, pride, fear, security, belonging), which are revealed only when there is a high level of trust.

Of course, whenever you seek action from a person or group, your comments must be framed in terms of *their* basic motivations, yearnings, ambitions, and interests.

3. INTRODUCING NEW PROPOSALS

Having spent time discussing commonality and building confidence, the climate may be right for pioneering new ideas or proposals.

However, before going further, let me give you the three basic ground rules for maintaining trust and playing the game:

Number 1: Flexibility should always be displayed.

Number 2: Concessions must always be reciprocated in one form or another. Not so fast. This does not mean that your concession has to be equal in magnitude. In some instances, a promise to merely consider their idea is sufficient.

Number 3: Never impugn the motives of anyone. This is the prohibition against attacking face. Which means that if a third party is present, you must be especially sensitive about what you say.

One change that you might want to institute is the use of *creative problem solving* (integrative bargaining) to achieve win-win outcomes. This would replace the more competitive approach of *positional bargaining* and its potential for spawning losers. Certainly, if your relationship involves continuity, this is in the interest of both parties.

As you attempt to unveil the novel, there are other *commonsense principles* that you should incorporate in your approach:

1. Realize that resistance is more often about when or how the new arrangement was initiated, not about content per se.

2. When launching a new proposal, publicly concede that some adjustments may be necessary.

3. Fractionate the issues, so there is gradual implementation on a piecemeal basis over an extended period of time. (A common collective bargaining technique used by unions is to negotiate for management's acceptance of a new concept that will not cost them anything in the contract under discussion. Then, three years later in the next go-round, they bargain to activate this dormant provision.)

4. Don't spring any idea that is a departure from the norm or what is expected without some warning.

5. Make use of probing questions to sift for alternatives similar to your own before you casually reveal it (for example: "Gee, I was just thinking, what if . . .").

6. When strong opposition is encountered, sound a temporary retreat. As my Aunt Helen, a French war bride, used to say, "It's sometimes necessary to step backward in order to go forward."

7. If you can bring into play new information, facts, or circumstances previously unknown, it greases the skids for the other side to alter their outlook.

8. Try to understand why the other side is really saying "no." Always validate their feelings and reshape and refashion your new proposal to deal with these underlying apprehensions.

9. Finally, time is required for people to adjust their mind-set, as well as to go back to their organization, which also has to adapt and reconcile themselves to the new reality.

4. GET INVOLVEMENT

Formerly, I said that individuals who are actively involved and participating in generating or verifying facts and ideas are more likely to support the new conclusions that have evolved. In sum, they feel a sense of ownership.

So if you are doing some computations, ask the other side to help you. Get them into the act, rather than just giving them the total.

Years ago, stand-up comics would throw out the names of cities and ask the audience to partake with a show of hands. Coming from this tradition, Jay Leno, when he enters from behind the curtain on NBC's *Tonight Show*, does something very similar as he physically greets his fans.

As you know, *it's not an easy task to help people change, even when it's in their interest to do so.* And if they have already expressed a contrary position publicly, it's even more difficult. So if at first you don't succeed, keep reminding yourself that stumbling isn't falling and certainly not failing.

The *key to persuading is patience and posture.* Which brings us to our next topic: the power of a gaming attitude.

6

A GAMING ATTITUDE

The winning attitude is to be physically loose and mentally tight.

ARTHUR ASHE

By this time I hope you realize that seeing negotiation as a game can help you develop a psychological shield between your self-esteem and the aggressiveness of others. And with this outlook will come the perspective and detachment of an outsider.

If you have this gaming spirit, you won't try too hard to make a deal happen. Allowing some slack, you'll let events unfold on their own.

Why? Because if you are overanxious and push too hard, people are more likely to resist.

Remember the boys that Tom Sawyer ultimately conned into whitewashing his fence? At first, he came on too strong, so they thought of the effort as work. Only when he backed off and lightened up did they see the task as play and gladly undertook it.

You know this: The best way to get a merchant to lower his or her price is to care about the item for sale, but not t-h-a-t much. Previously, I called this attitude one of conscious inattention.

When I made my first visit to Japan decades ago, I was surprised to see very few cash registers in retail stores. In its place, shopgirls used the abacus, the ancient calculating instrument.

These cashiers seemed almost absentminded as their fingers flew over the wooden beads until the correct total emerged. Much like the expert archer who affords the arrow some life of its own.

What I'm saying is that one of the most important determinants of producing successful negotiating outcomes is your attitude. *The same is true in life, where it's not primarily what you make it, but how you take it.*

Hence, train yourself to regard almost all of your social exchanges, interactions, and life situations as games. Step back a little, enjoy the moment, and have some fun.

Even when things look like they are falling apart and your children are driving your crazy, invoke the sacred question: "Will I remember this in twenty years?"

If the answer is "no" or "unlikely," then . . . fuhgeddaboudit!

Life, for all of us, is a roller-coaster ride, continuous ups and downs and tos-and-fros. As the Arab proverb says, "The dog barks but the caravan moves on."

Some have said that this is my own interpretation of the ancient Chinese yin and yang philosophy, where what first appear as opposites are really complementary. If there were no men, there would be no women and vice versa. Without experiencing failure, we would not enjoy success, and if we weren't aware that death lies in wait for all of us, we could not appreciate life.

Whatever. But this I believe: Life contains few permanent absolutes.

Certainly, we all know the bad things that can leave us devastated—the loss of a loved one, sickness, pain, suffering, depression. Among these, there are no nuances or grays. It's all black dog—the dumps.

However, most everything else is yin and yang—not necessarily good or bad but transient. It all depends on how you look at it.

Let's take the case of money, which has always been around. It just changes pockets.

For some who believe you are what you have, it's the drug of choice or the sine qua non. They spend their life trying to get it, so they can obtain stuff they don't need, to impress people they don't like.

On the other hand, for others it's a means or a necessity to fulfill their obligations and responsibilities.

As a practical matter, money itself is neutral. In fact, if you want to know what God thinks of money, just look at some of the yahoos he gives it to!

When I was in my late teen years, I went to the jazz club Birdland in Manhattan. At the time, our friend Bob Benton was dating the owner's daughter. While there, a musician sat down at our table and philosophically remarked, "You know, man, what you see depends upon who or where you be."

Many years later, his wise observation came alive for me when Ellen had the responsibility for finding us a new home, as we relocated from Libertyville to Glencoe, Illinois.

Although I've told this tale before, there were specific portions that I deliberately omitted—primarily to save myself from personal embarrassment.

The essence of the story is about how Ellen found a home she wanted, and before I ever saw it had obtained the commitment of everyone in my "organization" (aka family). Presented with a fait accompli, I in effect ratified a decision that was already made by the people who were important to me.

Never previously revealed was that after we both signed the contract for the purchase price of $135,000, I matter-of-factly inquired, "By the way, what was it listed at?"

"Same," she said.

"No, Ellen, I mean what was the asking price?"

"Oh, it was $135,000."

"No," I said, "that can't be, 'cause that's what we're paying."

"Well, Herb, you got that right."

Grabbing my chest, I gasped, "I don't believe it. You paid the asking price? Nobody does that!"

"Well we just did," she said.

Attempting to stay calm, I tried to reassure myself. "Well you must have had a good reason. There's gotta be something I don't know—some justification?"

"Well, there was," she said. "It was a vacant home."

"What? Ellen, you don't understand. Vacant homes always go for less."

"Not in this case," she replied.

Incomprehensible and trying to maintain calm, I implored her for an explanation.

"Okay, I'll tell you. If the home were occupied, we would have to wait for the owners to move out. Because that takes time, we wouldn't be residents of the school district until two months into the school term.

"So our kids would come into a new school after classes have been going on. Socially, they would be in an alien world and academically they would be struggling to survive. As a result, their self-esteem would diminish, their grades would drop, and they would be miserable. Who knows if they would even be able to go on to college after such a horrendous experience—struggling constantly to make friends and catch up?

"But now, they can begin with their peers, make friends, get a good educational foundation, and feel good about themselves. They now have a chance to go on to college, professional school, careers, and good lives.

"Well, Mr. Negotiator, isn't it worth a lousy $10,000 to ensure that your children have good lives?"

You know, I had never really thought about it that way. The woman is not wrong—she's right.

Thus, what is a liability for one person (a vacant house) is, in reality, an asset for another. After all, "What you see depends upon who or where you be."

This brings us to the remaining sources of power. For the most part, they have been touched upon in the previous pages. For that reason, what follows is a synopsis of these points of potency. My intention in completing this list is to give you the confidence that comes from knowing you have more power than you might believe.

1

EXPERTISE

Unfortunately, too many of us never question the opinions and statements of those we *believe* have some specialized or esoteric knowledge. Whether it's an auto mechanic, an attorney, a stockbroker, a TV psychologist, a tax accountant, or even a medical doctor, these people are not infallible.

The main thing is not to be overly impressed by advanced degrees or alleged credentials. So, don't hesitate to make inquiries, ask for explanations, and when appropriate say, "I don't understand. Could you simplify that for a lay person?"

If you need more courage, remind yourself that respect for experts started with wizards, conjurers, and witch doctors. Moreover, when someone is getting paid for expertise, shouldn't that affect his or her objectivity?

8

KNOWLEDGE OF NEEDS

Throughout this book, we have discussed the difference between expressed positions (demands) and underlying interests (actual needs).

There are two ways to ascertain what the deal makers or breakers really are:

One is before you even go out to meet your counterpart, obtain information from someone who's done it before. Certainly, experience is the best teacher, but it's more cost effective to use the experience of someone else.

Then, when you interact with the other side, ask questions listen, and probe. In doing so, if you are just slightly sensitive, you'll learn how you can rearrange and restructure your offer to make the deal.

9

INVESTMENT

Already discussed at length, this element of power is one of the most crucial. Getting the other party to spend time, money, or energy in resolving a conflict or solving a problem provides the foundation for closure.

Every experienced negotiator knows that there is a direct correlation between the extent of investment and the willingness to compromise. If for no other reason, it's why you should always begin every strategic interaction in a cooperative manner, putting off the more contentious, emotional, and zero-sum issues for later.

10

REWARDING OR PUNISHING

When people think of power, what usually comes to mind is the capacity to compensate, or the alternative, to coerce.

If the potential target believes that they are vulnerable to being hurt or amenable to being helped, those with the capability to bring this about have power relative to such a person, institution, or nation.

To reiterate, because power is a relational concept, it's not the attribute of a single person or group, but embedded in a social relationship. Hence, if I had a crust of bread it could be sustenance for a starving person. Yet, to a wealthy individual who just consumed a big meal, it's only a gigantic crumb.

Obviously, when we talk about rewards we are referring to the entire range of carrots, from providing psychological sunshine to financial remuneration. By the same token, sticks might include physical harm, impeding career progress, financial penalties, or anything that you wouldn't want to happen.

Behavior tends to be shaped by the explicit or implicit reward and penalty system. For example, in the defense industry, major government contractors traditionally had staggering cost overruns. Why? The system never disciplined or punished these outcomes.

Perhaps one of the most vivid portrayals of how carrots and sticks fashion conduct was given to us by David Mamet in his 1984 Pulitzer Prize–winning play, *Glengarry Glen Ross.*

When the drama opens, we learn that four salesmen who peddle real estate to reluctant buyers are in the midst of a contest. The one who sells the most plots of land will be given a Cadillac and the runner-up a set of steak knives. Presumably, finishing third enables you to keep your job and last place gets you fired.

Operating in this context of cutthroat competition, we see these characters cajole, connive, dicker, intimidate, threaten, and wheel and deal to gain an edge. They are always "closing." After all, jobs, monetary rewards, and families are riding on the results.

The relevant point is that people's behavior can be transformed by the system under which they operate.

11

IDENTIFICATION

Often called "referent power," getting others to identify with you or your situation transmits empathetic vibes that cause others to feel that they share your feelings and aspirations.

This is an acquired characteristic, evident from your style and demeanor. It's a manner of conduct that inspires cooperation and respect.

Before beginning a social exchange of some import, ask yourself these questions:

- "What can I do or say at the outset to build a trusting relationship?"
- "How can I best approach them so they emotionally identify with me and my position?"

12

MORALITY

When dealing with those who have similar values and ethical standards the final fallback position is always to beseech them to do what's fair.

If without defense or pretense, you humbly ask for justice, people often respond positively. Although far afield, the surrender tactic has been used in the animal kingdom to insure survival. When two wolves are involved in deadly combat, the one about to be killed will expose his throat to the victor. Faced with this choice, the triumphant wolf invariably will not exploit the opportunity.

Years ago, when I was first employed by a particular governmental agency, they asked for my fee schedule. At the time, I really wanted this assignment, but we both knew there was no way they could afford my regular price.

Then, during a face-to-face meeting, I said, "Honestly, I want to work with you on this. Since I trust you 100 percent, I know you'll get me as much money as you can. Whatever that amount is, I'll still do it."

Two months later when I arrived at their headquarters, I learned from a third party that my negotiating partner had spent endless time and energy looking for ways to increase my fee. Finally, he had to go into the next year's budget for additional funds.

13

PRECEDENT

When something previously done or said is advanced as an example or justification, it tends to carry weight. And where customs, traditions, and long-standing practices are held sacred, invoking them is overwhelmingly persuasive.

In the United States, Great Britain, Australia, and Canada, routine buying and selling at fixed prices occurs because we simply follow habits. For instance, if you never negotiated with a "one-price store," why would you believe it could be done? So by not trying, you won't succeed. Which goes to prove you were right after all in believing you can't negotiate with a "one-price store." In essence, your personal precedence has created a self-fulfilling prophecy.

But if you try, you can overcome the past barrier. Just showing where your current situation is different from the facts upon which the original precedent came into being was established.

For heaven's sake heed this message: *You Can Negotiate Anything!*

14

PERSISTENCE

Never give in, never give in—never—in nothing, great or small, large or petty—never give in except to convictions of honor and good sense.

WINSTON CHURCHILL

Sustaining ourselves in any endeavor where initial effort goes unrewarded requires that what we're striving for is worth the sacrifice. Manifestly, in the case of Churchill's World War II crusade, history has validated that his goal was worth the trying and dying.

Obviously, few of us today are embarked upon such a noble cause. Still, most people are not persistent enough as they pursue worthwhile objectives. I have seen many negotiators, upon having an idea rejected, all too willing to drop their proposal and move on. Somehow they have forgotten that "No" is an opening bargaining position and that it always takes time to get comfortable with anything unexpected.

Therefore, force yourself to be more tenacious and persevering. Even though your approach or proposal receives a cold reception, bring it up again at a different time and in a different way. Remember, "with the withering of the last no, the yes cometh."

Not only in negotiating, but in life, when you go that extra mile, the traffic diminishes.

The moral: Keep on truckin' and tryin'.

15

A CONCLUDING POINT ABOUT POWER

To underscore all of this, let me share an experience that I had many years ago. At the time, I was involved with contract negotiations for the installation of cable television for several of Chicago's North Shore communities.

One of the villages was Kenilworth, an affluent prim-and-proper suburb that borders Lake Michigan. As it happened, town residents invited Ellen and me to a small dinner party at their home.

During the course of the evening, I was impressed by the sumptuous elegance of the surroundings and the graciousness of our hosts, Margaret and John Fitzgerald. Coming from old money and somewhat straitlaced, they were very nice people.

After dinner, we retired to the library for cognac, and in the course of conversation Margaret mentioned that she was having a problem with her three-year-old son, Johnny.

"What is it?" I inquired.

"Well, he uses foul language," she said. "You understand?"

"What specifically do you mean?"

"You know . . . you can appreciate this . . . it's the vulgar four-letter word."

"Which one?" I asked.

Hesitantly, she stammered, "Well, it's . . . the . . . one descriptive of . . . or synonymous with . . . you know . . . intercourse. It begins with the letter F. You know?"

At the time, I thought: "Oh boy, I certainly know that one. I've heard it myself and maybe even used it a few times."

Actually, it's not surprising that most three-year-olds utter that vulgarism. Why? Because the word happens to be orally pleasurable. In fact, psycholinguists have been studying that four-letter vernacularism for decades and determined that it's in the 97th percentile of oral pleasurability. Kids just love to pucker their lips and tingle as they slap that word off their alveolar gum ridge. It's an enjoyable feeling. It's why kids don't go around saying, "Goat you."

Ever hear *that* expression? Of course not. It doesn't produce the same delightful tingle. (Parenthetically, it might be noted that words or language become popular because the speaker enjoys saying them. This may explain why so many Yiddish words have infiltrated the English language.)

Certain words seem to tickle the American funny bone, especially words starting with the letters "sch" or "sh." Think for a moment, what we have appropriated in our daily usage. There's schlepp (to drag oneself around), schlock (goods of low quality), schmooze (to converse informally), and the epithets of schnook, schnorrer, and schmuck. What about the bumbling schlemiel who spills soup on the unfortunate schlimazel. All these are found in *Webster's* dictionary.

Moving back to the mother's tale, I asked her how she reacts when this happens.

The grandfather clock was chiming midnight as she started to respond. But she didn't have to. Suddenly, all eyes were diverted to the upstairs hallway, where little Johnny stood at the top of the stairs in his bunny pajamas.

"Johnny," she shouted, "do you know what time it is? Get yourself back to bed."

Disregarding his mother's instructions, Johnny kept walking down the steps. As his parents beseeched him to return to bed, he pursed his lips as if about to deliver his favorite expression.

Abruptly, Mr. Fitzgerald interjected, "Hey Johnny, come on down. It's good seeing you. Can we get you something to drink? Come meet the Cohens."

Indeed, I had the feeling that if little Johnny wanted a martini he could probably get it.

So, if the capability to produce an intended effect is power, who's got it in that family? Johnny, at the age of three, had already established himself as the person who would determine what happens next.

Many years later, when Illinois elected a man named Fitzgerald from the North Shore to the U.S. Senate, just for a fleeting moment I thought, "Oh my God, it's him."

Obviously, it wasn't. My kid is still out there, probably building a business or political empire.

PROMINENT POINTS

- If you're a seller of products, services, ideas, or proposals, generate competition for what you have.
- As a buyer or consumer, realize that vendors know that money talks and sometimes walks. The only thing it doesn't say is when or if it's coming back.
- Progress requires that you occasionally break from the herd and question symbols of legitimacy.
- Develop a reputation as someone who is willing to risk and even incur loss for the sake of core values and principles.
- To positively affect the behavior of your counterpart, start out by telling them what they would like to hear and then express your ideas simply, using examples from *their* experience.
- The best way to deal with a direct threat is to ignore it, play dumb, claim a lack of authority, or just laugh it off.
- Watching the process unfold, develop the gaming spirit of caring, but not t-h-a-t much by lightening up and giggling more.
- Whenever you feel powerless and running on empty, it's time to fill 'er up, by rereading these pages.

CHAPTER XI

NEGOTIATING THIS . . . AND THAT

Almost every human transaction (sex, marriage, politics, for example), and even human traffic with the divine (religion), is a form of negotiation, the everlasting mating dance of the quid pro quo.

LANCE MORROW, *TIME* MAGAZINE

Throughout this book I have tried to illuminate the negotiating process by furnishing provocative examples, anecdotes, and tales. Along the way, however, there are subjects that I have not directly covered. Hence, this chapter intends to remedy this by dealing with some of these areas.

1

TERRORISM—A NEGOTIATION BY VIOLENT MEANS

During the late 1970s I became concerned about the threat that international terrorism posed for Western democracies. Familiar with the Prussian military strategist Carl von Clausewitz's dictum that "war is politics by other means," it struck me that terrorism was an extreme and unconscionable form of negotiation.

WHAT IS TERRORISM?

Terrorism is a staged act of violence against innocent people designed to gain maximum media coverage in order to produce shock and dread in the viewing public. This widespread fear is intended to put pressure on the authorities to grant the wishes of these barbarians.

In sum, the public is supposed to blame themselves ("Why do they hate us?—What have we been doing wrong?—What are the root causes of their anger and frustration?"). Regrettably, for decades and even now, there are some who have been susceptible to this stratagem.

Terrorism, then, is asymmetrical warfare in the service of a cause: The relatively powerless deliberately commit atrocities against civilians attempting to extort concessions from a much more powerful government. Instead of using time, information, and power to affect behavior, they employ the maiming and mayhem of noncombatants to get what they want.

Precisely, it's the willful choice of civilians as targets for political purposes. Thus, when I heard someone say on television that George Washington was a "terrorist freedom fighter" without being challenged, I was incensed and appalled. Indeed, Che Guevara and Fidel Castro, who are not among my favorites, never stooped to acts of terrorism.

When TWA Flight 847 was skyjacked in 1985 and Robert Stethem, an off-duty Seabee, was murdered, I was contacted by the CIA director. This resulted in a meeting with Bill Casey and President Reagan, and my writing "The Scourge of International Terrorism"—July 10, 1985. (Included herein as Appendix 4, it affords my thoughts and recommendations at that time.)

TERRORISM AND THE MEDIA

If you read this document you will realize that I believed then that the Western media and our government were neglecting the potential danger posed by transnational terrorism. In fact, a month later I submitted an op-ed piece to the *New York Times,* "Terrorism and the Media," August 1986 (Appendix 5), which was never published, but which you may find of interest.

Please don't get me wrong; I'm a Jeffersonian democrat when it comes to the issue of a free press. Moreover, I do not subscribe to theories that the media operates in concert or has a deliberate bias. Rather, I suspect that many of those on television and their producers lack historical perspective or perhaps are overly concerned with what will produce instant ratings.

How else can one explain the countless hours of programming devoted to Internet kidnapping, shark attacks, road rage, and carjackings? What about the endless time given to O. J. Simpson, Gary Condit, and Susan Smith? Of course, these matters should be covered, but journalists should have a sense of priorities as to what is most important to the health and well-being of the nation.

TERROR ATTACKS OF 9/11

In September 2001, however, the calamity resulting from the attacks on New York City's Twin Towers and the Pentagon brought into focus the repugnance of terrorism. While the rest of the world had been exposed to this type of carnage for at least three decades, albeit not of this magnitude, Americans believed themselves immune.

In retrospect, it's easy to fault governmental agencies and the media for this tragedy, which washed the nation in images of horror and heroism. But in truth, the vicious dimension of these attacks was simply unimaginable to the rational Western mind-set.

Habitually, we ascribe our values and beliefs to others—even those evildoers who would do us harm. In this regard, I am reminded of author Rich Cohen's (who coincidentally is my son) portrayal of Joseph Gens in *The Avengers*.

In 1941 after the German invasion of Lithuania, Gens was put in charge of the Vilna ghetto. Though there was evidence that those rounded up for relocation were being murdered, he could not bring himself to believe that this was happening. Thinking as a civilized person, he assumed that the Nazis would act in their own self-interest. And this meant using those that they deported as laborers to help them win the war.

Therefore, from the perspective of those who brought us the terror of 9/11, this was an extension of negotiation by extraordinary means. Their goal was to extract foreign policy concessions from the United States, who they thought could be taken on with impunity. If they could cause us to sustain considerable loss of human life and produce sufficient fear, over time they would undermine our confidence and sense of purpose.

At this writing, I am hopeful that the American public understands what is at stake. For to grant favors to terrorists will only embolden them and cause more civilian deaths.

This means that, on occasion, the United States may find itself at odds with some of our traditional allies. History has shown that too often world opinion is influenced by commercial interests, appeasement, and fear. But as Winston Churchill knew in 1939, sometimes to do what's right requires that you stand alone.

From the macrocosm of terrorism we now move to the microcosm of a more familiar subject . . . parenting.

2

RAISING CHILDREN

I have 42,000 children. And not one comes to visit.
MEL BROOKS'S 2,000 YEAR OLD MAN

Happy families are all alike," wrote Tolstoy at the start of *Anna Karenina*. "But every unhappy family is unhappy in its own way." During the *sturm und drang* of being a parent I often thought of Tolstoy and wished Howard Baker had asked him, "What did you know and when did you know it?"

Certainly, politics and parenting are the only important jobs for which no formal education is required. Perhaps that's why truly happy families seem as rare as sunny days in Seattle.

THE EDUCATION OF A FATHER

After Ellen and I married we had three children. That's the way they used to do it. Although I traveled a great deal, when I was home I spent virtually all my time with our children, especially the oldest.

Sharon was a perfect little girl and young woman—until she got into high school. After an outstanding freshman year, she suddenly became apathetic and indifferent to the world around her. It wasn't that she was doing anything bad, she just wasn't doing anything. Most of her time seemed to be spent staring out the window or looking at her fingernails.

When I complained to Ellen about *her* daughter, she tried to make me feel better. "What are you talking about?" she said. "She doesn't smoke or drink, she's not taking drugs, and she's not even going out with boys."

"That's the problem," I said. "If she were doing any of these things I could hope that she'd stop. But she's not doing that stuff, so I have no hope."

Eventually, Sharon's lethargy got to Ellen too, and in a moment of frustration Ellen remarked to me, "You know, raising kids is like making pancakes—you ought to be able to throw away the first batch."

As I continued watching Sharon watch the wall, I began to think about Ellen's philosophic remark.

Hmm, she's right 'cause the first batch is hardly edible. The second lot of pancakes is not bad. But the third batch is downright delicious.

So the problem cannot be the batter, but the grill. Which means that it may not be the kid, but us, her parents.

Maybe we were overmanaging her or watching her too closely. Perhaps, I thought, she needs more freedom—some separation from us to grow into herself. Sure, I was too emotionally involved—caring too much.

Accordingly, I hit on a scheme to get rid of the kid—at least for the summer. By divine guidance or luck I discovered a program, the Experiment in International Living, which would take her off our hands for at least two months. And the country I selected to send her to was France. Truly, I felt they deserved each other.

Undeniably, one of the memorable moments of my life was when the plane door closed and Sharon was on her way to Paris. Buoyed by the thought of two months without aggravation, Ellen and I skipped out of O'Hare Airport, arm in arm. Never have we been so close.

Be assured that after two months, Sharon returned and Ellen and I met her at the gate. She looked well and we all walked downstairs to wait for her luggage. Eventually all the baggage came out and the carousel stopped.

While I was looking for her bags, Sharon just stood there gazing into space.

"Where are your bags?" I asked. "Well I know you checked two when you left," I said, "but you stopped off in Paris, so maybe you have three?"

"No, not really," she said.

"But where are the original two?" I asked.

"I guess they're not here," she replied.

"Don't tell me the airline lost your bags. How did they manage that?"

"No, not really," she said.

"What happened? Were they stolen? Why would anyone steal a kid's duffel bags? Oh my God, you got mugged! Were you robbed in Paris?"

"Uh, it was in Paris all right," she said. "I was walking on the Champs-Elysées and I was *so* tired. The bags were *so* heavy and my arms hurt *so* much. So, I just left them there on the sidewalk."

During the rest of her turbulent teen years things didn't get much better. Because I felt that she was not sufficiently productive and responsible, I got involved in micromanaging her life. This meant that I reviewed her homework, got her a part-time job, and laid out rules of conduct.

For the most part, Sharon humored me, practicing what I later termed "malicious obedience." Somehow in her readings she came across the Spanish proverb, "Se obedece pero no se cumple" (One obeys but does not comply) and this helped her play the game. So most of the time we got along.

Fast-forward now to the time when high schoolers apply to the university of their choice. Since I believed she didn't understand how important this decision was, I again took over. After considerable research and study, I had her make applications to some of the finest women's colleges in the United States. Not only that, but I personally drove her to visits and interviews at Wellesley, Williams, Mount Holyoke, Vassar, Smith, Radcliffe, and Bryn

Mawr. And would you believe, she was actually accepted to three of these distinguished institutions of higher learning? My strategy had paid off!

When it came time to make her decision among these three, we were sitting at the kitchen table. Suspense had been building as we awaited word on her choice.

"Mom and Dad," she said, "I made my selection."

"What is it? Which one?"

"I decided I'm going to Newcomb," she replied.

"Newcomb what?" I said. "That's not on our list. In fact, that's not a school. It's a baseball player: Don Newcombe of the Dodgers."

"No, it's a college that's part of Tulane," she responded. "It's in New Orleans."

By this time, I realized that her needs and my needs were not the same and that she would be more committed to succeed in the school *she* selected. Moreover, Sharon's persistence was wearing me out and I still had two younger children who needed my attention. From their standpoint, I suspect they were grateful for what up to now had been my benign neglect.

Four years later, Sharon graduated from Newcomb College and the entire family was at dinner in New Orleans celebrating the occasion. Although sitting around the table in a festive mood, the inevitable question was raised.

"So, Sharon, what do you intend to do now?"

"What do you mean?" she said.

"Are you getting a job?" I interjected.

"Oh no," she said. "I'm not ready for full-time employment. I need time to think."

"So what are you going to do?" I asked.

Without pausing she replied, "I'm going to law school."

"I never knew you wanted to be a lawyer," Ellen remarked.

"Well actually I don't," Sharon said, "but I need a lot of time to contemplate what I'm going to do with the rest of my life. I thought of getting an MBA but that's only two years. A JD, however, takes three, so I'll go to law school."

Though I was slowly burning inside by her flip attitude, I inquired offhandedly, "Oh, have you decided on a particular law school?"

"Yes, of course. I'll go to the University of San Diego Law School."

"Is that right?" I snapped. "I didn't even know that they had a law school. If you want California, what about Boalt, Hastings, Stanford, USC, or UCLA? Those I heard of."

"Well it came down to one thing," she said.

"What was that?" Ellen asked.

We all leaned forward anxiously waiting to hear this "one thing"—this sole criterion for her decision.

Sharon paused and then uttered the word . . . "Climate."

Sharon graduated from the University of San Diego Law School and was accepted into the honors program at the U.S. Department of Justice, where she was a trial attorney in the civil division. Thereafter, she became a federal prosecutor and today enthusiastically works in that capacity in a highly responsible position.

During this time she married Bill and they have four children. Besides being wonderful loving parents, they both are active in many charities and programs, including, of all things, the mentoring of teenagers.

Why have I shared this lengthy story with you?

First, with the perspective of time I realize that this tale of passing parental disappointment is more about me than our daughter. Suffering from what I consider historical amnesia, Sharon hardly remembers any of this.

Clearly, in those days as a dad I was too emotionally involved—caring much too much about the insignificant. Now, in negotiating with offspring, I am finally mastering the proper balance between "irrational exuberance" and utter despair.

Second, as you go through the frequently exasperating experience of parenting teenagers, I hope that you will recall "Sharon's saga." In moments when you are disappointed and dispirited, take heart that things will work out well. It just takes time for your foundation of love to surface.

Lastly, this chronicle of my credentials will establish that I'm far from an expert on the subject of raising children. Most of what I know I have learned from the experience of negotiating with Sharon and her siblings, Steve and Rich.

Having gone through this process, however, I'll share with you what I have picked up.

The joy of the young is to disobey.
JAMES M. BARRIE

Whenever our teenage kids complained about the established order of things it always reminded me of the 1954 movie *The Wild One*. In one scene, Marlon Brando, the menacing leader of a motorcycle gang, rides into a small town in Middle America. There, he is approached by a local teenage girl who asks him, "What are you rebelling against?" And his reply was, "Whaddya got?"

For decades, Madison Avenue and media mavens have been trying to categorize and label demographic groups: baby boomers, Gen X, the Millennials. They might even have us believe that birthdates are destiny.

Obviously, living at a time of great change, youngsters of today are different from their parents and, certainly, grandparents. But hasn't this always been true?

My mom and dad's generation knew that living required struggle, sacrifice, and deferred gratification so their children could have a better life. Presently, kids raised in relative prosperity amidst greater acceleration and transience are more focused on the here and now: their own happiness and immediate desires. Yet, they are also more accepting of individual differences and tolerant of other races, religions, and sexual orientation.

Most notable, from a parental perspective, this generation of kids, like all their predecessors, has their own style of dress, music, and even language. Indeed, they have enriched our culture with such phrases as, "don't go there," "talk to the hand," "hello?," "Whatever," "yadda, yadda, yadda," and "Yeah, yeah, sure, sure."

Significantly, though, in too many instances the responsibility of character formation has moved from the family to peer group celebrities who appear in the mass media.

Still, we know that the first ten years of a child's life are what shape self-esteem, instill confidence, and furnish values. If you don't believe me, just ask psychiatrists, whose adult patients declare that in their heads they still hear voices from childhood telling them, "Shame on you," "Don't embarrass me," "You're not smart enough," "You can't do that," "Sex is dirty," "Your sister's so much prettier than you," "You're getting fat," and on and on.

My purpose in saying all this is that the unconditional love you give your child in the formative years stays with him or her forever. Sometimes it vanishes from sight during the tempestuous teens, but it will always reemerge.

ITEM: Young children also engage in negotiating. From the time they are toddlers we have seen them attempt to play one parent against another, hold back affection, and make demands when it's time to go to sleep.

If very determined, they complain about monsters under their bed and, as a last resort, might even force themselves to throw up.

PARENTAL NEGOTIATING NUGGETS

Which brings us to the revelation of my personal negotiating nuggets for interacting with children. Here are some of my credos and concepts, which I suspect were in part influenced by the wisdom of Chaim Ginott.

Number 1: Distinguish Between Morality and Propriety

Human beings all have behavioral preferences and tastes. There are things we favor and those that we frown upon.

In my case, I had at least a hundred ideas and opinions as to how my children should act and comport themselves. These ranged from the way they dressed to what was ingested into their bodies.

But I learned early on that if I attempted to impose all my predilections upon them, the result was a total loss of credibility.

So I separated the handful of moral issues from the multitude of behaviors that I preferred. This core of righteous items was nonnegotiable because they involved the child's health and welfare and the consideration of others. Among this group were: no drugs, no driving if alcohol was consumed, respect for the dignity of people.

Beyond this small nucleus of rules, there were at least one hundred other matters where I expressed my opinion as to what was suitable and appropriate. With respect to these, the child was expected to listen to my sensible advice, take into account my experience and the strength of my convictions. Then, after weighing all this and thinking about the consequences, he could do whatever he wanted.

As a result, this meant that our son Rich for years wore jeans with holes in both knees and occasionally one near his crotch. Did that bother me? Of course. But this was an area where he was able to express his creativity and air out his body.

Another subject where there was a difference of opinion was music. Being from a different time, I favored Frank Sinatra, Perry Como, and Dean Martin, but Steve went for hard and loud rock—music whose lyrics were unintelligible to me.

The point is that by making this distinction between the absolute and the advisable, teenagers have a sense of freedom. It's like the difference between the attitude of a penitentiary inmate and a cloistered monk.

NUMBER 2: MINIMIZE PEER GROUP PRESSURE

Previously, I mentioned that too many children identify more with their peers than with their family. To reduce this dangerous trend, we had a family rule that if a child did something stupid and gave the excuse that "everyone else did it," he would be punished commensurate with the offense.

On the other hand, if a child informed us that before making this unfortunate decision, he contemplated the risks and effects, and was not incited or impelled by others, this would be a mitigating factor.

In the end, you want to develop individualistic-thinking children who are not afraid to go against the grain.

NUMBER 3: OBTAIN TIMELY INFORMATION

Insist that you or your spouse be the first to know. Your child should be informed that you want to know bad news immediately. No surprises. In that case, punishment would be minimal or none.

On the other hand, if you learn disappointing news from someone else or discover it yourself, the penalty would be compounded.

For example, let's say your child borrows the family automobile, scrapes the fender and walks in, and says, "Dad, I just damaged the car pulling into the garage." Under these circumstances, my response would be, "Thank God it's only physical damage. Are *you* okay?"

What you're doing is establishing a reward and penalty system that reinforces candor and open communication.

NUMBER 4: USE DESCRIPTIVE "I" LANGUAGE

Earlier, I mentioned the importance of being nonjudgmental and not overreacting to the things you are told. Naturally, this applies to children as well.

While keeping calm and cool (not accusatory), substitute the word "I" for "you."

Let's assume your kid is playing the TV very loud or bouncing a ball against a wall in the living room. Instead of saying, "You're playing that too damn loud" or, "You have a lot of nerve throwing the ball inside the house," I would personalize my annoyance.

"I'm disturbed by the TV (or the ball)," I might say. "I think I'm getting a headache. I'm really bothered. I know I shouldn't, but I find myself getting very upset and angry."

At this point, the savvy child, receiving the message, will cease and desist.

NUMBER 5: LESSEN SIBLING RIVALRY

When children have differences and disputes, don't play the role of a mediator or act like King Solomon. Try to have them resolve their disagreement themselves.

During the teenage years, my daughter, Sharon, would sometimes run to me with news: "Steven just punched me." Before I could even react, Steven appeared. "I didn't hit her," he protested. "I was just making a fist and she ran into it."

Rather than separating the combatants or rendering a judgement, I did the opposite. I brought them together for a full hearing of the dispute.

First, I gave Sharon five minutes to tell her story, which included the incident and what led up to it. Then Steve got five minutes to present his case and contradict anything that his sister had said.

Then it was Sharon's turn to rebut her brother's contentions. Again, it was back to Steve for his counterargument. By now they were developing commonality. Both of them were especially bored by me and this entire process.

All at once, they stood up and walked toward the door together. One of them usually said, "Forget it. Where's Mom?"

What does this technique do? Certainly, it saves you a lot of time in the future. But more, it teaches them to solve their own problems and become more self-reliant.

A coincidence no doubt, but Sharon and Steven became attorneys.

NUMBER 6: LET THE OFFENDER DETERMINE HIS FATE

Inescapably, it is the nature of things that children will lapse or misbehave. When this occurs, they generally recognize that they overstepped the bounds and expect to be disciplined.

In these instances, the offender and his parents convene around a dining table, only he's installed at the head, where a parent would normally sit.

"Okay, I want you to act as the mom and dad," I say. "What do you think a fair punishment should be?"

Surprisingly, the child almost always comes up with a very severe penalty. On these occasions, his mother and I confer and his recommended disciplinary action is surely reduced.

This approach has the benefit of having the parents appear understanding and compassionate. Additionally, the child is more committed to accepting the outcome because of his involvement.

NUMBER 7: LEARN TO FORGIVE— ESPECIALLY YOURSELF

There are some parents who act as though raising well-adjusted children depends upon the right conjunction of happenstance, luck, and, perhaps, the alignment of stars. Thankfully, they are in the minority.

The vast majority of us, however, take this responsibility seriously. Perhaps too seriously. These dedicated Moms and Dads, dealing with kids who procrastinate, obfuscate, and infuriate, may on occasion feel a sense of failure and disappointment.

There was a time when I was so baffled and frustrated by a child's behavior that I was inconsolable. Heartsick as I was, I remember listening repeatedly to Jerry Herman's Broadway musical score from *Mame*. Over and over again, I played cut thirteen of the recording, "If He Walked into My Life Today," about the nagging doubts and guilt of childrearing. It only depressed me more.

The timeless truth, though, is that children need missteps and setbacks in order to grow and develop. They learn from these, so they can find their own way. Helping me with this idea was our son Steve, the so-called neglected middle child, who taught me that the more I know about this subject, the less I think I know.

Once I was counseling him about the importance of getting more As on his report card. After listening politely and actually taking notes (knowing how to play the game), he gave me his perspective.

"Dad," he said, "while high school encourages hyper-competition for grades, I think this should be the time for discovery and exploration." How could I argue with that?

More pointedly, parents who give much to their children blame themselves if something goes wrong. Truly, we all need to remember that in this wacky world you can't control everything. Unexpected stuff happens! All you can do is your best and that's more than enough.

Further, Moms and Dads always evaluate their efforts prematurely, because the process has not yet run its course. Indeed, where love has been given without having to be earned, things invariably work out.

Bruno Bettelheim, the eminent psychologist, had this to say: "The primary measure of parenting can be seen in how your children raise their children."

Above all, remember that compassion, forgiveness, and grace come from the strong, whereas only the weak are callous, cruel, and indifferent.

PROMINENT POINTS

- Terrorism, an unconscionable form of negotiations, is a staged choreography of violence directed against innocent people, designed to influence the behavior of a powerful government.
- Today's children are affected by peer group pressure. Occasionally, though, they express a desire to be different—by dressing exactly like their friends.
- Although raising kids may be akin to making pancakes, we don't have the luxury of throwing away the first batch.
- Our greatest challenge as parents is negotiating with our offspring in ways that produce win-win outcomes.

CHAPTER XII

THE GAME OF LIFE

The real voyage of discovery consists not in seeking new landscapes, but in having new eyes.

MARCEL PROUST

Having come this far, I hope the journey has been both informative and enjoyable. More significantly, perhaps you are now viewing this game from a slightly different perspective. I have always believed that things for the most part don't change, but outlooks can.

All we are given in life are possibilities and options. But the ability to recognize them and transform dreams into actuality depends upon us.

THE OUTSIDER'S PARAGON

In the history of North America, one of the most successful groups in achieving their goals were those we call immigrants. Even today, one of every six Canadians are immigrants as are one out of fourteen in the United States.

By and large, they arrived on these shores with very little in the way of tangible assets (money, education), yet so many of them achieved their objectives. In many instances, they surpassed the native-born. How did these outsiders do it?

Certainly, they did not stride down gangplanks, immaculately attired, announcing their desire to achieve the big time. No, I don't think so.

These were people who came here in the bowels of over-crowded vessels, with tags around their necks. For the most part, they didn't know the English language. Or if they did, they spoke with a brogue, a lilt, a rhythmic cadence, or a heavy accent.

ITEM: Of particular interest is what religious and secular scholars have told us about Jesus, one of the most influential figures in the history of the world. Doubtlessly, he did not have the impressive physical stature of a Hollywood action hero.

According to the Gospels, he dressed shabbily and wore a beard. But more, he was an outsider from Nazareth, easily identifiable by his accented speech.

So, newly arrived immigrants knew they didn't know—which is the requisite attitude for acquiring knowledge. They asked questions, actively listened, and were not afraid to say, "Help me."

Not knowing the new language, they tried to read the nuances and cues, understanding that "meanings aren't in words but in people."

Better yet, immigrants came here with great, maybe unrealistic, aspirations. People told them that they were expecting too much. But they went ahead anyway. Remember, these were individuals who didn't fully understand what was being said or just figured that this is America, where the impossible wasn't what it used to be.

In times of rapid change, we all are immigrants in our once familiar world. Perhaps if we were to see ourselves in that light, we would be less literal in obeying things that don't make sense. Which means occasionally questioning authority, reality testing, probability estimating, and using our own judgment more.

As Erich Fromm has said, "If the danger of the past was that men could become slaves, the danger of the future may be that men could become robots."

Using the skills and senses of the immigrant, you can obtain more information, aim higher, and take calculated risks. This will enhance your ability and effectiveness, not only as a negotiator, but also as a manager, leader, parent, consumer, and even as a relationship partner.

THE ROLLER COASTER MODEL

There are those who see life as a game, to be won or lost—akin to a race up a staircase. Their goal is to overcome others in order to reach the top first.

But a more realistic paradigm is a roller coaster ride, where we go up and down—but always moving forward. To get the most out of this journey, one needs some overarching system of values or ethics that gives meaning to living. As Dostoyevsky said, "If you've got a *why* for your existence you can live with almost any *how*."

James Stockdale, while a captive in North Vietnam, proved that resistance and dignity could be maintained under the worst conditions. In his incandescent triumph of spirit, he afforded a luminous example for all of us.

Moving toward the end of this work, I don't presume to know what destiny holds for any of us. One thing, however, is certain: "None of us are getting out of this world alive."

Knowing this, allow me to conclude with some suggestions for playing the game of life. Although mentioned in this book in one form or another, they are worth repeating.

1

THE BALANCE OF CARING, BUT NOT T-H-A-T MUCH

Outside of a dog, a book is a man's best friend. Inside of a dog, it's too dark to read.

GROUCHO MARX

My explicit theme throughout has been the value of detaching ourselves from immediate desires. For a compelling or overwhelming need will not produce a good deal. As Alexis de Tocqueville cautioned: "Never abandon mature design to gratify a momentary passion."

Certainly, the best way to get a merchant in the Istanbul bazaar to lower his price is to appear to have little interest in what he's selling. By seeming to be devoid of desires, or have other options, you can exert considerable leverage over anyone who wants something from you.

A case in point: With our first two children, we employed the successful strategy of rewarding behavior we desired with end-of-the-meal desserts. Then along came the youngest, Rich, who could not be bribed with cake, pastry, or ice cream. By necessity, another prize had to be found.

This incantation to care but not t-h-a-t much applies to abstract ideas as well. Take the concept of freedom, which works only if there are some voluntarily accepted boundaries. But this is true with children too: To keep them close you've got to give them space.

We are all here for a relatively brief time. So in this same spirit of balance, I wish the Almighty will take a liking to you—but not t-h-a-t soon.

2

THE FORCE IS WITHIN YOU

The only limits of power is the bounds of belief.
HAROLD WILSON

By any measure, you have more power than you think. Don't suffer from the fear of trying. If you have never sustained a setback, I suspect it's because your aim has been too low.

Too often, what prevents us from attempting more is in the invisible images in our minds. This is what I call the tendency to focus on the 4Fs: faults, flaws, foibles, and failure. Should this be the case, your last frontier is not outer space, but inner space. It's you yourself and the artificial barriers that you've established that limit your potential.

If the meaning of life is that it should have some meaning, only action can bestow significance upon your existence. And that requires striving and expending yourself in a worthy cause.

3

DIFFERENTIATE YOURSELF

Insanity is doing the same thing over and over again, but expecting different results.

RITA MAE BROWN

We all know that in many Pacific Rim cultures (China, Japan) conformity is encouraged and expected. Children are told that the protruding nail is the one that gets hammered down, just as the rock that stands up in the river is worn away by the current.

In America, on the other hand, unique people and exceptional events are savored in the nooks and crannies of our minds. President John F. Kennedy remains a living memory, whereas President Calvin Coolidge has faded into oblivion. When someone told Alice Longworth Roosevelt that the latter was dead, she is reported to have said, "How can they tell?"

When you endeavor to do what's right against all odds, even if you don't at first succeed, there's nobility and even majesty in such setbacks. After all, you're not here to do what's already been done.

In an expanding world, patience and persistence are on the side of the unorthodox, idealistic outsider. If nothing else, the rapid pace of change can cause those who once dwelled in the suburbs of ideas to find that without moving, they are suddenly living downtown.

4

CELEBRATE EACH DAY

I have no yesterdays,
Time took them away,
Tomorrow may not be—
But I have today.
PEARL YEADON MCGINNES

Implicitly, one of the messages of this book is the need to find more joy, fun, and laughter in our everyday strategic interactions. If nothing else, this will reduce anxiety, worry, and lend perspective.

Many years ago I was reminded of all this while in London on business. It was especially memorable because I was at the St. James's Club. Up to then, this was the first time I had ever been admitted to a private club.

The night before my departure I went to sleep about 3:00 A.M. and asked the operator to call me in three hours. I figured I would nap on the flight back.

Coming from the United States I had expectations about wake-up calls. In my experience about half the time, they are perfunctory recorded messages that do the job. On other occasions, it's usually an impersonal female voice that tells you the time and recites, "Have a nice day."

When the call came, I was startled from a sound sleep. I didn't know where I was. Instinctively, I picked up the receiver and heard a booming imperial voice that seemed to be coming from above.

Resonant with authority and in an impressive British manner it said, "Mr. Herbert Cohen, this is your final day. You're checking out."

My first reaction was, "This is it"—the BIG Checkout—but I was not ready to go just yet. Awed and alarmed, it took me at least five seconds to realize where I was and what had just happened.

Eventually, that morning I was on my way to Heathrow Airport. But I couldn't shake that Lordly 6:00 A.M. checkout call. Maybe this was the way those who departed were actually notified? What if this *were* my last day?

As my taxi proceeded to the airport we unexpectedly hit a traffic snarl. The gridlock was so bad that we hadn't moved in at least five minutes.

Ordinarily, fearful of missing my flight I might have asked the driver, "Can you get off this road and go a different way?" or, "What if we traveled on the shoulder?" Who knows, maybe I might have gotten up on the roof of our vehicle to see what the problem was.

At this particular moment, however, having experienced "the Lordly checkout," I decided to relish the moment.

Instead of just sitting there, I got out and personally introduced myself to other drivers and passengers. One woman was playing her car radio very loud and I asked her if she wanted to dance. Her partner smiled and lent encouragement: "Go ahead, dance with the crazy Yank." We were doing a lindy hop on the highway and others were joining the festivities.

Unfortunately, the fun lasted for only about ten minutes, until the traffic finally started to move. Those who were there probably still remember it.

Continuing the trip, and reflecting on what transpired, it seemed that *what we regret most in life are not the things we did, but the things we didn't do.* Perhaps the lesson for me was that life should be lived not only for length but breadth too.

So let me close with the advice I remember hearing from Leo Buscaglia, who once said, "Live each day like it's your last, because one of these days you're bound to be right."

PROMINENT POINTS

- Not being overly attached to the status quo can enable you to gain perspective, obtain more information, aim higher, and take calculated risks.
- With all due respect, learning negotiation solely by reading a book is like making love via e-mail. Thus, get out there and dare to begin.

APPENDIX 1

Carter Went Against All Logic in Ruling Out Hostage "Expert"

To help get the hostages back from Iran, the Carter Administration called upon Herb Cohen, an internationally respected negotiator. He not only told Jimmy Carter's people what they were doing wrong—while they were doing it—but he predicted the release of the hostages almost to the exact hour.

There was only one problem: The Carter strategists paid no attention to him. They sought his expert views, then excluded him from their deliberations. Not until Ronald Reagan's advisers consulted Cohen, ironically, did anyone listen to him.

He submitted his conclusions in writing to Reagan's campaign manager, William Casey, on Oct. 25—10 days before the election. "Khomeini and his mullahs know that they are talking to an anxious buyer," advised Cohen. "Therefore, the maximum price that they can extract from this administration will be just prior to the election. . . .

"To put it bluntly, any experienced negotiator or bazaar vendor knows that on Nov. 5 the Iranians will have to put their 'illegally obtained merchandise' on sale at a cut-rate price."

Although the anxious Carter might be willing to pay the maximum price, Cohen predicted, there wouldn't be time to cut a deal

An article by the syndicated columnist Jack Anderson, dated Thursday February 12, 1981.

before Election Day. The release of the hostages would come too late, therefore, to bail out Carter. "And so, it is probable that Gov. Reagan will be the President-elect on Nov. 5," wrote Cohen.

With Reagan the winner, this would put Carter "in an excellent position to negotiate a palatable agreement" before the transfer of power. "If by word of deed the President-elect and his spokesmen make clear that there will be a radical departure from the existing policies with respect to government-sponsored terrorism," Cohen advised, "the Iranians will view Inauguration Day as their final deadline.

"As a result, they will select the option of dealing with Carter, the Satan known, rather than Reagan, the Satan unknown," Cohen added prophetically. "There is a negotiating truism that most concession behavior and all settlements will occur at the deadline."

Reagan issued statements calculated to exploit the Iranian apprehension about him. Cohen correctly calculated that the statements would impress the Iranians because, he wrote, they saw Reagan as "a person who means what he says." Thus Reagan responded as Cohen recommended, and the Iranians reacted as Cohen predicted—on the exact deadline he had foreseen.

From the beginning, Cohen studied the Koran for clues to Ayatollah Khomeini's behavior. He also brought to the hostage crisis his experience in dealing with other hostages, as a consultant to the Justice Department and the FBI.

He advised Carter's people to abandon their "passive policy" and take the offensive. His plan was simple. He listed two dozen new sanctions to impose on Iran—embargoing food and medicine, expelling Iran from the satellite communications network, cutting off all commercial flights, sealing the borders against smugglers, etc.

The idea was to impose these penalties, one at a time, five days apart. This would put the United States in the position of acting instead of reacting, Cohen argued, keeping the Iranians off-balance, wondering what was coming next.

The plan was rejected if it was ever considered. Then on Oct.

23, when the Republicans were still nervously wondering if Carter would pull an "October Surprise" to get the hostages out and himself re-elected, Reagan's campaign manager flew to New York City for a five-hour talk with Cohen that lasted until 2 in the morning.

Casey asked him to put his views in writing, and two days later, Cohen offered this analysis: "Since January, the Carter administration caused the 'Iranian Hostage Crisis' to become mired in Wonderland, where the Red Queen is the sickly, senile Khomeini, the drowsy dormouse an American President and Alice, the figure of reason, has been out on a prolonged coffee break."

Cohen said the Carter administration had failed to grasp—and exploit—the key point in the hostage seizure: It was a criminal act, and the Iranian mullahs were kidnapers. Cohen faulted Carter for having "no coherent and consistent strategy," commenting: "This uncertainty and impotence have given even ineptitude a bad name."

APPENDIX 2

The Mishandling of the Iranian Hostage Crisis

For almost a year President Jimmy Carter has been enmeshed, entangled and exasperated by the enigma known as, "The Iranian Hostage Crisis." Throughout this period, despite well-publicized gestures, considerable activity and efforts, he has been unable to bring this tragic episode to a successful conclusion. Indeed, given all the media coverage of movement without progress, dashed hopes and unrealized plans—all amid the staged background spectacle of thousands of chanting marchers—this lingering affair has taken on a theatrical quality. So, we are still mired in Wonderland, where the Red Queen is the sickly, senile Khomeini, the drowsy dormouse, an American President and Alice, the figure of reason, out on an extended "coffee break."

From the outset, we have been negotiating with a tough, cynical and criminal adversary, who has been trying to extract an extortionary price for the return of our illegally detained diplomats. The arena may be International Diplomacy and the stakes human lives, but Khomeini and his mullahs, have been operating like rug merchants in the classic Persian Rug Sellers Bazaar. To them, these innocent Americans are merchandise or "rugs for sale" and

A Confidential Memorandum to Governor Ronald Reagan and William Casey, dated October 25, 1980, presenting a background analysis and strategic approach for use in facilitating the release of the Americans held captive. This document is the memorandum referred to by Jack Anderson in Appendix 1.

they have consistently manipulated our media, our emotions and more significantly, a United States President, in their attempt to secure a maximum selling price.

Since January, the Carter Administration has vacillated and zigzagged, without any coherent or consistent strategy to secure the release of the hostages. Displaying more symbolism than substance and an embarrassing incapacity to manage the flow of events, the Administration's overall handling of this matter has even given ineptitude a bad name. The President himself has been the embodiment of irresolution, seemingly unable or unwilling, to exercise and maintain the initiatives necessary to induce responsible civilized behavior on the part of Iran's Revolutionary Regime. More pointedly, his response to this outrage has been so erratic and incongruous that it serves to underscore an unfortunate but growing public perception that he may be willing to compromise national values, principles and interests, to secure re-election to office.

To fully understand the present Presidential predicament, it is necessary to go back to the underlying dynamics, which gave rise to the continuing crisis:

By October 1979, it became evident to Khomeini and his fundamentalist followers on the Revolutionary Council that the success of their "divine mission" was being threatened short of its goal—a return to the "golden Age of Shi'ism." From the Imams' perspective the revolution was beginning to flounder. Bogged-down by the reappearance of pre-existing attitudes and life styles, religious fervor and radical zeal were abating. Mismanagement of the economy was causing disaffection among secular elements and the ruling clergy were being challenged on several fronts by separatist and ethnic groups.

Suddenly, Khomeini and his disciples were confronted with an unacceptable possibility. What they had believed was a Pro-Islamic movement, might actually have been primarily an Anti-Shah uprising. Thus, they were looking for an issue that could be used to revitalize the flagging spirits of the people and restore unity and purpose to the revolution—which in their eyes still had a long way to go. Fortuitously, the Shah's entry to the United States for medical treatment provided a convenient focal event that could be used to meet these underlying concerns, interests and needs.

Clearly, the Shah was a vulnerable target, who could be accepted and used as the personification of evil. For that reason the mullahs' strategy was to focus all attention on him. Their initial implementing tactic was the simultaneous seizure of the United States Embassy in Teheran and the Statue of Liberty in New York Harbor. Although reported as "spontaneous acts by students," it should have been evident from the outset that this was government-sponsored terrorism by surrogate soldiers—carefully planned and coordinated operations. In effect, this was "The Persian Version of *Dog Day Afternoon*," intended to create an international audience before whom they could air their grievances and extract concessions.

In the main, Khomeini and his medieval-minded mullahs were behaving quite logically (considering their mindset), in pursuit of the following objectives:

1. To unify a fragmented nation and encourage greater personal sacrifice by fueling a common hatred of the Shah and his "agents" held captive in the Embassy.

2. To exorcise all Western (American) cultural influences from Iran, as modern life styles and material conveniences were seen as major obstacles to the restoration of a mullah-dominated Islamic State.

3. To further radicalize the revolution, purging secular and moderate elements in the process, thereby insuring the passage of an Islamic Constitution.

4. To publicize their magnified grievances against the Shah, which could be used to justify future revolutionary excesses, economic deprivations and gross human rights violations.

5. To ignite the Middle East with Khomeini's brand of revolutionary and fundamental Islamic Shi'ism.

President Carter's initial response to this outrage was an admirable exercise of restraint and patience. It took courage not to react in knee jerk fashion in the face of this provocation.

Still, once the Iranian holidays passed in mid-December and the physical safety of the hostages virtually assured, the president could have managed events to secure their release without compromising national interests. But to his surprise, the captivity became a political advantage, helping defeat Senator Edward Kennedy's bid for the Democratic nomination. Playing upon the concern of the American people, Mr. Carter unknowingly made the hostages the "centerpiece" of his administration. This was underscored by the unprecedented media attention, which revealed that the Commander-in-Chief was consumed by this issue, praying for the detained diplomats and their captors morning and night. Yet, this myopic focus, combined with the "Rose Garden Strategy"—an unwillingness to leave the White House to campaign and debate Senator Kennedy, further emphasized the importance of this matter and the value of hostages.

While this approach may have caused President Carter to temporarily soar in domestic popularity, it shocked our allies, but even worse, it resulted in increased demands. Keep in mind, that we were, and still are, dealing with people possessed of a "bazaar mindset," who view our diplomats as valuable merchandise, to be sold back to us at a price. So, this pervasive need of our "Chief Buyer" only caused the value of the "rugs" to increase in the eyes of the Iranian mullahs and their surrogate student-terrorists.

Playing to the concerns of the American people and his own rising political fortunes, Mr. Carter publicly announced that we had no options in this situation. By mid-January we were doing nothing and proud of it, expressing impotency via a policy of "watchful waiting." In essence, we removed any incentives (either positive or negative) that the Iranians might have had to negotiate with us, allowing the situation to drift from emergency to permanency.

From the mullahs' perspective, the detriments of retaining the hostages were now minimal, but the advantages substantial. Ergo, the virtually risk-free captivity could be used by them to achieve many of their objectives. As a result secular elements were purged from government and the Islamic Constitution was ratified over-whelmingly. The hostages served them well, as a rallying point for national unity, that is, until the Iraqi invasion conveniently came along. They had succeeded in gaining internal and external pub-licity for their complaints against the Shah and the holding of the hostages settled into routine, with little perceptible protest by the world as a whole.

Accordingly, the hostages became central pawns in the struggle for power taking place among Iranian Revolutionary Groups. Rival factions and personalities maneuvered for dominant influ-ence, each trying to gain the attention of Khomeini, the country's supreme power. And with the failure of the United Nations Com-mission, it was evident, that he threw his weight behind the advo-cates of continuing chaos in their conflict with those who sought a return to normalcy.

The captors and their supporters came to believe that they had this Administration over a barrel. As President Carter's policy soft-ened, their position became tougher, using the old "Rug Sellers' Negotiation Ploy" of raising the price each time a bid was made for the hostages' release. For the student-terrorists and their chant-ing supporters outside, the crisis became a school holiday, a com-plete vacation from responsibility and authority. As Bani Sadr and a few others realized, this continued festival was in reality, a diver-sion from the real work and sacrifice required to build a nation.

We should have known there was little chance appealing to fun-damental Shia Muslims through *our* value system. There is noth-ing in Khomeini's Koran about détente, compromise or reasoning. While we were defensive, apologetic and forgiving, he was aggressive, confident and inflexible. In expecting kindness and compassion from Khomeini or his clerics, we should have re-membered the Old Persian Proverb; "There are three things I have never seen—the eye of an ant, the foot of a snake and the charity of a mullah." Fundamentally, we were "reading from a dif-ferent hymnbook."

Though recognizing the Iranians have some grounds for bitterness and that ultimately, they will need a graceful way out of this dilemma of their own devising, we should not have precluded the possible exercise of power to shape their decision-making. This was a negotiation from the outset and it was hurting our bargaining position by continually eliminating options and displaying a reluctance to act in the face of government-sponsored terrorism.

The recipe of "watchful waiting" could only produce a dish of justification for the politics of international terrorism. We have always owed it to the hostages to make sure that the terms of their release did not legitimize their capture and put Americans all over the world in peril. Continued American passivity in the face of the criminal behavior, has been seen as a loss of nerve with the obvious conclusion that we can be taken on with impunity. If we were not willing to act and take some risk in this situation where we were certified by the United Nations and the International Court as being in the right, for the sake of what, might we be expected to do so?

The issue at stake was never the Shah or Iran versus the United States in a contest of wills. Rather it was Iran versus the civilized world in a criminal breach of International Law. From the beginning, President Carter should have said to the Iranians that our standards of asylum would not be dictated by the illegal seizure of hostages. We should have been seen as standing clearly on principles that command respect.

Instead of keeping the focus on Iranian outlawry, we became publicly involved in the Shah's whereabouts and medical condition. We would not let him in, then we would, then he would have to move, then we would not let him stay, then we promised that if he left he could come back and then we did not want him to leave Panama. In this absurd sequence of events, we compromised our principles and displayed a policy of accommodation that was perceived in Iran and the rest of the world as weakness.

Each concession made to these criminals, without getting anything in return, has only whetted their appetite and caused them to raise the ante. We have gone from dispatching Ramsey Clark, beseeching Kurt Waldheim, embracing Valerian Cappuci to involving all sorts of unpredictable and risky third party amateurs. We have been grasping at straws, practicing accommodation and compromise in a futile attempt to appease enraged outlaws.

As any competent negotiator, leader, politician or consumer knows, in order to get anyone to negotiate with you in good faith they must believe that you can, and just might, bring about intended effects, which they perceive might help them or hurt them.

Neither a potential seller, nor the current Iranian Regime, will change their negotiating posture unless they understand that we are capable of giving them something that they want, or *just might do something to them now or later, that they regard as detrimental to their interests and objectives.*

Therefore, to publicly rule out options such as military force or even retribution, was to eliminate incentives for negotiation. It was no way to break the impasse. On the contrary, it invited the student-terrorists to hang on to their captives and milk the situation for everything they could get. Instead, these adversaries should have been made to feel that they have something to gain in negotiating in good faith and much to fear if they don't.

The real power in Iran has always been Khomeini and he is a tough bargainer, who sees "concession behavior" as a sign of weakness. We should never have made payments-in-advance. Alternately we should have put pressure on Iran, to strengthen the hand of the realists on the Revolutionary Council, and give, even the unreasoning, an incentive to put the crisis behind them. America could have speeded the process by acting in ways that gave the realists and true revolutionaries cause for concern. By incrementally increasing the pressure on Iran through measured and calibrated actions, we would have forced a confrontation between the militants and some emerging government that wanted to prove that it was really a government.

What President Carter never exhibited was a comprehensive "game plan" and consistent implementing tactics to achieve the release of the hostages. If he wanted to break the stalemate, Iran should have been given a message from our coherent behavior, that the longer the impasse existed, the greater would be the risks for them. Our actions should have been consistent and there should always have been follow-through. While incrementally building pressure on Iran, President Carter should have preserved and cultivated "back channels" of communications, as a safeguard against misreading of signals and to insure that no opportunity was lost for fruitful negotiation.

Since this was not done, it has raised questions of judgment on the part of our Chief Executive Officer. Certainly, President Carter wants to get the hostages back, but he has done nothing for almost nine months. The only departure from our public display of impotence was, "The Jimmy Carter Desert Classic" (the botched rescue attempt), an action that may have undermined the commitment of the Western alliance and shook the nation's confidence in our defense establishment.

As noted previously, Khomeini and his mullahs realize that they are selling hostages to an anxious buyer. From their mindset, they know the maximum price that can be extorted from this administration will come just prior to the election, when a politically ambitious incumbent might conceivably pay a top price to assure his re-election. To put it bluntly, any experienced negotiator or bazaar vendor recognizes that, on November 5, the Iranians will be forced to put their "illegally obtained merchandise" on sale at a cut-rate price. In short, after the election (regardless of outcome), bargaining leverage will shift, causing the hostages to go on sale—at 40 precent off!

Should an agreement be reached prior to the election, the cost of freedom for the fifty-two hostages will come high. The Iranian leaders will get their best possible payoff from an act of terrorism. Yet, if the agreement is not consummated within the next week, there will be a shift of power that will enable us to buy back our hostages, at a cost that will *not* approximate the paying of blackmail or ransom to criminals. Hopefully, President Carter will recognize this reality and wait patiently until after the election to negotiate from greater strength.

There is a negotiating truism, that most concession behavior and settlements occur at "the deadline." Accordingly one of the reasons that this crisis has dragged on endlessly, has been the passive (reactive) policy of the Carter Administration, which never caused the keeping of the hostages to become so burdensome, that the Iranians felt the need to put a deadline on themselves. President Carter's handling virtually told them that in retaining the hostages they'd run no risk and incur no cost. Thus, the assets or advantages of maintaining their criminal behavior (using the hostages—as pawns in their internal power struggle, as a rallying point for national unity and to keep their revolution rolling) always exceeded the liabilities or disadvantages.

Now, however, the Iraqi invasion has not only magnified the detriments of keeping the hostages (the need for hard currency and spare parts), but it has given the mullahs a "new Satan." Fundamentalists can use this "holy war" as a rallying point to consolidate and stabilize their revolution, while at the same time bludgeon Bani Sadr and the moderates for improper conduct of the fray. Of course, these factors will still be in existence after our election, when the current administration can finally resolve this crisis.

It should not come as a shock that the ruling mullahs have a different timetable in mind. From their perspective, the "fifty-two hot rugs" will bring the highest price this coming week, prior to our Presidential election. In fact, all indications are that the Ayatollah had this timing in mind, when he deliberately stalled the announcement of his "Four Conditions" until September 12. This carefully calculated date would have given Iran and U.S. negotiators a full six weeks to conclude the buy-sell transaction, at a time more favorable to the seller. Therefore, any "October Surprise" was never Carter's, but Khomeini's. Regrettably, our "Purchasing-Agent-President" has not realized the role he's been playing in Khomeini's drama. Succinctly put, Jimmy Carter has been on an emotional roller coaster ride with the rest of the American people—only he was riding in the first car.

From all appearances, Khomeini's scheme was to "cut the deal" when his bargaining leverage was at a maximum. It might have worked had the unexpected not occurred. This was not just Iraq's full-scale invasion of Iran, but Saddam Hussein's widely publicized news dispatch that Khomeini released the fifty-two hostages in return for American support. Since the "morally-directed Ayatollah" could not be seen as being in league with "the great Satan," informal contact and negotiations were broken off, thereby dispelling any rumors that an agreement was, or might be, "in the works."

However, the two or three week hiatus, taken to invalidate the Iraqi news dispatch, may well bury Khomeini's carefully planned scheme. It seems inconceivable, that the short negotiating time remaining, can permit the extensive and complicated bargaining necessary to come to a binding agreement that would return the hostages. Furthermore, there are at least three other factors that preclude any possibility that the current "informal negotiations" might prove fruitful, prior to Election Day—November 4, 1980:

> *First*, the unfreezing of Iranian assets presents enormously complex problems, involving a multitude of financial and governmental institutions, that will take time to work out.
>
> *Second*, it is unlikely that Khomeini would be willing to negotiate formally with the United States. So, additional delay must occur in the selection and use of a third party intermediary that will be acceptable to all sides.
>
> *Third*, the fragmented student terrorists, the Majlis, and the general public, have not been adequately prepared for such a sharp reversal or departure from what they have been hearing and believing was Khomeini's policy. As Machiavelli has said, "It takes time to get used to a new idea."

Thus there should be no "October Surprise" that might influence the outcome of the election. And so, it is probable that Governor Reagan will be the President-elect on November 5.

Should this scenario transpire, the Carter "lame duck" administration will be in an excellent position to negotiate a "palatable agreement" to secure the release of the fifty-two hostages. This probability will occur if the Iranians come to believe that the new Republican Administration will take a much tougher approach to this criminal breach of international law. If, by word of deed, the President-elect and his spokesmen make clear that there will be a radical departure from existing policies with respect to government-sponsored terrorism the Iranians will view Inauguration Day as their final deadline. As a result, they will select the option of dealing with Carter, "the Satan Known," rather than Reagan "The Satan Unknown."

Although the internal political circus in Iran cannot be predicted with absolute certainty, if President-elect Reagan comes on strong the mullahs will be faced with a "Good-Guy-Bad-Guy" choice, imposing a deadline on themselves of January 20 at 1:00 P.M. for the resolution of this crisis. Following is the rationale for this denouement date:

1. Doubtlessly, it is the intention of Khomeini and the mullahs to prolong the war with Iraq, which means they will need to strengthen the Revolutionary Guards and obtain badly needed hard currency.

2. Khomeini's four conditions, which omit the demand for a U.S. apology, indicate a softening of terms and a willingness to settle this matter.

3. Iranian Prime Minister Rajai lacks the political courage to make the decision himself now, but he can syndicate this risk by going to the Majlis, which will take a few months.

4. The failure of Bani Sadr as commander in chief, to make progress against the Iraq invaders has given the mullahs an issue that can be used to undermine the moderates—a convenient substitute for the hostages.

5. In the past, the Mujahadeen (whom the mullahs do not control), prevented Bani Sadr from transferring the hostages from the student-terrorists to the government, when in April 1980, they massed in great numbers outside the Embassy. This blocking ma-

neuver is no longer possible, since the hostages have been dispersed to locations unknown.

6. The Iranian perception of Ronald Reagan is that he comes from a "fast draw cowboy tradition" of shooting first and asking questions later. Assuming that as President-elect, this image is maintained and even enhanced (e.g. by making reference to the Embassy takeover as intolerable criminal behavior), when he is about to take the oath of office Khomeini will do a fast cost-benefit analysis of the situation and take what by contrast, the reasonable but outgoing Jimmy Carter has offered. From their viewpoint, with the departure of the current incumbent, America's Chief Buyer, will go his offers and their investment in the relationship. At best, they will have to start all over again—back to square one—with a new, albeit combative President—an unpredictable and potentially dangerous top Purchasing Agent. Moreover, the Iranian experience with President Jimmy Carter causes them to view him as an indecisive "paper tiger," who can be mapped and manipulated with ease, whereas Ronald Reagan is seen in Iran as a person who means what he says.

Finally, the Carter Administration's handling of the drawn-out crisis has resulted in the steady erosion of our bargaining position, giving the Iranians a kill as well as a chase—as they engaged in the sport of "Diplomat Hunting." A *prolonged* policy of watching and waiting and public declarations that we have no options was and is a bankrupt strategy. From the outset, the health and well being of fifty-three innocent Americans and their families, required that we operate as experienced negotiators and not as amateurs. Ultimately, the success of this "buy-sell transaction" will be determined *not* just by whether we secure the safe release of the hostages. But there are other fundamental questions, perhaps even more important, that only history can answer:

1. Will our passivity serve to encourage future criminal undertakings of this nature and embolden international terrorists?

2. Has our handling of this matter gained the respect of our Allies and Third World Nations?

3. How will our unwillingness to take risk, sustain casualties and exercise power be perceived by future antagonists?

4. To what extent, have we abandoned our traditional concepts of honor and principle in the face of this terrorist extortion?

5. Will the concessions made to Iran adversely affect our relationship with the Arab nations and the balance of power in the Middle East?

Admittedly, President Carter's initial restraint after the Embassy seizure was commendable. Nevertheless, in the following ten months, this patience was needlessly prolonged and transformed into a policy of paralysis.

His mishandling of this crisis has shaken the confidence of the American people, as well as our allies in other parts of the world. The only beneficiaries from the failure to manage this geopolitical negotiation have been the Iranian mullahs, the Kremlin leadership and the temporary political fortunes of Jimmy Carter himself. Essentially, he has pursued a policy of patience without pressure, which was perceived as paralysis in Teheran. Obviously, a nation that is unwilling or unable to take risk to manage its destiny will inevitably become manipulated against its own interests.

On November 5 there still will be time to look at this tragic crisis realistically, to stand up for what we believe before the world and if necessary, give our goodness some muscle. Above all, we must stop all the ignorant and futile self-recrimination, which only saps our self-confidence and our will.

If, as Dickens said, "We forge the chains we wear in life," then resolve, combined with a sustained negotiating strategy, are the shears that can finally set the hostages and all America free.

APPENDIX 3

The Reality of Adversarial Negotiations

When the Oslo accords were signed on the White House lawn in September 1993, many believed that the road for Mideast peace had at last, been found. Indeed, enthusiasm was so high, that it resulted in the awarding of the Nobel Peace Prize to Yitzak Rabin and Shimon Peres of Israel and Yasser Arafat of the Palestine Liberation Organization.

Basically, this agreement called for the Palestinians to renounce terrorism and accept the legitimacy of the Jewish state. To reciprocate, Israel was required to turn over land and this formula was supposed to move the parties from a climate of hostility to one of harmony. To enforce these provisions, Arafat's Palestinian Authority (P.A.) was allowed a 24,000 man police force which were given rifles and side-arms by the Israeli government.

Subsequently, while Israel was making territorial withdrawals, Chairman Arafat still maintained his commitment to "holy war," but only when he spoke to his followers in Arabic. Allowing the area he controlled to be used as a haven for those who attacked Israeli civilians, he glorified suicide bombers by calling them "martyrs."

Moreover, as the years passed, Arafat's "police force" would grow to 40,000 men armed with heavy weapons that were smuggled into the country. From all indications, he intended that Oslo was to be the first step in a multi-phased plan to eliminate the

A Memorandum to the Honorable Colin Powell, Secretary of State, dated February 1, 2001.

State of Israel. This message was unmistakably communicated on the Palestine Authority's website, official maps, in student's textbooks, etc. which showed their country made up of the entire West Bank, Gaza Strip, Jerusalem and all of pre-1967 Israel.

This was the reality that served as a backdrop to Israel's national election in 1999. During his campaign against Benjamin Netanyahu, Ehud Barak vowed that if he became Prime Minister, he would withdraw the nation's military forces from Southern Lebanon and try to make a final peace with Chairman Arafat and the Palestinians.

When Barak became Prime Minister his first order of business was to fulfill his promise. Israel, after 22 years pulled its troops from the security zone in Southern Lebanon without getting anything in return.

How was this unilateral concession seen by its adversaries?

First, Haffez al Assad, the Syrian dictator said, "It's the first Israeli military defeat since the creation of the state in 1948." Thereafter, when Barak said he would return virtually all of the Golan Heights held since 1967, his offer was rejected out of hand.

Then, all the terrorists groups from Hezbollah to Hamas came to believe that Israel's soft spot was that they placed too high a value on human life. Thus, it reinforced the strategy that the maiming and murdering of civilians was Israel's Achilles heel. In sum, handing over territory, a gesture of good will intended to elicit good will in return, was instead seen as a sign of weakness.

This brings us to July 2000, when "lame duck" President Bill Clinton summoned Ehud Barak and Yasser Arafat to Camp David. Having survived the Monica Lewinsky relationship and the ordeal of impeachment, Mr. Clinton wanted to leave office on a high note. Clearly, the resolution of this long running conflict might bring him a Nobel Peace Prize and re-establish his place in history.

What Bill Clinton brought to this negotiation was his considerable persuasive skills. He is one of the unique people who has the ability to communicate sincere concern and compassion in the time span of a handshake.

Casting himself as an "honest broker," the President and his Secretary of State Madeleine Albright, believed they had a special relationship with the P.A.'s chairman. After all, he had visited the White House more than any other "head of state" and in an unprecedented gesture, was entertained at the home of the Secretary. As for Mr. Barak, a military hero who had known the horrors of war, his past concessions indicated an eagerness to deal for a final peace. Moreover, they knew he was determined to avoid a clash with Israel's closest ally, making sure he would not be blamed if negotiations failed.

Despite Mr. Clinton's confidence that he could succeed where so many others had failed, the odds were stacked against him from the outset. His fundamental mistake was to assume that Arafat's past-intransigence and indecisiveness was a psychological problem that could be overcome by creating an atmosphere of trust. And this attitude adjustment could be accomplished by unprecedented Israeli territorial concessions.

The reality, however, was this was a bitter adversarial negotiation where differing perceptions, motives, interests and constituencies had to be taken into account.

By way of explanation let me deal with some of these items:

1. THE TIME WAS NOT RIPE FOR A SUMMIT

In order for negotiating to succeed, both sides must perceive that they are better off with an agreement than the status quo.

This was not the case with Arafat, who enjoyed his chosen role as the leader of the "victimized" Palestinians. This guise gave him access to Western leaders, Western financial support and Western media. He had become a celebrity in fashionable places in New York, London, Paris and Washington, D.C.

What was needed to get him to negotiate in good faith, was a change in his cost-benefit calculus. By that I mean, the detriments of no agreement would have to outweigh the benefits of a stalemated status quo.

2. MAKING UNILATERAL CONCESSIONS

When trust does not exist, concessions that are not worked for and do not require reciprocation are not appreciated.

At the Camp David Summit, Ehud Barak made unexpected and unanticipated generous concessions. To Arab militants and apparently Yasser Arafat himself, this was seen as a sign of Israel weakness and desperation. As a result, the P.A.'s chairman never bothered to even respond with a counter-offer.

3. DIFFERING TIMETABLES

In all negotiations, concessions and agreements occur in proximity to the deadline. Where timetables differ, the side with the tighter time constraints is disadvantaged.

President Clinton's need to make a deal before the November elections, or at least before he left office, was common knowledge. Barak also was facing Parliamentary elections in Israel. Of the three players, only Mr. Arafat was free from the pressure of time.

Having not prepared his constituencies for the possibility of a concluding peace agreement and under no time compulsion, the Chairman would have rejected whatever was offered. From his viewpoint, anything tendered or given was to be regarded as the starting point for the next round of negotiations.

4. DISPARATE INTERESTS

Although negotiating often begins with positional bargaining, agreements are achieved by satisfying underlying concerns and interests.

Considering that militant Arabs view the State of Israel itself, irrespective of size, as a trespass on "holy" Muslim soil, any territorial concessions at this time would not be enough. So what Barak and Clinton believed was an exceptionally magnanimous first offer (94% of the pre-1967 land), only whetted Arafat's appetite.

5. DISSIMILAR PERCEPTIONS

In geopolitical negotiations, courageous leaders like Anwar Sadat and Yitzhak Rabin, understood that it was sometimes necessary to compromise in order to avoid needless bloodshed. Certainly, Ehud Barak has tried to carry on in that tradition.

Yasser Arafat, on the other hand, seems to take his cue from the "Arab street" and the more radical Islamic militants. Over the years he has been a corrupt and authoritarian ruler, manipulating violence to serve his political ends. Looking at his track record, it is evident that he has an 11th century sense of the value of a child's life with a 21st century sense of public relations. Regrettably, the media plays right into his hands in this regard.

Although Arafat has been credited with putting the fate of Palestinians on the world agenda, let us not forget that he did this by terrorist skyjackings and murdering American civilians and diplomats. An enigmatic figure, he has always chosen the past with its religious wars over the future.

From all indications, he has now embarked upon a strategy that combines low-magnitude guerilla warfare, terrorism, and international media coverage. Its purpose is to destroy Israel's morale and sap its will.

Using Israel's hurried "Saigon-like" retreat from Lebanon as a model, his plan is obvious:

A: Use media-covered violence to bring international criticism of Israel.

B: Cause Israel to sustain military casualties in the West Bank and Gaza.

C: Keep Israel mobilized which will consume resources, affect its economy and impoverish its will and determination.

D: Encourage Hamas, Islamic Jihad and Hezbollah to extend terrorism to pre-1967 Israel (Tel Aviv, Haifa, West Jerusalem, Hadera, etc.).

E: Use Western European nations and our so-called Middle East allies to press the United States, who in turn, will pressure Israel to come back to the bargaining table—only this time in a state of weakness and despair.

All this is not to say that Israel's policies have always brought them closer to a permanent peace with their neighbors. For instance, since the Oslo accords they have continued to build or extend settlements on the West Bank. Citing military necessity; from all appearances, these activities are the result of domestic political considerations. But their existence in such numbers and in some places like Hebron are an impediment to normalizing relationships and building trust. Primarily, they play into the hands of the militant factions who are oblivious to the loss of human life.

However, there's little doubt that by acquiescing to the second intifada, Arafat may have let loose forces that he will find difficult to control. More significantly, this military intifada has further radicalized the Palestinian populace, virtually destroyed the Israeli consensus for an agreement and will bring about the election of Ariel Sharon. Thus, as a new administration takes office in Washington, if the peace process is not dead, it's at least, comatose.

6. CONSTITUENCY SUPPORT

Despite the human tendency to want certainty and remove ambiguity, where there has been long-existing hostility, interim agreements are the way to go.

During the Camp David Summit, two heretofore-taboo subjects were discussed in detail: the plight of the refugees and the status of Jerusalem. While some progress was apparently made on the first issue, Jerusalem was a stumbling block.

Actually, by linking this emotionally charged religious matter with the return of other territories, it expanded the negotiation to a Pan-Arab issue. Once this occurred, Arafat needed support and cover from the more moderate Islamic regimes (Egypt or Saudi Arabia). Indeed, when the summit broke-up, he visited these countries but no help was forthcoming.

This should have been expected, since in Egypt and Saudi Arabia all criticism of the rulers is deflected against Israel, which is portrayed in the vilest terms. Perhaps more surprising, is that Hosni Mubarak and the Saudi Royal Family also encourage their media and radicals to denounce the United States, as a way of diverting attention from their own stagnant economies and corrupt regimes.

Simply put, Saudi Arabia and Egypt, who receive considerable aid from us, have no great interest in resolving the Palestinian issue at this time. They need Israel as an enemy, in order to serve as a convenient scapegoat—an outlet for the frustrations of their people.

Having raised these issues, here's what the new Bush administration should be doing:

First, do not welcome or subsidize Arafat as the prior administration did, until he cracks down on Hezbollah, Islamic Jihad and Hamas. He must be made to use his power to stop terrorism that operates from the territory he controls.

Second, Arafat must prepare his constituency for peace with Israel. This means educating Palestinians that Israel is here to stay.

Third, do more to persuade the Western allies to stop funding Arafat in his luxurious lifestyle, until he negotiates in good faith.

Fourth, crack down on charities within the United States who funnel the money they receive to the families of suicide bombers and international terrorists.

Fifth, put pressure on Saudi Arabia to stop funding Wahhabi Islamic schools which are petri dishes for transnational terrorists.

Sixth, use our close relationship with the new Israeli government to encourage them to adopt policies and take action that strengthens the "silent majority" of Palestinians who truly want to improve the life of their people.

Finally, it's time to recognize that the world is a dangerous place. This is especially true in the Middle East, where the last few decades have witnessed the growth of Islamic militancy. During this time they have been picking off Americans overseas and killing our people (Riyad, Khobar Towers, African Embassies, USS Cole, etc.) with impunity.

Because we delivered pinprick retaliations or none at all, they see us as risk averse. In twenty years we have never done anything to bring to justice those like, Imad Mughviyeh and Osama bin Laden who have been murdering American citizens. Before it's too late, it's time to put some muscle behind our diplomacy. Let us not forget that in the Arab world it's power and a willingness to use it that commands respect.

APPENDIX 4

The Scourge of International Terrorism:
Its Threat to America

History is replete with episodes of "hit-and-run terrorism," staged acts of mayhem, enacted for the purpose of producing calculated effects on a viewing audience. Deplorable and destructive as these violent incidents may have been, they were predictably performed by small groups of extremists who had few supporters and very limited resources. Consequently most of these vintage scenes of violence, confined as they were in duration and geography, had little effect on the political vitality and stability of the societies in which they occurred.

But, over the past two decades a new and more virulent strain of the violence has emerged. No longer bound in time, or by place, it has become a widespread contagion of epidemic proportions. Sponsored and supported by sovereign states, as a weapon of proxy warfare, the malignancy of modern international terrorism, has grown to the point where it can threaten the well-being and health of democratic institutions everywhere.

Fortunately, we in the United States were spared much of the savagery and chaos that came with the dawning of the "Age of Global Terrorism." Unaffected, unaware and uninformed as we were at the onset in this international plague, it's not surprising,

A Confidential Memorandum to President Ronald Reagan and CIA Director William Casey, dated July 10, 1985.

357

that the tragic mini-drama of the TWA Flight 847 in Beirut, like the epic-saga of the Iranian Hostage crisis, filled Americans with incomprehension, frustration and even fascination.

Certainly television ratings indicated that the drama-filled re-play of democracy's impotence was a source of viewer enthrall-ment but there's reason to believe that Lebanon's Shia version of *Play It Again Sam*, also produced considerable feelings of agitation, indignation and maybe even humiliation. There, in living color were two "Beirut Bag Men," cowardly criminals in pillowcases, taunting, threatening and terrorizing the world's greatest nation.

How do we react to this provocation? From the public's per-spective we responded immediately, airlifting network camera crews to the scene and canceling the vacations of Tom Brokaw and President Reagan—in that order. Then we deliberately raised the stakes by placing all personnel of the four major networks on alert status throughout the Middle East and Europe. Next we took the crisis to the brink by wearing down antagonist Nahbi Berri with round-the-clock television interviews. From break-of-day bargain-ing on *Good Morning America* to nocturnal negotiating on *Nightline*, he was forced to stare into a camera lens until he finally blinked. In the end a novel "Doctrine of Media Retaliation" had delivered the message "Mess with us and next time you'll not only have to deal with Bryant Gumble by day but Larry King all night."

Admittedly, this is an exaggerated and perhaps a surrealistic chronicle, nonetheless beneath the hype and hyperbole, is a cru-cial issue of causality.

Virtually accepted as dogma, for almost four decades, has been the tenet that the credibility of America's retaliatory capability has constrained the Soviet Union from direct aggression against members of the NATO Alliance. Indeed, this conceptual premise is the foundation for Mutual Deterrence which posits that no sane government would start a nuclear war if it believed that such an action might trigger unacceptable retaliation in kind.

Simply put, as long as the Kremlin leadership cannot perceive the benefit of a favorable exchange ratio, no incentive exists for a surgical first strike. Therefore, Moscow's decisions may be affected more by their assessment of America's resolve and determination to match its words by deeds and less by our stated policies or rhetoric. Tersely formulated: Will the Soviet Union interpret our prolonged passivity in the face of recent terrorist provocations as a sign of diminished resolve?

For their part the President and Secretary of State seem ahead of Congress and the media in anticipating this question related to "credibility carry-over effect." Like the words of a Chinese proverb, "When you pluck a flower you disturb the stars," foreign policy is a complex tapestry, where a multitude of threads are inextricably intertwined. To be sure, Mr. Reagan knows first hand that his swift response to the PATCO Strike and the decisive invasion of Grenada had worldwide reverberations.

Unfortunately, Byzantine bloodletting in the labyrinth that is modern Lebanon is not conducive to immediate and effective reciprocation. Delayed reactions, on the other hand, always cause problems in communication and raise doubts about motive. Take as an example NATO's decision to deploy Pershing II and Cruise missiles as a response to the Soviet installation of SS20's. Since there was a five-year time interval between the decision and its actual implementation, when it did occur it created the impression among many Western Europeans that the move constituted an American escalation of the nuclear arms race.

So before the memory of the skyjacked Beirut hostages, the recent killings of six Americans in San Salvador, and the murder of two Americans aboard a Kuwaiti Airliner in Teheran last December fade from the public agenda, the United States must act to protect its citizens at home and abroad. In essence, tomorrow's non-combatant victims of terrorism will be the result of today's flaccid response to terrorism.

We must match our words with the capability to thwart and punish these criminals. The tying of Yellow Ribbons is not a strategy of deterrence but rather the substitution of symbol for substance, words for deeds—the snare in whose coils a President's credibility can be destroyed.

When viewed strictly in numerical terms, the amount of casu-

alties produced by terrorist acts, pale when compared to the
bloodletting in Lebanon, the continuing carnage from the Iran-
Iraq war, or even the nation's homicide rate. Still, the spreading
plague of international terrorism portends peril far greater than
statistics alone might imply. Although the most visible crime of
our time, the true nature and significance of this new brand of political violence has failed to register with the public at large.

What is Terrorism? It is the calculated menacing and maiming
of innocent civilians for the purpose of producing fear and anxiety in the viewing audience in order to gain political ends. By trying to change our thinking, actions and policies through fear these
criminals are engaged in a form of mental rape. What is new is
that to their megalomaniac recipe has been added the stock of
state sponsorship, a dash of high technology and a great deal of
theatrical seasoning. Indeed, as practiced today it's a form of show
business, which combines spectacle, fear, excitement and a message.

Consequently the criteria for measuring the success of a terrorist operation depends almost entirely upon the amount of publicity it receives. By this criterion, if you can get the United States
of America by its networks, its heart and mind will follow. In the
final analysis the most likely location for terrorist spectacles in the
years or decades to come would be places where the media exists
in great numbers such as New York City, London, the Olympic
Games or even the Academy Awards.

Wittingly or unwittingly the media are the spokesmen of the
Terrorist transmitting their message, the instrument through
which the world audience instantaneously knows the excitement
and drama of their deeds. Television journalists and commenta-
tors who cover these events are not the proverbial flies on the wall,
but co-producers in a theatrical extravaganza. Like it or not they
are not objective observers but players in the game.

By indiscriminately menacing, maiming or murdering innocent
people, the Terrorist attempts to disorient and intimidate the
viewing audience. What appears as a random atrocity is so frightening to our own sense of personal security that we virtually need

to assume the existence of an understandable reason, motive or explanation behind it. In short, we are already predisposed and conditioned to learn the "underlying grievances," which must have caused the frightening effect. The next stop, of course, is to blame the victim.

Having said all this, the question is what can we do now to curb the scourge of Terrorism, which at its current rate will become the growth industry of the future?

1. TIMELY RETALIATION

For too long we have been reluctant in responding to Terrorism. About a decade ago when those who had real or imagined grievances against the United States began picking-off Americans overseas (military personnel, diplomats or civilians) we delivered pinprick retaliations or just did nothing. We said we did not want to risk harming innocent people in striking back, but that only gave license to those nations that harbor known terrorists. Now the time is long overdue to inform these sponsor countries (Iraq, Syria, Libya, Yemen, Lebanon, etc.) that if you do not rid yourself of these Terrorists and their bases we will do it ourselves.

As someone once said, "If you want to win the fight against malaria, it will take more than swatting at mosquitoes. You've got to drain the swamps where they breed."

2. EDUCATE THE MEDIA ABOUT THE THREAT

We must try to get the American Electronic Media to avoid the "knee jerk reporting reflex" which causes journalists to convey terrorists' grievances, threats and promises along with the pleas of hostages. Only if they exercise some self-restraint can we save our national government from the paralysis of its will.

Moreover, it would be helpful if journalists understood the difference between terrorists and freedom fighters, between cold-blooded murder and executions and between the innocent victim and criminal perpetrators. In the world of the terrorist, words and impressions are more real and sometimes more deadly than guns and bombs. In short, the "striving for balance" and moral blindness may aid and even encourage these criminal thugs.

3. USE DIPLOMATIC AND ECONOMIC LEVERS TO OUTLAW TERRORISM

In the past the United States has made half-hearted attempts to get the United Nations to pass such a proposal only to be thwarted by a coalition of Muslim nations, who insisted that the term "terrorism" be drastically redefined. In effect, that's like a Doctor saying that he would be willing to take out your appendix providing it is redefined as your daughter. Clearly we must use all the "chips" available and persist in this goal.

4. TIGHTEN AIRPORT SECURITY

On all flights, both international and domestic airports should install state-of-the-art security baggage detectors—including three-dimensional scanners that can spot plastic explosives and weapons. Further, all checked baggage should be x-rayed to guard against time-release or remote control bombs.

In addition, the Federal Government should consider subsidizing the airlines to improve the capability and quality of airport security staff. We should also ban flights to overseas airports that we know are easy targets for terrorists (Karachi, Athens, Manila, etc.).

5. EXPAND AND INTENSIFY INTELLIGENCE GATHERING

Clearly we have been relying too much on technical intelligence collection systems at the expense of the difficult challenge of penetrating terrorist groups with human sources. From all indications, the President will soon sign the necessary ISA finding that will enable us to recruit and train Arab agents to infiltrate suspected terrorist groups in Iran, Syria and Lebanon. This should only be the first step since we are sorely lacking in human intelligence collection both overseas and domestically.

Beyond this we must get better coordination among all of our intelligence agencies and greater cooperation with all the civilized nations who stand with us against this threat to progress, modernity and Western Civilization.

APPENDIX 5

Terrorism and the Media

"Asleep in the same bed, but with different dreams"

Terrorism in its current form is the willful maiming and murdering of civilians to produce fear in a large viewing audience for the purpose of pressuring a government to change its policies. Yet, despite the awesome increase in this barbaric activity, the ominous nature of this new brand of terrorism has failed to register with the public at large, democratic governments and certainly the media.

Although the most visible crime of our time there is no evidence that the United States and its Western allies have a coherent strategy to combat its menace. Rather, by our own ignorance and inaction, we have made this form of political violence cost effective as we acquire the reputation as a target that can be struck with impunity.

What are the salient features of this new strain of terrorism? First of all, with sponsorship and financing from sovereign states,

A paper dated August 1986.

this modern brand of criminality has become international in character. Once the exclusive weapon of isolated idealists, fringe fanatics or political anarchists, terrorism has emerged as a career path to privilege and prestige. Accepted and protected by national governments, terrorists live a life style of travel, fame, financial security, excitement and even respectability.

Henceforth the new terrorists will no longer come just from the urban poor and illiterate but will be recruited from the more educated middle class. This means they will have the capability to stage more spectacular acts of mayhem that produce more victims and engender more worldwide publicity.

Second, the current strain of terrorist violence ignores the traditional distinction between civilian and combatant. Indeed, one of the most frightening aspects of contemporary terrorism is that innocent victims, selected either for their symbolic value or mere availability, are treated as potentially disposable objects. As Claire Sterling has said in her book, *The Terror Network,* "what matters is not the identity of the corpse, but its impact on the audience."

Third, while terrorism was once used as a strategy of last resort, employed against tyrannical regimes, nowadays from the outset, it is aimed primarily at constitutional democracies. Undoubtedly, states committed to freedom of information and sensitive to shifting public opinion are much more vulnerable to propaganda and extortion than closed and repressive societies. For the most part, this accounts for the conspicuous absence of terrorism in totalitarian regimes.

Finally, today's terroristic acts are "tria juncta in uno," requiring along with a perpetrator and a victim, the public, for who it is all carefully choreographed, to gain maximum attention. Grievance claims, self-display and propaganda all come together in a theatrical performance for an audience, whose participation is solicited.

Since advertising terrorism increases its effectiveness by drawing attention to the insurgents and their announced cause, publicity is essential. However, publicity, important as it is, is not the only goal being sought. Also significant is the establishment of terrorists as political actors, which acceptance of their adversary role in a negotiation process necessarily implies. In other words, the ultimate achievement for the politically powerless terrorist, is to gain recognition of the legitimacy of their grievances and victimization by taking part in government sanctioned bargaining.

Accordingly, the mass media is an intrinsic element of international terrorism. For it provides the oxygen that gives life, to what otherwise would be a stillborn event. Driven primarily by competitive zeal, the television reporter especially, "has camera and will travel." As a result, from the Iranian hostage crisis, to the hijacking of the *Achille Lauro,* we have seen too many instances where electronic journalists have shown deference to the criminal captors, or usurped the legitimate role of government. For example, David Hartman on *Good Morning America* concluded an interview with Nahbi Berri of the Shi-ite Amahl, by asking, "is there anything else that you might want to say to President Reagan?"

Obviously it would be unrealistic to believe that the networks might avoid covering these potential dramas. However, is it too much to ask, that they not cast themselves in a collusive role, in what ultimately takes on the appearance of a made-for-TV docudrama?

Responding to this loaded question, network representatives react in knee-jerk fashion, with The Cosell Cliché, "We're just telling it like it is." But we all know that you cannot separate the observer from what is observed, for the mere act of covering an event changes its very nature. Since all human beings respond to events as perceived, not necessarily to objective reality, the media's active involvement in these terrorist spectaculars has the effect of shaping both its own, and the audience's perception. In sum, they give us a map, but in most cases, it does not correspond to the territory.

By indiscriminately menacing, maiming or murdering innocent people, the terrorist attempts to disorient and intimidate the viewing audience. What appears as a random atrocity, is so frightening to our sense of personal security, that we virtually need to assume the existence of an understandable reason, cause or explanation behind it. So we are already predisposed to learn the "underlying grievances" or "root causes," which we think must have produced this frightening effect.

Living in "An Age of Alibi" we find it easy to mistake an antecedent event for the proximate cause (i.e. using George Will's illustration . . . "The rooster crows so the sun rises"), while at the same time making us more susceptible to the righteous self-justification of criminal thugs, especially if they proclaim a political motive.

There's no doubt about it, television especially, can and does shape the way we think. It sapped our will to continue the Vietnam War. It held all of us hostage on a 444-day emotional roller coaster ride after our embassy was seized in Iran. For most of us, it supercedes any first hand knowledge and experience that we might have about situations involving domestic or international conflict. It guides us in formulating models and judgments, helps us determine credibility and by its very nature and structure, conveniently frames the issues at stake.

Unfortunately, despite an awesome increase in visual coverage, the ominous nature of the new variety of terrorism has failed to register with the media at large. It may even be argued that the major networks' attempt at "balanced reporting," has only served to perpetrate a mythology of terrorism and contribute to the "take a terrorist to lunch mentality."

Harsh as this judgment may seem, evidence exists that coverage of "terrorist theatricals," have been a contributing factor to the current state of muddled thinking, which is legitimizing terrorism and even elevating it to respectability.

First, is the media's tendency to adopt the terminology of terrorists: For example, how often have we heard felons referred to as "commandos," "guerillas," and "freedom fighters." Since words define and limit our thinking, this corruption of language must be resisted. In sum, brutal torture should not be called "trials" or "interrogations" and criminals do not "execute," but murder their victims.

Second, is the application of a doctrine of moral equivalency, whereby those on our side are often given equal weight with the perpetrators of indiscriminate violence. Because of the adversarial relationship between the news media and government, there is a presumption an administration will attempt to conceal anything which might cause their actions to be questioned. So the media somehow feels obligated to contact academicians, foreign nationals and those with strange sounding names, to serve as a counterweight to the "official line." Of course, there are not always two sides to each and every conflict. Sometimes some things are just plain evil and cruel and fairness might require "one-sided reporting."

Lastly, the media must make every effort to avoid justifying the criminal acts of individuals because of purported noble causes. This "Officer Krupke Cop-out" would have us believe that terrorism stems primarily from political or socio-economic injustices. In reality, when we examine specific cases, the root cause seems to be psychological and pathological. Illustrative of this point would be the Japanese terrorists responsible for the Lod Airport Massacre of May 1972. According to the lone survivor, Koza Okamoto, he and his cohorts were recruited by North Korean agents, trained in Lebanon and Syria, financed by West Germans, armed in Italy, and given their instructions by members of George Habash's People's Front for the Liberation of Palestine.

Reviewing the more recent terrorist episodes, such as the skyjacking of TWA Flight 847, the occupation of the *Achille Lauro*, the explosives planted on commercial airlines by Sikh and Tamil nationalists and the Berlin disco bombing, it is noteworthy that none of these crimes had a military or economic motive. What they have in common, is that all of these horrible actions were carefully designed and orchestrated to gain international publicity for hopeless causes. In each case, the media, albeit unwittingly, supplied the vehicle by which this primary objective was achieved.

It should be obvious that the quality of our lives has already been altered and degraded by the disgraceful phenomenon of international terrorism. Yet, most of the media has been slow to recognize its complicity in this growing threat to our culture and survival. One notable exception has been syndicated columnist,

David Broder, who has written, "If we thought about it more and understood its essence, we would probably stop writing about it, or we would cover it with considerably more care and respect."

Still, accepting the danger presented by international terrorism does not mean any less commitment to a free and independent press. Rather the media itself must balance the public's right to know with related responsibilities: Its obligations to safeguard human life and to ensure the preservation of a democratic society, if only for its own self-interest.

BIBLIOGRAPHY

During the last half century, there has been a veritable explosion of literature relating to the field of negotiating. For those who wish to read further, I have attempted to categorize this substantial body of knowledge, which ranges from the practical to the theoretical. Of course, these selections represent my own limited awareness, preferences, and biases.

HIGHLY RECOMMENDED

Brandenburger, A., and B. Nalebuff. *Co-opetition.* Doubleday (1996).

Bazerman, M., and M. Neale. *Negotiating Rationally.* Free Press. (1992).

Cialdini, R. *Influence.* William Morrow (1984).

Cohen, H. *You Can Negotiate Anything.* Bantam (1980).

Filley, A. *Interpersonal Conflict Resolution.* Scott, Foresman (1975).

Fisher, R., and W. Ury. *Getting to YES.* Penguin (1981).

Ginott, C. *Between Parent and Child.* Avon (1956).

Haley, J. *The Power Tactics of Jesus Christ and Other Essays.* Avon (1969).

Hoffer, E. *The True Believer.* HarperCollins (1951).

Iklé, F. *How Nations Negotiate.* Harper & Row (1964).

Lewicki, R., and J. Letterer. *Negotiation.* Irwin (1985).

McDonald, J. *Strategy in Poker, Business and War.* Norton (1950).

Milgram, S. *Obedience to Authority.* Harper & Row (1974).

Schelling, T. *The Strategy of Conflict.* Harvard University Press (1960).

Shapiro, R., and M. Jankowski. *The Power of Nice.* John Wiley & Sons (1998).

Trump, D., and T. Schwartz. *The Art of the Deal.* Random House (1992).

Zartman, W., and M. Berman. *The Practical Negotiator.* Yale University Press (1982).

CLASSICS IN THE FIELD

Most of these works are significant and influential. Still, some may be dated and too technical for the lay reader.

Alinsky, S. *Rules for Radicals.* Vintage (1972).

Blau, P. *Exchange and Power in Social Life.* Wiley (1964).

Boulding, K. *Conflict and Defense: A General Theory.* Harper & Row (1962).

Chamberlain, N. *Collective Bargaining.* McGraw-Hill (1951).

Douglas, A. *Industrial Peacemaking.* Columbia University Press (1962).

Druckman, D. *Negotiations.* Sage (1977).

Goffman, E. *Strategic Interaction.* University of Pennsylvania Press/Ballantine (1969).

Guetzkow, H., ed. *Simulation in Social Science: Readings.* Prentice Hall (1962).

Heider, F. *The Psychology of Interpersonal Relations.* Wiley (1958).

Kelman, H., ed. *International Behavior.* Holt, Rinehart & Winston (1965).

Maslow, A. *Motivation and Personality.* Harper & Row (1954).

McClelland, D. *Power: The Inner Experience.* Irvington (1975).

McGregor, D. *The Human Side of Enterprise.* McGraw-Hill (1960).

Peters, E. *Strategy Tactics in Labor Negotiations.* National Foremen's Institute (1955).

Rapoport, A. *Fights, Games and Debates.* University of Michigan Press (1960).

————. *Strategy and Conscience.* Harper & Row (1964).

Schelling, T. *Arms and Influence.* Yale University Press (1966).

Shubik, M. *Game Theory and Related Approaches to Social Behavior.* John Wiley (1964).

Siegel, S., and L. Fouraker. *Bargaining and Group Decision-Making.* McGraw-Hill (1960).

Stevens, C. *Strategy in Collective Bargaining Negotiation.* McGraw-Hill (1963).

Von Neumann, J., and O. Morgenstern. *Theory of Games and Economic Behavior.* Princeton University Press (1944).

Walton, R., and R. McKersie. *A Behavioral Theory of Labor Negotiations.* McGraw-Hill (1965).

RELATED BOOKS OF INTEREST

For those who wish to make their own choices, here is an eclectic group of books that both complement and supplement those previously mentioned.

Alexrod, R. *The Evolution of Cooperation.* Basic Books (1984).

Bacharach, S., and E. Lawler. *Bargaining.* Jossey-Bass (1981).

Baldwin, D. *Paradoxes of Power.* Basil Blackwell (1989).

Bartos, O. *Process and Outcomes of Negotiations.* Columbia University Press (1974).

Bazerman, M., and R. Lewicki. *Negotiating in Organizations.* Sage (1983).

Bell, D. *Power, Influence and Authority.* Oxford University Press (1975).

Brams, S. *Negotiation Games.* Routledge (1990).

Burch, G. *Resistance Is Useless.* Headline Publishing (1994).

Churchill, W. *The Gathering Storm, Vol. 1.* Houghton Mifflin (1948).

Coddington, A. *Theories of the Bargaining Process.* Aldine (1968).

DeBono, E. *Conflicts: A Better Way to Resolve Them.* Harrap (1985).

———. *Tactics.* Collins (1985).

Deutsch, M. *The Resolution of Conflict.* Yale University Press (1973).

Deutsch, M., and R. Krauss. *Theories in Social Psychology.* Basic Books (1965).

Dixit, A., and B. Nalebuff. *Thinking Strategically.* Norton (1991).

Druckman, D. *Human Factors in International Negotiations.* Sage (1973).

Druckman, E., ed. *Negotiations—Social-Psychological Perspectives.* Sage (1977).

Frankel, V. *Man's Search for Meaning.* Simon & Schuster (1959).

Goleman, D. *Vital Lies, Simple Truths.* Simon & Schuster (1985).

Gordon, T. *Parent Effectiveness Training.* Plume (1975).

Gulliver, P. *Disputes and Negotiations.* Academic Press (1979).

Hoffer, E. *The Ordeal of Change.* Harper & Row (1963).

———. *The Passionate State of Mind.* Harper & Row (1955).

———. *The Temper of Our Time.* Harper & Row (1967).

Janis, I. *Victims of Groupthink.* Houghton Mifflin (1972).

Kahn, H. *On Escalation: Memoirs and Scenarios.* Praeger (1965).

Lall, A. *Modern International Negotiation.* Columbia University Press (1966).

Lax, D., and K. Sebenius. *The Manager As a Negotiator.* Dimensions (1986).

Levin, E. *Levin's Laws.* M. Evans (1980).

Mastenbrock, W. *Negotiate.* Basil Blackwell (1989).

McCormack, M. *On Negotiating.* Dove (1995).

Mnookin, R., S. Peppet, and A. Tulumello. *Beyond Winning.* Belknap-Harvard (2000).

Morley, I., and G. Stephenson. *The Social Psychology of Bargaining.* London: Allen Unwin (1977).

Murninghan, K. *Bargaining Games.* Morrow (1992).

Poundstone, W. *Prisoner's Dilemma.* Doubleday (1992).

Pruitt, D. *Negotiation Behavior.* Academic Press (1981).

Raiffa, H. *The Art and Science of Negotiation.* Harvard University Press (1982).

Rowny, E. *It Takes One to Tango.* Brassey's (1992).

Rubin, J., and B. Brown. *The Social Psychology of Bargaining and Negotiations.* Academic Press (1975).

Shea, G. *Creative Negotiating.* CBI Publishing (1983).

Strauss, A. *Negotiations.* Jossey-Bass (1978).

Swingle, P., ed. *The Structure of Conflict.* Academic Press (1970).

Ury, W. *Getting Past No.* Bantam (1991).

Woolf, B. *Friendly Persuasion.* Putnam (1990).

Young, O., ed. *Bargaining.* University of Illinois Press (1976).

Zaleznik, A., and D. Moment. *Disputes and Negotiations.* Wiley (1964).

Zartman, W. *The Negotiation Process.* Sage (1978).

Zartman, W., ed. *The 50% Solution.* Anchor (1976).

INDEX